W9-BMT-699

ERNIE PYLE'S WAR

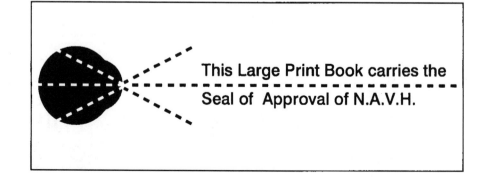

This Large Print Book carries the
Seal of Approval of N.A.V.H.

ERNIE PYLE'S WAR

★★★★★★★★★★★★★★★★★★★★★★★★★

America's Eyewitness to World War II

James Tobin

G.K. Hall & Co. • **Thorndike, Maine**

Published in 1999 by arrangement with Free Press,
an imprint of Simon & Schuster, Inc.

G.K. Hall Large Print American History Series.

The text of this Large Print edition is unabridged.
Other aspects of the book may vary from the original edition.

Set in 16 pt. Plantin by Al Chase.

Printed in the United States on permanent paper.

Library of Congress Cataloging in Publication Data

Tobin, James, 1956–
    Ernie Pyle's war : America's eyewitness to World War II / James
Tobin.
      p.   cm.
    Originally published: New York : Free Press, c1997.
    Includes bibliographical references (p. 515)
    ISBN 0-7838-8571-7 (lg. print : hc : alk. paper)
    1. Pyle, Ernie, 1900–1945. 2. War correspondents — United
States — Biography. 3. World War, 1939–1945 — Journalists.
I. Title.
PN4874.P88T63 1999
070.4′333′092 — dc21
  [b]   99-18826

For Leesa

Contents

PROLOGUE
★★★★

"And So It Is Over"

APRIL 18, 1945

Ernie Pyle's body lay alone for a long time in the ditch at the side of the road. Men waited at a safe distance, looking for a chance to pull the body away. But the machine gunner, still hidden in the coral ridge, sprayed the area whenever anyone moved. The sun climbed high over the little Pacific island. Finally, after four hours, a combat photographer crawled out along the road, pushing his heavy Speed Graphic camera ahead of him. Reaching the body, he held up the camera and snapped the shutter.

The lens captured a face at rest. The only sign of violence was a thin stream of blood running down the left cheek. Otherwise he might have been sleeping.[1] His appearance was what people in the 1930s and '40s called "common." He had often been described as the quintessential "little guy," but he was not unusually short. In fact, at five feet eight inches, his frame precisely matched the average height of the millions of American soldiers serving in the U.S. Army. It was his build that provoked constant references

7

to his size — a build that once was compared accurately to the shape of a sword. His silver identification bracelet, inscribed "Ernie Pyle, War Correspondent," could have fit the wrist of a child. The face too was very thin, with skin "the color and texture of sand." Under the combat helmet, a wrinkled forehead sloped into a long, bald skull fringed by sandy-red hair gone gray. The nose dipped low. The teeth went off at odd angles. Upon meeting Pyle a few months earlier, the playwright Arthur Miller had thought "he might have been the nightwatchman at a deserted track crossing."[2] In death his hands were crossed at the waist, still holding the cloth fatigue cap he had worn through battles in North Africa, Italy, France, and now here in the far western Pacific, a few hundred miles from Japan.

A moment later the regimental chaplain and four non-commissioned officers crawled up with a cloth litter. They pulled the body out of the machine gunner's line of fire and lifted it into an open truck, then drove the quarter-mile back to the command post on the beach. An Associated Press man was there. He already had sent the first bulletin:

COMMAND POST, IE SHIMA, April 18, (AP) — Ernie Pyle, war correspondent beloved by his co-workers, G.I.'s and generals alike, was killed by a Japanese machine-gun bullet through his left temple this morning.

8

The bulletin went via radio to a ship nearby, then to the United States and on to Europe. Radio picked it up. Reporters rushed to gather comment. In Germany General Omar Bradley heard the news and could not speak. In Italy General Mark Clark said, "He helped our soldiers to victory." Bill Mauldin, the young soldier-cartoonist whose war-worn G.I.'s matched the pictures Pyle had drawn with words, said, "The only difference between Ernie's death and that of any other good guy is that the other guy is mourned by his company. Ernie is mourned by the Army." At the White House, still in mourning only six days after the death of Franklin Roosevelt, President Harry Truman said, "The nation is quickly saddened again by the death of Ernie Pyle."[3]

One of Pyle's editors at the Scripps-Howard newspapers, George Parker, spoke on the radio. "He went into war as a newspaper correspondent among many correspondents," Parker said. "He came back a figure as great as the greatest — as Eisenhower or MacArthur or Nimitz." Parker spoke of "that strange and almost inexplainably intimate way" in which Pyle's readers had known him.[4] Indeed, people called newspaper offices all day to be sure Ernie Pyle was really dead. He had seemed so alive to them. Americans in great numbers had shared his life all through the war — his energy and exhaustion; his giddy enjoyments and attacks of nerves; his exhilarations and fears. Through Pyle's eyes they had watched their "boys" go to distant wars and become soldiers — green and eager at the start, haggard and worn at the end. Through his eyes they had glimpsed great vistas of battle at sea and they had stared into the faces of men in a French field who thought they were about to die. So no one thought it strange for President Truman to equate the deaths of Franklin Roosevelt and a newspaper reporter. For Pyle had become far more than an ordinary reporter, more even than the most popular journalist of his generation. He was America's eyewitness to the twentieth century's supreme ordeal.

The job of sorting and shipping Pyle's personal effects fell to Edwin Waltz, a personable and efficient Navy man who had been working as the correspondent's personal secretary at Pacific Fleet headquarters at Guam. There wasn't much to go through — a few clothes and toilet articles; books; receipts; some snapshots and letters. Here was Pyle's passport, stamped with the names of places he had passed through on his journeys to war — Belfast and London; Casablanca and Algiers; and on the last page, "Pacific Area." Waltz also found a little pocket notebook filled with cryptic jottings in a curlecue script — notes Pyle had made during his last weeks in France in 1944.

9 killed & 10 wounded out of 33 from D-Day to July 25 . . .

... drove beyond lines ... saw orange flame & smoke — shell hit hood — wrecked jeep — dug hole ... with hands — our shells & their firing terrible — being alone was worst. ...

Blowing holes to bury cows — stench everywhere.

Waltz also found a handwritten draft of a newspaper column. Knowing the war in Europe could end any day, Pyle had collected his thoughts on two sheets of paper, then marked up the sentences with arrows and crossings out and rewordings.

"And so it is over," the draft began. "The catastrophe on one side of the world has run its course. The day that had so long seemed would never come has come at last." He was writing this in waters near Japan, he said, "but my heart is still in Europe ... For the companionship of two and a half years of death and misery is a spouse that tolerates no divorce." He hoped Americans would celebrate the victory in Europe with a sense of relief rather than elation, for

in the joyousness of high spirits it is easy for us to forget the dead.

... there are so many of the living who have burned into their brains forever the unnatural sight of cold dead men scattered over

11

the hillsides and in the ditches along the high rows of hedge throughout the world. Dead men by mass production — in one country after another — month after month and year after year. Dead men in winter and dead men in summer. Dead men in such familiar promiscuity that they become monotonous. Dead men in such monstrous infinity that you come almost to hate them. Those are the things that you at home need not even try to understand. To you at home they are columns of figures, or he is a near one who went away and just didn't come back. You didn't see him lying so grotesque and pasty beside the gravel road in France. We saw him. Saw him by the multiple thousands. That's the difference.[5]

For unknown reasons Scripps-Howard's editors chose not to release the column draft, though V-E Day followed Ernie's death by just three weeks. Perhaps they guessed it would have puzzled his readers, even hurt them. Certainly it was a darker valedictory than they would have expected from him. The war had been a harsh mistress to Ernie. First it had offered him the means of escaping personal despair. Then, while his star rose to public heights he had never imagined, the war had slowly driven him downward again into "flat black depression." But he kept this mostly to himself. Instead he had offered readers a way of seeing the war that skirted de-

12

spair and stopped short of horror. His published version of World War II had become the nation's version. And if Ernie Pyle himself had not won the war, America's mental picture of the soldiers who *had* won it was largely Pyle's creation. He and his grimy G.I.'s, frightened but enduring, had become the heroic symbols of what the soldiers and their children would remember as "the Good War."

1

★★★★

"I Wanted to Get Out . . ."

ROOTS AND RISING, 1900–1935

Outside the little town of Dana, the table-flat plain of western Indiana rises ever so slightly to form what natives still call "the mound farm," a small cluster of white buildings on eighty acres of grain. The thin boy who lived atop this modest elevation in the early 1900s gazed over fields whose peaceful monotony was interrupted only by the little oasis of Dana a mile to the northwest. Only one image would have captured his attention — the tiny silhouette of a wagon or an automobile traversing the horizon on State Highway 36. In other words, the landscape's most notable feature was the means to escape it. In one way this seems fitting, for the goal of escape possessed the boy from an early age. In another way he never escaped this place.

"That long, sad wind . . ."

Sadness verging on bitterness always colored Ernie Pyle's memories of his early years. When he was a traveling newspaper columnist in the

14

1930s, he once found himself on a remote country road where he felt the dry breeze of his childhood brush his face, awakening a haunting mental picture of small men straining against circumstance and time. "I don't know whether you know that long, sad wind that blows so steadily across the hundreds of miles of Midwest flat lands in the summertime. . . ." he wrote in his column. "To me [it] is one of the most melancholy things in all life. It comes from so far, and it blows so gently and yet so relentlessly; it rustles the leaves and the branches of the maple trees in a sort of symphony of sadness, and it doesn't pass on and leave them still. It just keeps coming. . . . You could — and you do — wear out your lifetime on the dusty plains with that wind of futility blowing in your face. And when you are worn out and gone, the wind, still saying nothing, still so gentle and sad and timeless, is still blowing across the prairies, and will blow in the faces of the little men who follow you, forever." This was "just one of those small impressions that will form in a child's mind, and grow and stay with him through a lifetime, even playing its part in his character and his way of thinking, and he can never explain it."[1]

"Melancholy . . . worn out . . . gentle and sad . . . little men" — this was a description of Pyle's father, a carpenter at heart, who farmed because he could not make a steady living from his true vocation. "He's very meek and no trouble," Will Pyle's son once told friends. He might have been summing up Will's life.[2] Ernie depicted him in later writings as a kind but hapless figure, "the man who put oil on his brakes when they were squeaking, then drove to Dana and ran over the curb and through a plate-glass window and right into a dry-good store." Will's face would break into a brilliant, sparkling smile when he was pleased or amused. But he spoke little, even to his family. "He has never said a great deal to me all his life, and yet I feel we have been very good friends," Ernie once told his readers. "He never gave me much advice, or told me to do this or that, or not to."[3]

The formidable Maria Taylor Pyle, not Will, filled the role of family protector and leader. Always called Marie, she stood no taller than her husband, but she gave the impression of being much the bigger of the two. She was a woman of ferocious dedication to the practical tasks at hand — raising chickens and produce, caring for her family, serving her neighbors. She "thrived on action," her son remembered. "She would rather milk than sew; rather plow than bake." Ernie's closest boyhood friend recalled her as "a woman of unusual character — she was husky of build, [with] red hair and florid complexion, an unusually hard worker, even for a farm woman, a strict disciplinarian, very considerate of other people."[4] Devout and abstemious, she liked a joke and laughed easily and heartily. She could doctor a horse and play the violin. When the neighbors' children were born she always at-

16

tended their mothers, and those children grew up to obey her as readily as their parents. With adults she could be devastatingly blunt. "Marie Pyle didn't wait to tell my dad what she thought of him," recalled Nellie Kuhns Hendrix, who grew up next door and was close to the Pyles for many years. "If he done something she didn't like, she'd tell him about it."[5] No one doubted that, as Ed Goforth, another neighbor, put it later, "She wore the pants in the family." Goforth remembered arriving one morning to help Will with some work. "She looked over at Mr. Pyle and said, 'Will, take Ed and go shear the sheep today.' Well, Ed and Will sheared the sheep that day."[6]

She raised her only child, whom she always called Ernest, with a mixture of toughness and tenderness. One of Pyle's strongest memories captured the contradiction. On a summer day when the boy was four or five, he was walking behind his father's plow when he stopped to fetch some wild roses for his mother. Cutting the stems with his father's penknife, he suddenly saw a long snake approaching swiftly through the grass. He screamed, bringing his father on the run, and Will sent him back to the house a half-mile away. Ernest came to a patch of high weeds rising between himself and the house. Fearing another snake might be lurking there, he called to his mother, who appeared at the door and summoned him to come ahead through the weeds. He froze and began to cry, whereupon

17

Marie came and whipped him for his apparent stubbornness. "That evening," her son wrote thirty years later, "when my father came in from the fields, she told him about the crazy boy who wouldn't walk through the weeds and had to be whipped. And then my father told her about the roses . . . and the snake. It was the roses, I think, that hurt her so. My mother cried for a long time that night after she went to bed." For the rest of her life she retold the story on herself, as if to expiate a sin.[7]

The other woman in Ernie's life possessed a will to match his mother's. She was Mary Taylor, Marie's older sister, who lived with the family until she married a neighbor, George Bales, at the age of forty, when Ernest was six. "Tall and straight" with "more energy than a buzz saw," she dominated Bales as Marie dominated Will Pyle. Uncle George was likable and smart but he was a dreamer, preferring grand, unrealized schemes to the myriad small tasks necessary for success on his farm. So it was Mary Bales who put in the long days of labor, raising enough chickens, hogs and cattle to get by. As a boy, Ernie saw a great deal of her. Later, after Marie Pyle and George Bales died, Aunt Mary and Will Pyle lived on together in the Pyle farmhouse.[8]

Though not prosperous, the Pyles were respected, hardworking, churchgoing people. To their son they passed on decency and compassion, sensitivity toward others and a capacity for

18

hard work. Yet there was some obscure unhappiness in this small family that planted in Ernie the seeds of a lifelong melancholy. It drove him to flee not only Dana but all spheres of safe, straitened routine, to assay large achievements far beyond Dana's field of vision. The exact sources of these drives can only be guessed at. But they had something to do with Ernie's enduring image of his small, silent father — and perhaps his uncle, too — toiling with little pleasure or worldly success in the shadow of the two strong-willed sisters. In Ernie's mind, his father would always be the "little man" straining against "the wind of futility." And so, Ernie feared, might he become such a man himself. The image persisted in his life and writings. His low points would always be shadowed by the fear that he was nothing but an ineffectual man striving mightily to no purpose, and governed by the whims of a powerful woman. Yet the endearing character Pyle established for himself as a writer, and the subjects of his legendry in World War II, were common men transcending the grinding circumstances of everyday existence. Will Pyle's memory cut both ways.

Ernie grew up as a keenly intelligent child in a home and a town where intellect and big dreams were not especially esteemed. Homely, small for his age, and fussed over by a strong-willed mother, he tended toward self-pity in a world of boys who all seemed bigger, more easygoing, and blessed with fathers who cut a wider swath than Will. Being a "farm boy" instead of a "town boy" exacerbated his itchy sense of inferiority. "I was a farm boy," he wrote nearly thirty years later, "and town kids can make you feel awfully backward when you're young. . . . Even today I feel self-conscious when I walk down the street in Dana, imagining the town boys are making fun of me."[9] While the other kids in the schoolyard wrestled and roughhoused, "I always sat under a tree and ate my apple."[10] His closest friend, a boy one year older named Thad Hooker, often urged Ernie to try sports. But Thad would be pushed away with a bitter "Aw, hell, you know I'm no good at games."[11] Because his voice cracked when he spoke loudly or excitedly, he developed a lifelong habit of clearing his throat before speaking, then using a low and even tone to lessen the chance of a humiliating squeak. At some point he grew anxious about his teeth, cleaning them constantly with twine.[12] Intelligence and insecurity fought in Ernie's mind, pushing him to the role of the outsider looking in, unsure whether to test himself against the big boys or feign disinterest and wish them all a short trip to hell.

Certainly a farmer's life held no appeal for him. When Ernie was nine, Will led him into the fields and showed him how to use the harrow and plow. From that point on, Ernie remembered, "I worked like a horse," an animal he came to despise. He once estimated he rode five thousand miles to school and back on the Pyles' nag, and he trudged for many more miles behind horses in the fields. That was more than enough. During his years of constant cross-country travel, he refused to stay at farmhouses that rented rooms to guests, saying simply, "I've had enough of farms." "Horses were too slow for Ernest," Will remembered later. "He always said the world was too big for him to be doing confining work here on the farm."[13]

He cherished his glimpses of that wider world. Whenever a postcard arrived in the Pyle mailbox, he would snatch it and paste it into a scrapbook. He read as much as he could — mostly newspapers and adventure tales. On a trip with his father to Chicago about 1910, he got his first impression of the big-city newspaper trade amid the noisy traffic of autos and street vendors. "I remember as a kid . . . how impressed I was with the ads I could see on the sides of huge trucks hauling loads of newsprint for the *Chicago Herald-Examiner*," he once told a friend, "the pictures and names of the writers, and the colored pictures of the comic-strip heroes."[14]

One species of hero just then emerging into public consciousness held a special allure. In Ernie's early teens, the walls of his bedroom sprouted sketch after sketch of race cars — the boxy, big-wheeled behemoths of racing's earliest days. His inspiration was the Indianapolis 500, then in its infancy but no less redolent of masculine glamour than it is today. One year his parents allowed Ernie to attend the race. He was enthralled by the giant crowd lining the two-and-a-half-mile brick oval, the spectators' black Model T's jamming the grassy infield, reporters rushing in and out of the speedway's five-story "press pagoda," the howl of engines and the glimpse through the smoke of drivers in their helmets and goggles. The annual race, which he witnessed several times, excited his imagination for many years. Even in his thirties, he daydreamed of racing at Indianapolis — a clue to the yen for glory that stirred beneath his self-deprecating facade. "I would rather win that 500-mile race than anything in this world," he confessed in 1936. "To me there could be no greater emotion than to come down that homestretch, roaring at 130 miles an hour, those 500 exhausting, ripping miles behind you, your face black with grease and smoke, the afternoon shadows of the grandstands dark across the track, a hundred thousand people yelling and stomping their excitement, and you holding up your proud right arm high in the Speedway tradition of taking the checkered flag — the winner! I have dreamed of myself in that role a thousand times."[15]

Not surprisingly, the boy who longed for speedway heroics also longed to join the Army when, in 1917, President Wilson committed American forces to the Allied cause in World War I. Too young for service by more than a year, Ernie watched in frustration as other Dana boys left for Europe, including Thad Hooker, who was permitted to leave school early in 1918 to join up. At the high school commencement that spring, a flag-draped chair took Thad's place among the graduating seniors. "I could hardly bear to go to commencement, I was so ashamed that I wasn't in the Army, too," Ernie recalled later.[16] In October 1918 he enlisted in the Naval Reserve, hoping to see action eventually. But that hope burst only a month later, when the warring powers announced an armistice.

With no war to escape to, Ernie searched for alternatives. After the prospect of battle, college seemed a pale second choice, but at least it promised a route away from the farm. So, in the fall of 1919, he left for Bloomington with a single suitcase and an aimless ambition. "He always had big ideas," said Nellie Kuhns Hendrix, for whom Ernie, ten years older, was a big brother figure, telling the neighborhood youngsters of faraway places and imagined adventures. "He wanted to do things."[17]

"We aspire to become journalists . . ."

The war's end brought Indiana University its biggest enrollment to date in the fall of 1919: 2,229 students, more than twice the population of Dana. Among the young veterans flooding the campus was Paige Cavanaugh, a wisecracking iconoclast from the small town of Salem, Indiana, who would become Ernie's lifelong surrogate brother. The two could be serious or raucous together, and they shared many likes and dislikes, though Ernie never could share Cavanaugh's contempt for war veterans who paraded their special status. "Ernie had a hero complex," Cavanaugh said later. "He and I both had a good eye for phonies around the campus, and we used to sit around and mimic them. But nobody who had been overseas could do wrong in Ernie's eyes, no matter how big a blowhard he was."[18]

Cavanaugh later enjoyed claiming credit for launching Ernie's newspaper career, if only by suggesting they enroll in journalism as sophomores because the course was reputed to be easy. In fact, Ernie had expressed a strong interest in the field as a freshman, but university rules prevented him from taking the introductory course until his second year. Cavanaugh later told the story this way: on registration day in the fall of 1920 the country-boy team of Cavanaugh and Pyle tiptoed into a silent classroom where a professor in horn-rimmed glasses sat waiting over his enrollment book, appraising his disheveled scholastic suitors without a word. In the stillness Ernie finally cleared his throat and announced: "We aspire to become journalists, sir."[19]

Though he majored in economics, journalism occupied most of Ernie's remaining years at I.U. Classwork was dispatched quickly; "he had such

24

a memory he didn't need to study much," a friend said.[20] Instead he invested his energies in the *Daily Student.* Though "he had periods of mental lowness . . . when he was certain he wasn't worth a damn," he won the approval of editors who rewarded his industry with a demanding beat, the university administration.[21] He was appointed editor-in-chief of the summer *Student* in 1921 and served as city editor the following fall. In a comment echoed by many a later editor, a *Daily Student* superior recalled: "He was a shy boy but worked hard and made friends quickly."[22]

One night about this time, as Ernie typed phoned-in dispatches from the Associated Press, the story of a soldier killed in battle brought tears to his eyes. It was the Pulitzer Prize–winning work of AP reporter Kirke Simpson, whose subject was the interment of the Unknown Soldier at Arlington National Cemetery in 1921. Simpson's style trembled under the weight of patriotic melodrama — "Alone, he lies in the narrow cell of stone that guards his body; but his soul has entered into the spirit that is America" — but it affected the youngster so deeply that he could quote from the story many years later, when he told a reporter that Kirke Simpson had given him a goal to aim at.[23]

If Ernie had found a vocation in newspapering, his passion was to see as much of the world beyond Indiana as he possibly could. In his first college summer he leaped at the chance to labor in a Kentucky oil field. He toured the Great Lakes on a Naval Reserve cruise. "I wish I was a good ball player so I could get to make some of those trips [with the I.U. team]," he wrote Aunt Mary one spring. "They went all thru the south this spring on their training trip, and went to Ohio the other day and got to go all thru the state penitentiary."[24] He bummed rides into neighboring states, following the football team — "He wasn't so damn much interested in boosting the morale of the team as he was in seeing the country," Cavanaugh said — and finally joined the team as manager in order to secure train tickets.[25] But his midwestern rambling paled in comparison to the remarkable stunt he pulled in the spring of 1922, when he and three fraternity brothers wangled permission to accompany the I.U. baseball team by ship to Japan. Working as cabin boys, Ernie and his comrades survived a typhoon in the North Pacific only to find their papers prevented them from disembarking in Japan. To Ernie's delight, they were forced to journey on to China and the Philippines before rejoining the team for the cruise home. "I never felt better in my life," he wrote his parents from Shanghai.[26]

By the middle of his senior year, the outside world looked so inviting that Ernie bailed out of college altogether. On the morning of January 28, 1923, Ernie reported for work at the daily *Herald* in LaPorte, Indiana, a factory town squeezed between Lake Michigan and the

Indiana-Michigan border. The newspaper's editor, an I.U. alumnus, had asked the chairman of the university's journalism department to recommend a promising youngster to fill a reporting vacancy. The chairman had recommended Ernie enthusiastically, but he made his usual first impression in LaPorte. "Small, frail and sandy-haired . . . bashful and unimpressive," the newcomer "didn't look like a newspaper man" to the city editor. "But he was there, and we needed a man, so . . . he went to work."[27] And he prospered, covering a variety of assignments effectively and winning friends quickly, though "he had an inferiority complex . . . and would never let anybody forget that he was a 'country boy' and a 'poor devil.' " Ernie wrote his outstanding story, which demonstrated rare courage, after infiltrating a Ku Klux Klan rally, then defying the thugs who trailed him out of the meeting and warned him not to publish his account.[28]

To leave Bloomington just one semester shy of attaining his degree must have grieved the Pyles. Yet he had spurned their wishes. Precisely what he was thinking is guesswork, as the record is bare on this point. He did solicit the opinion of his faculty mentor, Clarence Edmondson, dean of men at I.U., who advised him to take the job. Still, Ernie's decision must have served as a harsh declaration of independence from Dana. Certainly he was thumbing his nose at propriety. When even Paige Cavanaugh, who was no stick-in-the-mud, warned Ernie he might amount to little without his diploma, his friend had only laughed and said, "We'll see."[29]

There was another factor involved in his departure: Harriett Davidson, a red-headed native of Bloomington who was "one of the most highly respected girls in school," as Ernie proudly informed his parents. Throughout college he had dated regularly, but he fell hard only for Harriet. At the time he left for LaPorte the romance apparently remained intact, but soon Ernie began hearing tales of a young doctor who collected Harriett for dates in a sparkling red Buick. When Ernie's colleagues on the *LaPorte Herald* heard of his quandary, they teased him and noisily predicted his fraternity pin would soon be returned. Then, sometime in the spring of 1923, "the pin did come back," one of them remembered, "and all of us felt like first class heels. . . . Ernie was broken-hearted. . . . He did not want to stay in Indiana any longer. . . ."[30]

A piece of lucky timing then bestowed a mercy on the miserable twenty-two-year-old. It arrived in the form of a telegram that invited Ernie to a meeting with Earle Martin, a high-ranking editor with the Scripps-Howard newspaper chain. Searching for talent, Martin had just visited Bloomington, where Ernie's friend Nelson Poynter (then editor of the *Daily Student*, later a distinguished editor and publisher) had recommended Ernie. Martin offered Poynter and Pyle $30 a week each to work for the *Washington*

Daily News, a new tabloid he had just taken over for Scripps-Howard.[31] Ernie didn't hesitate. Only four months after his arrival in LaPorte, he and Poynter boarded a train for Washington, where they pulled into Union Station early enough on a Sunday in May 1923 for Ernie to see his first major league baseball game.[32] Friends in LaPorte tried to persuade him to stay a while to gather more small-town experience before this quick and painless leap to big-city journalism. But Ernie would hear none of it. His editor wasn't surprised. From the moment Ernie arrived in LaPorte, Ray Smith remembered, "He . . . had 'sand in his shoes.' "[33]

"A good man, but not much drive . . ."

The *Washington Daily News* was founded in 1921, just eighteen months before Ernie's arrival, in the massive business expansion that made Scripps-Howard one of the nation's most powerful newspaper chains. Tabloid in format, the *News'* assigned mission was to woo the working man and woman away from the four established Washington dailies with short, snappy stories and aggressive local reporting. To accomplish this, Earle Martin recruited a staff of talented youngsters and set about creating a competitive tabloid without a tabloid's traditional reliance on sensationalism and pictures. He intended to showcase cleverly written stories whose main appeal to the reader would be their brevity and punch.[34]

For this kind of writing the stripling from LaPorte, with his four months of professional experience, proved amazingly well suited. His superiors immediately noted gifts of efficiency and simplicity. Dispatched to cover an explosion at the Bureau of Standards early in his tenure, he phoned in notes that were a model of clarity, prompting Martin to spout off in the city room about "a damn good story."[35] Soon Ernie was shifted from reporting to the copy desk, where he transformed other reporters' writing into the spare, readable style Martin wanted. Copy-editing suited Ernie. For a writer of his temperament — suspecting he was more gifted than others but fearful of showing it — the task held hidden satisfactions. One was the sheer fun of manipulating words into pleasing shapes and sounds. Another was the pleasure of putting to rights the mangled or dull prose of the reporters; they might outrank a timid copy editor in prestige, but he held the ax over their words. Indeed, some *News* reporters could barely recognize their handiwork after it emerged from under Ernie's quick pencil. But that was all to the good in the eyes of his superiors. After he converted one writer's droning account of a multiple hanging into a few taut paragraphs, Martin tacked the article to the city room bulletin board and pronounced it "the perfect tabloid story." Editors long remembered Ernie's technical skills as a beginner. "He was one of the fastest copyreaders I ever saw," said one, "and one of the cleanest writers . . ." Another said simply: "He had a very orderly mind."[36]

He persisted in presenting himself as the "poor devil," the aw-shucks kid from the sticks — a convenient refuge for a young man who nursed equal portions of ambition, irresolution and insecurity. Now and then he quietly offered articles to other publications — including, perhaps, the fledgling *New Yorker*, which he admired — but got nowhere. "A good man, but not much drive," was the verdict of his peers at the *News*, who remembered his tenure in the mid-twenties more for his signature belch, inventive profanity and eccentric clothes than his ambition.[37] They quickly became aware of a life-long crotchet: Ernie was perpetually on the verge of an illness, in the middle of an illness or getting over an illness. One *News* colleague later testified to his "wondrous hypochondria. The standing office gag was to ask Ernie every hour on the hour how he felt. He had only one reply through the years: 'Terrible!' And I believe the kid meant it. He always looked it."[38] Always acutely sensitive to cold, he would sometimes wander into the *News* for his 7:00 A.M. shift in a lumberjack shirt and a long, white stocking cap, which he wore all day. On one such day, Scripps-Howard president Roy Wilson Howard, who always dressed to impress, descended from his Park Avenue offices in New York for an inspection tour of the *News*. Catching sight of the apparition in the stocking cap, Howard glared at one of his editors and demanded, "What's *that?*"[39]

Throughout Ernie's life, new acquaintances, men as well as women, felt an urge to take care of him. Surely this was the quality that first appealed to a young woman who met him in Washington in the fall of 1923. Geraldine Siebolds, always called Jerry, had grown up in Hastings, Minnesota, a tranquil town, much less isolated than Dana, that nestled prosperously on the Mississippi River just a twenty-mile streetcar ride from St. Paul. The frame houses of Hastings all had wide, friendly porches — all, that is, but the Sieboldses' house. It was a strange affair, built deep into the slope of a hill, with one story nearly entirely underground and another story perched atop it, no door in front and no porch. Neighbors said that Jerry's father, a foreman at the nearby state insane asylum, was afraid of the tornados that swept through the region in summer, so he had built a house to protect himself, his wife and their four children. The odd house fed a vague notion that Siebolds himself was odd. "I got the impression from my own family that he was kind of a weird person," said Harriet Hendrixson, who grew up several years behind Jerry in school and later became a close friend. Jerry, by contrast, was vibrant and popular, acting in school plays and singing in the Presbyterian choir. She stood out from the crowd partly because she was attractive and vivacious, but also because she excelled in schoolwork and read serious books on her own. There was a hint of the rebel about her. "She used to wear the weirdest clothes," Mrs. Hendrixson recalled. "She'd tack them up herself and used to pin things here and there." She had gone to Washington as a Civil Service clerk in 1918. In secret, she and a friend had taken the government service exam, breaking the news to their parents only when plans for their departure were a fait accompli.

In Washington, her rebelliousness flowered into the Greenwich Village–style bohemianism then popular among young urbanites of an intellectual bent. She was petite, with an impish smile that was peculiarly attractive in a manner more than one friend described as "pixyish." Her clothes were tailored, though she seemed never to buy anything new for herself. She was bright, charming and provocative, displaying a fierce iconoclasm in flashes of wit. A friend remembered her "stubborn, almost . . . morbid, nonconformism."[40] For a time she was engaged to a dentist, but she soon threw him over as too stuffy. She and Ernie first met at a Halloween party in 1923; a year later they began to date in earnest.[41]

Ernie was proving unable or unwilling to devote himself to the long, patient haul that was necessary for advancement even in the harum-scarum business of newspapering where change was endemic. When he tired of his routine, he simply would leave. Before his first year at the *News* was out, he took off for a Caribbean fling, working his way to Puerto Rico and Panama as a seaman. After only two years on the payroll, he pronounced himself worn out at the age of twenty-four and retreated to Dana for two months of rest. During this time he missed Jerry desperately, and when he returned they were married by a justice of the peace just across the Potomac in Virginia. She scoffed at this bow to propriety, giving in only when Ernie insisted that he could not shame his parents by living in sin. For years they shared a private joke by telling friends they weren't really married. Jerry would neither wear a ring nor observe the anniversary of their wedding, which took place in the summer of 1925.

The following spring, wanderlust struck again. Pooling their savings of about $1,000, Ernie and Jerry bought a Model T and a tent, quit their jobs and fled the capital for points west. In three months they toured the rim of the country, sleeping on the ground and cooking over open fires. They fell in love with New Mexico and Arizona, then crashed Paige Cavanaugh's bachelor quarters in Hollywood. "They were young, wild, unconventional and neurotic," Cavanaugh remembered. "They were tearing across the country as if someone was after them."[42] The exodus ended in New York, where they landed, exhausted and broke, at summer's end. They sold the Ford for $150 to buy food.

They spent sixteen months in New York. Ernie's copyediting skills brought a paycheck, first at the *Evening World*, then at the *Post*. It was not an era he cared to recall. As he summed it up long afterward: "Lived in a basement and never had enough to go to a show, and hated New York."[43] In December 1927, a letter arrived from a friend at the *Washington Daily News*. This was Lee Graham Miller, a young Harvard man with screen-idol looks who was a rising star in Scripps-Howard circles. In Ernie's absence he had become managing editor. Now he wanted Pyle for his telegraph editor, in charge of all wire copy. On the day after Christmas, 1927, Ernie was back at his old desk.[44] It was better than a New York basement, but still no solution to Ernie's restlessness. Within weeks he asked Miller to let him write — in off-hours — a regular column on aviation, and Miller agreed.

Ernie's aviation column first appeared in the *News* in March 1928, only ten months after crowds of shouting Frenchmen had surged across a Paris airfield to greet a startled air-mail pilot named Charles Lindbergh as his *Spirit of St. Louis* taxied to a stop after thirty-three hours in the air. Lindbergh's solo crossing of the Atlantic — now the only well-remembered feat of early aviation besides the first flight of the Wright Brothers — was in fact only the crowning moment in a decade-long frenzy of competitive efforts to court public approval of aviation in general and various corporations in particular. Air races, spectacular crashes, mysterious losses over land and sea, wild stunts, handsome prizes for distance, speed and endurance records — all these drew intense public curiosity year after year, and close attention from the press. Most magnetic of all was the lone, windblown figure of the pilot, a heroic image that resonated powerfully with Americans' traditional love of the frontiersman and the cowboy.

Ernie conceived the notion that people would enjoy day-to-day coverage of this burgeoning new enterprise, not only in its grand advances but in its technical intricacies and amusing trivia. His column, probably the first in the United States to deal exclusively with aviation, was not unlike the early computer columns that appeared in newspapers and magazines of the 1980s, full of hope and excitement about a field of endeavor that promised (sometimes overpromised) to remake American society. Each afternoon, after an eight-hour shift on the copy desk, he would hop on a streetcar or flag a taxi bound for one or another of Washington's airfields.[45] There he would wander from office to office and hangar to hangar, chatting with anyone he found. Sometimes he would stay up half the night on a floodlit field, trading stories with pilots or mechanics and listening for the drone of distant planes approaching. There was no lack of material for stories. Washington, lying at the midpoint of the Atlantic seaboard, was then a center of aviation activity, with two of the country's leading passenger airports, Hoover and Bolling Fields, the Washington Naval Air Station, and a sprinkling of smaller fields nearby. Downtown, congressmen and bureaucrats were shaping the new rules that would govern the new industry and handing out the contracts that would determine winners and losers among hundreds of competing entrepreneurs. As a swiftly growing business, employing 75,000 people by 1929, aviation offered the reporter continuing controversies and developments. Ernie wrote of passenger safety, night flying, engine and airplane design, the founding and expansion of airports and the birth pangs of national airlines. He encountered and befriended any number of pilots, most of them World War veterans now scrambling to earn a living as crop dusters, aerial photographers, Army aviators, passenger and cargo pilots, mail pilots or, most colorful of all, the barnstormers who gypsied from field to field, delighting crowds with wing-walks and offering thrill seekers their first flights for fees of a dollar a minute.

In this crowd of adventurers, hucksters and the occasional genius, Ernie's face gradually became familiar and welcome. He gained friends and often beat competitors out of stories by seeming to be just another one of the fellows rather than a pushy, question-firing reporter.

"Ernie always was the least conspicuous of the lot in manner and appearance," an acquaintance of that era recalled. "He withdrew behind his cigaret, and instead of talking he for the most part smiled genially at one and all. . . ."[46]

His column appeared on an inside page of the *News* under a succession of titles — "D.C. Airports Day by Day," then "Airways" (with a thumbnail photo of Ernie and an enlarged byline), and finally "Aviation" — with several items of news in each day's offering. At first he was determinedly newsy, presenting such ho-hum fare as this: "Hiram Bingham Jr., son of the Senator from Connecticut, who is also president of the National Aeronautics Corporation, was a passenger in the Washington–New York Airline's Ryan this morning on its regular run to New York."[47] But soon Ernie settled into a looser, more descriptive style: "If you follow the movements of the air mail, day after day you will find graphic examples of some of the finest flying in the world. Perhaps you remember what a terrible day yesterday was — heavy black sky, rain pouring down, wind blowing little gales in gusts. Walter Shaffer was up in it — flying."[48]

Ernie's favorites were the anonymous and hard-drinking mail pilots, who were amassing a record of utilitarian service that gradually convinced American business of the advantages of high-speed delivery over long distances.[49] In a preview of things to come, Ernie made a specialty out of telling tales of the mail pilots' feats of bravery and improvisation. They flew under constant pressure to deliver on schedule, yet without radios or detailed flight charts. Instead, they relied on state highway maps and shared lore about the locations of golf courses, polo grounds and dangerously lofty church spires. Fears of freezing cold and bad weather accompanied the mail pilots constantly. Ernie found this stolid, workmanlike flying far more admirable than the record-seeking heroics of Lindbergh and his imitators. A typical Pyle hero was an Ohioan forced to fly double-duty to pick up the slack for a colleague killed in a crash.

[H]e has never been to the North Pole, or the South Pole, or flown across the ocean at midnight with a pig in his lap. . . . No, all he ever did was fly the night air mail between Cleveland and Cincinnati every night for 34 consecutive nights last winter. Two hundred and thirty-eight hours in the air in a month. . . . He did it by going to bed the minute he got out of his plane, and resting every second he wasn't in the air. Even then it almost killed him. There isn't enough money in the world to make him do it again. All of which goes to show that the boys who break into the papers every morning aren't necessarily the ones who are doing our greatest flying.[50]

This sort of tribute made Ernie as popular

with the pilots as they were with him, and they returned thanks — and courted further publicity — by calling him first with news. When an East Coast mail pilot had to ditch, it was said that he phoned the Post Office, then Ernie Pyle. As a close observer of Ernie's career put it, "He found that . . . he had a gift for becoming a member of a group while retaining his ability to explain it to outsiders."[51] Such membership exacted a price, of course. He could not write negative stories — or not many of them — and retain his member-ship. His criticisms were models of caution:

> With a bow to my many friends in the Air Corps, and a deeper one to the crew of the Question Mark [a record-setting airplane], some of whom I know and admire greatly, may I venture the dastardly remark that I be-lieve the recent endurance flight was a bit foolish, unimportant and greatly over-rated?[52]

This coziness troubled neither Ernie nor his editors. The watchdog's role did not dominate newsrooms of the 1920s.

When the pilots called Ernie, or when they told of their exploits in airfield bull sessions, he became skilled at turning their tales into minia-ture narratives. In twelve inches of column type he could create a compelling little story from the experience of a mail pilot flying blind in a dense fog, then finding his way to safety by the light of a burning barn. He picked up human interest items, too — for example, the boy who wrote a mail pilot asking him to fly higher so as not to hit the boy's kite. As time went by he included more of these items in the column, realizing many readers preferred them over traditional "hard news."

He soon understood that his "poor devil" personal style was a useful style for a writer as well. When he needed to explain a technical matter, he developed the trick of disarming the reader with an "aw-shucks" approach, as in, "I hope I can get this straight, altho it's going to be a little difficult. . . ." His allusions were admirably concrete. Why did pilots prefer private airfields to public? Because, Ernie explained, "at a private field you get the kind of treatment you get at a high-class hotel, and at most municipal fields you get the kind of treatment you receive at the traffic bureau when you go for a driver's permit." And he allowed himself (with his editors' acquiescence) to speak in a voice that was increasingly personal:

[Y]ou will never know what real despair is until you get a job on a newspaper and spend two hours trying to be funny in a column like this, and every time you read it over and revise it it gets worse, and finally you have to tack a paragraph like this on the end to let your readers know you don't think it's funny either. Not very funny, anyway.[53]

In newspaper offices and at airfields, it was clear that Ernie had succeeded. The *News* soon relieved him of his copy desk duties, freeing him to work full time on the column. Not long afterward he was named aviation editor for all of Scripps-Howard. When a high-ranking editor undertook to introduce Ernie to Amelia Earhart, the renowned aviatrix stopped him. "Not to know Ernie Pyle," she said, "is to admit that you yourself are unknown in aviation."[54]

Friends thought Ernie's four years on the aviation beat were the happiest of his life. His time was largely his own. He chose his own topics; wrote in a more personal vein than the average reporter; and enjoyed a lay expertise in an interesting field. He even enjoyed a certain prestige. He spoke regularly with senators, cabinet secretaries and congressmen. Important fliers such as James Doolittle and Ira Eaker, later commander of the Eighth Army Air Force in World War II, were personal friends. A diverse collection of acquaintances — pilots, reporters, cops on the beat — dropped in often at the Pyles' apartment in southwest Washington, filling the humid air with convivial talk of flying, newspapering and where to find bootleg whiskey. To most friends the Pyles' life appeared carefree and exciting, and their marriage a model of mutual devotion. "They were so concerned about each other's feelings always," Harriet Hendrixson remembered. "You just felt it — that they adored one another, were so careful about never doing or

42

saying anything that would displease the other. They were in harmony, let's face it. It was almost a spiritual thing."[55]

But the tranquil surface covered quiet tensions and anxieties. There was a strange, hothouse insularity about the marriage. To Paige Cavanaugh, who once stayed with the Pyles for several weeks, the atmosphere of sensitivity seemed ominous. Each, he realized, was watching the other. "Ernie and Jerry did live for each other," Cavanaugh wrote later in an unpublished memoir, "but always in a nightmarish tug of war. They were always on the alert for a change of mood." They lived in a state of apprehension, "trying to forestall any little incident which might affect either of them. Ernie might come home in a mood of black despair caused by a rebuff while attempting to get an interview, or by a slight change in his copy by the desk, and then Jerry would go to work. And with Ernie lying on his back on the sofa, hands behind his head staring at the ceiling, Jerry quietly and patiently would mentally massage him back into a state of well-being."[56] No doubt Ernie *was* needy in this way. But it seems likely that for Jerry, being needed so desperately filled a gaping hole inside herself as well.

Ernie brooded about what would become of him in a profession that often served the old unkindly. He feared that aviation was becoming the domain of corporate big shots and that public interest was fading. Now in his early thirties, he had been in the newspaper business long enough to see older men, even successful ones, shunted into second-rate jobs as younger men came up through the ranks. Cavanaugh believed Ernie dreaded becoming "old, sour-pussed, [in] ill health, in debt, kicked from one desk job to another — a desk that finally had to have a bottle of cheap gin in the lower right hand drawer so as a man could keep on his feet."[57]

In the spring of 1932, the *News'* editor-in-chief, Lowell Mellett, asked Ernie to become the paper's managing editor. Ernie was appalled. The job would put an end to his writing and traveling, the very things he loved about the business. Instead, he would be an inside man again, a news technician who sat down to a desk each day in a ritual that would only remind him how short was the tenure of most editors. Then would come the polite demotion, and he would be on his way down toward the dead end he dreaded.

He said yes.

He liked and respected Lowell Mellett, felt grateful to the *News*, didn't want to let down his employers. So he threw himself into the job for three years, working killing hours, planning each day's edition, overseeing staff and payroll, making policy decisions and troubleshooting. He turned out to be good at the work, but he hated it. "For Christ's sake don't ever let 'em make you editor of a paper," he advised a friend a few years later. "It's a short-cut to insanity."[58]

44

All around Washington the drama of the early New Deal was being played out, but the *News'* business was local coverage; stories of the federal government came from Scripps-Howard and the United Press. Ernie's mind was not on the great issues of the day, but on crime, snappy features and the latest local tidbits from the streets of the District. He prodded his reporters, demanding that they "jolt" themselves — not to work harder but to "work more keenly." One of his memos to the staff was a definitive statement of his own approach to reporting and writing:

We have to *make* people read this paper, by making it so alert and saucy and important that they will be afraid of missing something if they don't read it. . . . We are asleep. Dead. . . . Get alive. Keep your eyes open. There are swell stories floating around your beats every day that you either don't see or don't bother to do anything about when you do see them. . . .

You can hardly walk down the street, or chat with a bunch of friends, without running into the germ of something that may turn up an interesting story if you're on the lookout for it. News doesn't have to be important, but it has to be interesting. You can't find interesting things, if you're not interested. . . . Always look for the story — for the unexpected human emotion in the story. . . .

> Write a story as tho it were a privilege for you to write it. . . . You don't have to be smart-alecky or pseudo-funny. Be human. Try to write like people talk.[59]

As Ernie pushed himself to do a job he disliked, Jerry became more reclusive. Holing up with her books, playing sad songs on the piano and drinking, she resisted his pleas to develop more interests and get out of the apartment. He was her only interest in life, she told him; making him happy would sustain her. Remarks by Ernie to friends years later make it clear that by now he knew his wife was troubled in depths he could not fathom. He even began to worry that she might attempt suicide.[60]

At some point during this period, Jerry discovered she was pregnant and elected to have an abortion. The timing, the circumstances of the pregnancy, Jerry's reasons for the termination — all these are matters of conjecture. But when Ernie told friends about the episode later, it was clear he had been deeply disturbed by it. He had wanted the child; she had not.[61] Her decision could only have compounded his mounting sense of hopelessness about the future.

"I . . . have failed to achieve my ambition," he wrote an old friend. "In fact my life the past few years has gone in such a routine and deadening way that I am not sure any more just what my ambitions are. I think maybe I haven't any material ambitions — rather my ambition is to be free

46

enough of material and financial worries that I can just sit and read and think. But to do that one has to get rich, and the prospects of me ever being rich are very slim indeed. . . . I get no chance to do any writing. I think that is where my greatest satisfaction lies — in writing — in expressing my feelings in print, and I don't get a chance to do it now."[62]

A decade earlier, during his first months at the *News*, Ernie had piped up during a late-night bull session to say: "You know, my idea of a good newspaper job would be just to travel around wherever you'd want to without any assignment except to write a story every day about what you'd seen."[63] Now, a decade later, he got a chance to try the idea. Recuperating from an illness, he followed his doctor's suggestion to take a long, leisurely trip across the country. He and Jerry poked about the Southwest — for which they conceived a lifelong love — then caught a slow freighter from California back to the East Coast. Aboard ship they passed many hours talking with a pleasant old gentleman who did nothing but travel the world. Ernie said later the traveler was "one of the few old men . . . who, by mere example, take the horror out of growing old." It was "the happiest three weeks of my life."[64]

They returned to Washington, and that appeared to be that. But just then the syndicated columnist Heywood Broun took a vacation, leaving a hole inside the *News*. Ernie filled it with eleven whimsical articles about his trip, and the stories made an impression around town. One who took particular note was George "Deac" Parker, Scripps-Howard's editor-in-chief. Pyle's articles "had a sort of Mark Twain quality," Parker recalled later, "and they knocked my eyes right out."[65]

Encouraged, Ernie confessed his unhappiness with his job to Lowell Mellett and resurrected his old daydream of doing a roving reporter column. Such an assignment not only would satisfy his own longings for travel and self-expression; he also believed it offered Jerry a desperately needed hope of renewal through fresh experience and a dramatic — and perpetual — change of scene. He pestered Mellett and Parker until, as Ernie recalled later, Parker said, "Oh, all right, go on and get out. You can try it a little while as an experiment. We'll see how it turns out."[66] Lee Miller would be his editor. The *News* would run the column each day, six days a week. Other Scripps-Howard papers would be allowed to pick and choose.

"I didn't like the inside work," Ernie told a reporter later. "I didn't like to be bossed . . . I didn't like to be tied down, roped in. I wanted to get out . . . get away . . . keep going."[67]

2

★★★★

"A Nice Little Column"

ROVING REPORTER, 1935–1939

Ernie wandered the western hemisphere for nearly seven years, from 1935 until early in 1942. A tramp with an expense account, he explored cities, towns and crossroads villages in forty-eight states, Alaska, Canada, Hawaii, and Central and South America. He got out of his Dodge convertible coupe to talk with thousands of people — soda jerks, millionaires, death-row inmates, movie stars, cranks, cowboys, strippers, sheepherders, strikers, bosses, promotors, sculptors, mayors, hookers, teachers, prospectors, tramps and evangelists. He wrote two and a half million words that comprise a forgotten but magnificent mosaic of the American scene in the Great Depression.

And in the process he created "Ernie Pyle."

The actual Ernie remained a bundle of contradictions and anxieties, pressured by deadlines and perpetually worried. But "Ernie Pyle" came to life as a figure of warmth and reassurance, a sensitive, self-deprecating, self-revealing, compassionate friend who shared his sadnesses and exhilarations, his daydreams and funny stories, his ornery moods and nonsensical musings, his settled prejudices and deepest meditations. In 1935, Pyle was merely a skilled newspaperman. By 1942, he had become a consummate craftsman of short prose and simultaneously shaped a mythic role for himself: an American Everyman ready for war.

"The heart of the thing"

In the latter half of the 1930s, news broke in thunderclaps — Nazi and Fascist aggression; civil war in Spain; resurgent depression; great labor strikes; the political wars of the later New Deal. It was also a time of heavyweight newspaper columnists — political tub-thumpers like Heywood Broun, Westbrook Pegler and Hugh Johnson; the chattering scandalmongers Walter Winchell and Drew Pearson; and, watching from above, the austere, intellectual Walter Lippmann, guiding presidents and other mortals through "Today and Tomorrow." Amid such news and among such giants Ernie Pyle seemed a pygmy. The heavyweights ran in hundreds of papers; Pyle's whimsical wanderlogue ran only in Scripps-Howard's twenty-four outlets, and inconsistently even in those. The column simply did not fit conventional definitions of news, and some editors doubted the wisdom of running a thousand words of it day in and day out. "It wasn't flashy, provocative, pontifical or in any way sensational," observed George Carlin, the United Feature executive who later took charge of selling Pyle in syndication. "Editors would all allow as how they liked it; a nice little column to have around but it wasn't 'essential.' "[1] Gradually, editors began to see what their readers saw — a quirky charm and a cumulative power that sharply distinguished the column from dime-a-dozen human interest features. You read Lippmann for wisdom, Pegler for controversy, Winchell for gossip, but Pyle you read for sustenance in difficult times. In Washington, a newspaper deliveryman was overheard to say, "The trouble with these column guys is they want to organize the world . . . except Pyle. Throw the rest away, but gimme Pyle."[2] When readers were polled in Scripps-Howard towns, Ernie invariably stood atop the list of favorite features among young and old, hard-up and well-to-do. An editor in Denver once told him that "kids, Civil War veterans, capitalists, professional men, and WPA workers all read everything you write that they can get."[3] Fan letters flowed in from the homebound elderly, who loved to travel in Ernie's shoes, while in Evansville, Indiana, a poll showed him to be the favorite columnist of local teenagers. In Pittsburgh, the column was thought to be especially popular among college students. In El Paso, an editor reported that "Ernie Pyle's name is as well known . . . as the police chief's,"[4] but that was nothing compared to Cleveland, where "the impression

51

soon prevails in your mind that Ernie Pyle . . . is the president of the United States. . . ."[5]

People who read Ernie Pyle every day were treated to a study in American particulars, often celebratory but often skeptical as well. His datelines, which ranged from the great cities to the tiniest dots on the map, signified the triumph of his youthful wanderlust. He sought the exotic as well as the familiar, delighting in every return to favorite places such as New Orleans and Albuquerque. He took exuberant pride in tallying new feats of geographic mastery, as when he crossed the border of his forty-eighth state (it was Utah in the fall of 1936). He sought out geographical extremes and oddities — the Northwest Angle of Minnesota, that odd chunk of the United States that juts into Ontario; the nation's southernmost place (Key West); the lowest point in the nation (Death Valley, California; ". . . you could go stand in it if you wanted to wade in the salt marsh"); the extraordinarily gradual drop in elevation in the five hundred miles between the Rocky Mountains and Oklahoma City, "the longest and gentlest slope in the world." He relished the richness of place names — Mexican Hat, Utah; Tamazunchale, Mexico ("The closest an American can come to saying it is 'Thomas 'n Charlie' "); and an Indiana village that went by four different names, depending on whether one consulted the road map, the rail depot, the Post Office or the residents. His senses were keenly attuned to local idiosyncrasies, pleasing or not. "I know within five minutes after driving into a town whether it's any good or not . . . ," he wrote. "Some cities are grouchy, some are indifferent, some are stuck-up, some have a robbery complex." He was no mere booster. The Atlantic coast from New York to Portland, Maine, he said, was "one long hideous summer resort for 400 miles, with millions of unhappy-looking people running in and out of hot dog stands in their bathrobes." When Scripps-Howard's editors in Ohio pleaded to have Pyle dispatched to talk up their depressed industrial centers in hopes of spurring tourism, Ernie was privately furious at their thinly veiled attempt to enlist him as "an all-around Chamber of Commerce mouthpiece for the flat dismal state of Ohio." He went, but took his revenge with a couple of rabbit punches: "If there's anything in this world devised to give a motorist the flibbertijibbets, it's an old, worn-out, patched-up brick pavement. For some reason, Ohio is filthy with them," and: "In northern Ohio — Akron, Cleveland, Toledo — prices are so high you get indigestion eating your meal. Hotels are up too."[6]

The column breathed the air of democracy. Other national columnists wrote down to readers from the cultural heights of New York, Washington and Hollywood, but Ernie wrote "on the level," among and about ordinary people. His trademark topics were drawn from the concrete stuff of everyday life. He resented pretense and snobbery, prized individualism and eccentricity. "Goddam all big shots," he told a friend, a sentiment that pervaded the column.[7] He far preferred "regular" people, by which he meant people innocent of class-consciousness, people "you could talk to." He suspected the mighty and embraced the low, and he held that the distance between those social extremes was much shorter than either believed. At a press conference he once appraised the spirit of the New Deal in the person and manner of Harry Hopkins, the shrewd social worker who became President Roosevelt's right-hand man:

Mr. Hopkins, I liked you because you look like common people. I don't mean any slur by that either, because they don't come any commoner than I am, but you sit there so easy swinging back and forth in your swivel chair, in your blue suit and blue shirt, and your neck is sort of skinny, like poor people's necks, and you act honest, too.

And you answer the reporters' questions as though you were talking to them personally instead of being a big official. It tickled me the way you would say, "I can't answer that," in a tone that almost says out loud, "Now you knew damn well when you asked me that I couldn't answer that."[8]

There was always a twist in his portrayal of the common man. During and after World War II it was often said that Pyle's travel writings in the 1930s were about "the ordinary human being living his ordinary life," as a Scripps-Howard editor once put it.[9] That was wrong. Ernie, following the adage that news is what departs from the norm, knew the truly ordinary was inevitably dull. It is far more accurate to say he studied *unknown* people doing *extraordinary* things. Take the month of December 1935, when he wrote of a young woman who had defied the norms of her backwoods village by forcing her father to quit abusing her (she killed him); and of an Alabama man who so loved Roman history that he built a genuine Roman temple on a hill and fitted it out as a home for himself. Or June 1936, when he wrote of a semi-literate black man who made a fortune in the logging business; and of the solid, comfortable home an old squatter had built out of materials extracted from the Memphis city dump and daubed all over with paint the colors of the rainbow.[10] Subjects like these were an apotheosis of commonness, a transformation of the ordinary into the sublime. They brought to life the American myth of self-recreation — a myth that appealed to Ernie because it lay at the heart of his own life.

He spoke to the reader directly, using the pronouns "I" and "you" with a fresh sincerity that convinced people they knew Ernie Pyle as well as they knew close friends. Because he professed to be no better or smarter than anyone else — he was always referring to himself as "a screwball" or "puny Pyle" — he could deliver judgments without seeming to preach. And he gave opinions not to persuade or instruct but simply as a friend gives them — as a conversational aside, a small sharing of oneself. When Lee Miller chopped these small phrases, as he did occasionally in the column's early years, Ernie fought back, defending "the 'little stuff' in my copy — the little personal phrases and opinions and asides, the stuff that I know was responsible for the success of the aviation column, and which I know readers do like to see, maybe just a word here and there, but really the heart of the thing."[11] He fostered the sense of intimacy with columns about his mother, father, and Aunt Mary. Though he had fled small-town life, these affectionate bulletins about the Pyles' doings in Dana made Pyle seem a champion of country ways and homespun verities. Jerry was idealized as "That Girl Who Rides With Me," or, as readers became accustomed to this little game, simply "That Girl." He might repeat a funny line of hers, or quote her pithy remark about something they'd seen, but as a rule he portrayed her in affectionate but hazy anonymity, allowing readers to fill in the empty frame with a mental portrait of an amusing and steadfast companion.

He wrote in his own masterly version of the colloquial style handed down from Mark Twain and Ring Lardner. Asked why he liked Pyle's column, an Indiana junk dealer replied, "He comes as near writing like a man talking as anybody I've ever read."[12] That was apt: Ernie's prose did flow like comfortable conversation. But few people talking off the cuff can command images as fresh and real as his. He said the weird stone spires of Utah's Bryce Canyon looked like "ten thousand pink flagpoles."[13] In the Kansas Dust Bowl, he described "the sand-laden wind . . . shooting south in thick veins, like air full of thrown baseballs."[14] His style's virtues are captured in the praise he himself once gave to an unlikely source of literature — the pithy historical signboards that dotted the highways of Montana in the 1930s. "The message is not only easy to read," Ernie wrote, "but it says something."[15]

Yet clarity was not Pyle's only aim as a stylist. Few readers guessed how carefully he attended to the cadence of a sentence or the choice of a word. He was embarrassed to admit it, the tough overseers of daily journalism being infamously skeptical of artistic aspirations. In the summer of 1936, fighting an early battle against his editor's pencil, he told Lee Miller, "You'll probably think I've gone nuts . . . but lots of times when I'm describing some scene or feeling, I try to make it sound almost like music, and I think sometimes it does, and I think it does to readers, even though they may not be specifically conscious of it. And often the dropping of a word or the cutting of one sentence into two shorter ones destroys the whole rhythm of it."[16] Ernie's quest for something "like music" often succeeded, as in this meditation in the Berkshires: "I must come someday and roam New England with greater leisure, and really know the things that now I am only beginning to sense, as you might sense the odor of fresh earth after the thaw, too young yet to know that it portends spring."[17] Or this scene from the grasslands of Montana's Powder River country, once lovely but now devastated by overgrazing and drought:

> The beautiful rolling green hills are bare, the color of the graveled road. Only now and then do you see a bunch of cattle; the others have prematurely gone to market, lest they wither away. The squat, treeless houses sit in the pitiless sun, far from the road, as always. Around them you see long rows of rusty, motionless machinery. You see the few work horses huddled along a dry creek, swishing the flies. There is no work for them in the fields. The farmers and cattlemen patch fences, or do chores, or just sit and wait.[18]

To follow Ernie's daily column was to achieve a fleeting but satisfactory freedom. He offered Depression-era readers the vicarious experience of an ageless American act — to "light out for the Territory," in Huckleberry Finn's words, to cast off the confining cords of civilization and pursue an ever-receding frontier. The romance of the open road, running as deep in the American tradition as the westward movement, ran always through Ernie's writing. A reader confined to a dreary desk or farm always found Ernie in some new spot, nourishing the reader's vicarious pleasure with reports of his own delight in sighting a new horizon and setting off. "The happiest I am at any time on a long trip is when we have been laid up several days in one place and then finally one morning we pack up, check out, fill up with gas, and light out into open country," he wrote. "Once in that car and under way, we don't have to talk to anybody, keep up with events . . . answer letters, remember things, or grudgingly fit ourselves into other people's worlds. We are alone, and free."[19]

The column was often light and humorous, yet a vein of melancholy ran through it, revealing the obscure sorrows of the boy feeling the "wind of futility" against his face. When Ernie's editors sent him to the drought-stricken Dust Bowl regions of the upper plains in the summer of 1937, he came away awed by that "withering land of misery."

> You get to accept it as a vast land that is dry and bare, and was that way yesterday and will be tomorrow, and was that way a hundred miles back and will be a hundred miles ahead. The story is the same everywhere, the farmers say the same thing, the fields look the same — it becomes like the drone of a bee, and after a while you hardly notice it at all.

It is that way all day. It is only at night, when you are alone in the enveloping heat and cannot sleep, and look into the darkness, and things come back to you like a living dream, that you once more realize the stupendousness of it.

Then you can see something more than field after brown field. . . . You can see then the whole backward evolution into oblivion of a great land, and the destruction of a people, and the calamity of long years on end without privilege for those of the soil, and the horror of a life started in emptiness, knowing only struggle, and ending in despair.[20]

He showed a remarkable capacity for identifying with sufferers. In fact, it was more than a capacity; it was a compulsion. This was never more evident during his travel years than in the fall of 1937, when he visited the leper colony of Kalaupapa on the Hawaiian island of Molokai. At a time when leprosy bore the stigma of "uncleanness" and shame, it was a dreaded place. Journalists were not allowed there for more than a couple of hours, but Ernie received special permission to visit for several days. His columns about it breathed an otherworldly air. "Roaming Kalaupapa," he wrote, "I felt a kind of unrighteousness at being whole and 'clean'; I experienced an acute feeling of spiritual need to be no better off than the leper. It wasn't a romantic feeling, it wasn't drama — it was something akin to that sorcery that lures people standing on high places to leap downward. My feeling will likely impress you as ridiculous fiction. But I did experience it . . ."[21]

As Ernie circled the nation with his nose to his deadline, he had little time to notice the extraordinary number of writers, artists, moviemakers and photographers who were engaged in their own intensive study of their native land. They were part of what historians would later see as a great upsurge in cultural nationalism — an exploring of America's roots and a celebration of American culture. The movement was *Life* magazine's stark photographic portraits of southern sharecroppers and migrant workers. It was the craze for historical fiction such as Margaret Mitchell's *Gone with the Wind.* It was composer Aaron Copland's *Hymn to the Common Man* and Martha Graham's *American Document* ballet. It was the Federal Writers' Project's forgotten masterpiece, the magisterial, 378-volume *American Guide*, whose hero was the ordinary American multiplied by a million. It was the brooding cityscapes of Edward Hopper, who told his fellow artists that "a nation's art is greatest when it most reflects the character of its people."[22]

By the late thirties, the celebration of America was taking on a distinctly defensive tone. With each ominous advance by the legions of Hitler, Mussolini and Franco, the approaching world crisis increasingly overshadowed the nation's domestic life. Fears of home-grown fascism, fanned by the rise of demagogues like Senator Huey Long and Father Charles Coughlin, rattled nerves. Was democracy doomed? Only a few years earlier, American writers had been fired with a will to transform the nation in order to lift it out of depression. Now they became desperate simply to preserve the nation in preparation for war, "to see the real nature of the traditions that we are trying to save . . . in order to gain new strength for the struggles ahead," as the critic Malcolm Cowley put it.[23] For most socially aware writers, political and economic reform remained an ultimate goal, but "their primary emphasis," says the historian William Stott, "was on what they felt to be constant and valid in American experience."[24]

And what was constant and valid? By 1940, the answer was being trumpeted from movie screens, Post Office walls, and the essays of the literary elite: the People, the ordinary American of factory and farm, the Common Man. In great public murals, WPA artists enshrined the Common Man and Woman as custodians of folk wisdom, symbols of frontier strength and industry, sources of the nation's salvation. In *Our Town*, Thornton Wilder discovered deep wells of quiet resilience. The plain man of Main Street rose up as Frank Capra's Jefferson Smith in *Mr. Smith Goes to Washington*, a fiery preacher of American integrity. Henry Fonda became not only the downtrodden Tom Joad of *The Grapes of Wrath*, but also *Abe Lincoln of Illinois*, the archetypal common man.

With his keen ear for harmonies between the ordinary and the sublime, with his plain name and his country-boy style, Ernie Pyle would soon come to symbolize what the cultural nationalists meant when they wrote so feelingly of "the people." At a time when the rural/urban balance had tilted decidedly in favor of the cities, he reminded anxious city folk of the old farm ways. In an era of narrowed opportunities and disappointed hopes, he symbolized freedom and fresh starts. After December 7, 1941, the romantic ideal of "the People" would become a central symbol of the nation at war. The homespun wisdom, the small-town integrity, the clear-eyed vision — all would be distilled and focused into a single human image in combat garb, skinny and humble, the Common Man gone to war.

"The ogre this job has become . . ."

"I have no home," Ernie once wrote during this period. "My home is where my extra luggage is, and where the car is stored, and where I happen to be getting mail this time. My home is America."

This was no romantic exaggeration. He and Jerry lived as nomads. Jerry's piano and furniture sat in storage in Washington. Extra clothes hung in closets in Dana. Blankets and books were packed away in Jerry's sister's house in Denver. When Ernie checked into a hotel, he entered the address of the *Daily News* in the guest register. When he and Jerry set out in 1935, everything they needed fit into only six suitcases and satchels. Even as they accumulated more possessions over the years, they needed no more than ten bags, though a motley collection of extras accumulated in the cracks. As Ernie cleaned out the car in mid-1938 he hauled out "four double armloads" of stuff, including scores of old magazines, fifty or so road maps, several huge manila envelopes crammed with mail, some souvenir rocks, some Alaskan furs, and a stone fish they had bought in Wyoming.[25] The Pyles carried so many books they were sometimes mistaken for publishers' representatives. Their clothes were a hodgepodge, purchased as needed. Reviewing their combined wardrobe one day in 1937, Ernie found items bought in Maine, Arizona, California, Colorado, Minnesota, Manitoba, Alabama, Indiana, Mexico and New York City.[26]

The latest edition of the American Automobile Association's *Hotel Directory* sat close at hand. When they approached a new town, one of them would run a finger down the list in search of a medium-priced hotel. (The high-priced places were invariably "without individuality or warmth," Ernie believed.)[27] If they liked a place, a penciled checkmark was inserted next to the listing, a reminder for the next time they came through town.[28] They seldom found themselves in a room that didn't suit them, and they rarely paid as much as five dollars for a night's lodgings. By Ernie's estimate they stayed in some eight hundred hotels during their traveling years.[29] Some they visited so often that maids and desk clerks became old friends. Returning to a favorite such as the Hotel Hungerford in Seattle, where they often stayed in an eighth-floor suite overlooking the misted city and Puget Sound, was "just like getting back home."[30]

Luggage was carefully packed and arranged in the same way each morning by Ernie, the well-organized member of the pair. When they were staying somewhere for a few days, two bags and Ernie's typewriter went inside with them each evening. When the visit was for one night only, they wouldn't unpack at all, simply removing items from the bags as needed.

Hotel bills, meals, tips and other essential expenses were all paid by Scripps-Howard, and the Pyles held costs to a minimum, always worried lest the home office consider their roaming too expensive. Ernie's breakfast on the road was an unvarying ritual — orange juice, one medium-boiled egg, crisp bacon, dry toast, coffee or milk — for which he paid as little as 30 cents in Memphis and as much as $1.25 in Lake Louise, British Columbia, a price that flabbergasted him.[31] Lunch, an institution he disliked, often consisted only of fruit or a chocolate bar, and dinner for the couple seldom came to more than two or three dollars. Total costs for their first day on the road in 1935, including hotel, came to $5.80.[32] Ernie, choosing his routes from ordinary service station maps, rarely averaged more than 40 miles per hour. Sometimes he would cover three hundred miles in a day, but he was often content to drive only a small fraction of that distance.

In the early years of traveling the Pyles seldom minded the absence of a home or their own furniture and special objects of affection. "I don't think [Jerry] gave a darn about *things*," Harriet Hendrixson remarked.[33] Nor did Ernie. Yet many months passed before this strange, gypsy life seemed normal. At first "there were times when I'd have that terrible 'lost' feeling," Ernie confessed after eighteen months on the road. "We'd stop in a ratty hotel in a gloomy town in some thinly populated and drear part of the country, and at dusk I'd feel alone, and foreign, and blue."[34] But "constant wandering grows on a fellow," he said, and the uneasiness passed — though he did occasionally awaken in the night and have to retrace his route for the past several days to figure out where he was.

It was a hard life. "One story a day sounds as easy as falling off a log," he once told his readers. "Try it sometime."[35]

Friends kidded Ernie that he had things easy, that his life was a perpetual vacation. In fact, he toiled almost without letup, always struggling to build or maintain his precious "cushion" — the number of columns completed before his deadline. A big cushion meant he could breathe easily, or at least work less frenetically, for a few days. He almost never missed deadlines, but his cushion was seldom very thick. Other daily columnists wrote just as much, of course, but most of them wrote from a single city (Washington, New York or Hollywood) about a single inexhaustible topic (politics or celebrity gossip) relying on a stable of well-known sources. Ernie, by contrast, wrote on the run, changing locales constantly and digging up fantastically diverse topics among people he had never met. The ever present deadline hung over his shoulder like a malevolent schoolmarm, constantly accusing him of sloth and delay. In fact, a weekly workload of six columns — based not on off-the-cuff opinion but on real reporting — was just this side of impossible, and to tackle it month in and month out was a labor of Herculean proportions. His regimen, he once said, demanded "five halves to every day — half for digging up material, half to write it, half for visiting old friends, half for sleeping, and half for traveling."[36] Instead of growing easier with time and experience, Ernie told a reporter in 1937, "I find that writing this one story a day is harder now than when I began."[37]

It was one of the column's attractions, of course, that Ernie seemed to be leading a fantasy life of leisurely wandering. He encouraged readers to see him that way. Consider a stretch of nineteen columns published in the spring of 1939 after Ernie toured the Four Corners region of the American Southwest, the wild vastness of mountain and desert where the boundaries of Colorado, New Mexico, Arizona and Utah converge to form a cross on the map. Ernie's account of the trip was the diary of a man at ease, eager to sample every sight and sound along his meandering path, pausing to enjoy "sweeping vistas of sagebrush," the "deep, clean silence" of a mountain summit, the deserted cabin of a hermit, the weird magnificence of Monument Valley. He had time to seek out the isolated wooden post that marked the exact latitude and longitude of the Four Corners — "Nobody but some screwball like me would think of coming out here to write about it" — and he delighted in recounting his boyish feat of sitting in four states at once, eating lunch in four states at once, and littering four states at once. He had time to chat with an odd assortment of absorbing characters, including a ten-year-old cowgirl, an aging cowboy who had chucked civilization to retire to the desert, and one Parley Butt, an ancient Mormon settler, "ugly as a mud fence," who, upon being elected to the Utah legislature by the margin of a single vote, had declined to serve, saying, "if that was the best they could do, nuts to 'em." There was time left over to shoot the rapids of the San Juan River and to meditate on life beside the lonely gravesite of a desert Indian. But the picture of a man at leisure was an illusion. In readers' newspapers, the Four Corners trip stretched over nearly three weeks' worth of columns. In fact, the traveling had been crammed into just seven days of rough driving over a thousand miles of dirt roads, followed by a week in an Arizona tourist cabin where Ernie, feeling "goddam lousy" with a desert sunburn and a nasty cold, had produced a raw block of 30,000 words, then sculpted that mass down to 20,000, enough to fill fifty pages of a book.[38]

Sometimes he would drive and do interviews by day, then set his typewriter on some narrow hotel desk and write half the night. More often he would spend several days doing nothing but observing and interviewing, then spend several days just writing. In either case the words came with difficulty, sometimes with extreme difficulty. Once in the spring of 1936 he described his routine in the third person, saying that after a typical day of reporting, "he sits down to write, and doesn't feel like it, and keeps struggling away until midnight, and then tears everything up and says to himself 'Oh I'll write it tomorrow.' That's the way it is, day after day, and there are days when a fellow doesn't get anything done at all."[39] A few weeks later he wrote in a similar vein to Miller from aboard a cruise ship on Lake Erie: "This is a very fine boat and we're on a very fine lake. The people who think what a swell job I have should see me here in my stuffy little cabin, no shirt on, writing on a chair, turning out seven pieces in three days at sea, while all the other people read and walk and have fun. Goddamit. All the water I've seen is what comes out of the tap."[40]

"About one day in six months I really lead the kind of life my friends think I lead all the time," he told readers that summer. "That is — nothing at all to do."[41]

In bad moments he feared the columns weren't good enough. During his first trip to Mexico in early 1937, Ernie sent six "lousy" columns to Miller with a half-kidding vow to "start back as soon as we get ourselves squared away, then sell out and go back to the farm, which I never should have left in the first place."[42] Miller, Parker and Mellett immediately wired him back, saying, "YOUR STUFF EXCELLENT QUIT WORRYING ABOUT IT."[43]

"That was grand of you to send me that wire," Pyle responded. "I hate to think I have to be babied . . . but I suppose I do. I'm not worried about what anybody thinks of my stuff; I'm worried about the fact that when I sit down to write I haven't any emotion or enthusiasm. . . . I worry . . . that maybe I'm just a flash in the pan, and that I'm written out."[44] Sending Miller a plea to preserve the column's small colloquialisms, he apologized for his sensitivity to editing, saying, "I'm not trying to be any prima donna, as you must surely know, but I am so interested in the column, and I'm also cursed with such a touchiness and melancholia. I feel that my stuff at its very best is only just barely good enough. . . ."[45]

By 1937 it was obvious that Ernie's fears of cancellation were unfounded. What threatened the column was not official disapproval but Ernie's own exhaustion and self-doubt. Complaints and vows to quit became constant refrains in letters to friends. He daydreamed of doing nothing but sitting and reading for months, or of quitting to make and sell jewelry. It is an irony that Pyle, for all his mastery of his form, did not in the end have the temperament for the assembly-line production demanded of a daily columnist. Three years into his self-imposed hitch, he told close friends — E.H. Shaffer, editor of Scripps-Howard's *Albuquerque Tribune*, and Shaffer's wife, Elizabeth, a magazine writer — that his recent columns had been "inconceivably rotten." He was "just tired as hell of being alive, and writing columns, and looking at myself. I think if I don't get out from under this pressure of always a column tomorrow I'm going nuts. . . . I firmly expect them to suggest that I try reading copy on the Birmingham Post for awhile. . . . Do you know of any nice little business propositions out there for a broken down newspaperman?"[46]

Yet he continued, and his difficulties increased.

Fan mail became too great a chore for him to handle alone, yet even when a secretary was hired in Washington to help with routine replies, his own stack of unanswered correspondence tugged at his sleeve. Over the years the Pyles acquired a small army of acquaintances who assumed, whenever the Pyles returned to town for a new round of reporting, that Ernie and Jerry were free for socializing, and the Pyles could seldom say no to an invitation. At these times Ernie's cushion dwindled dangerously. During a two-week stay in Hollywood in 1938 they spent time — not just once but repeatedly — with, among others, a close family friend from Dana; an aviator friend and his wife; two old prospectors Ernie had befriended in Alaska; the parents of his goddaughter; Scripps-Howard's cartoonist and his wife; a woman Ernie had known at the Washington airport; a friend from New York days; a *Daily News* colleague; a Filipino friend whom Ernie had smuggled across the Pacific to enroll at Indiana University in 1922; and Paige Cavanaugh; not to mention new acquaintances from the movie studios. Ernie could have turned down the invitations, but he didn't, perhaps believing that Jerry deserved some fun after long periods of solitary confinement with only Ernie for company. After too many hours of talk and drink, Ernie would finally flee to some hotel room to catch up with his writing. "The thing is so damned hard because people can't realize that I actually have to work," he complained to Lee Miller. "[T]hey feel that I'm practically on vacation; they don't realize that I work at reporting all day and must have the nights for writing. The only way I could have full time for myself would be simply to refuse to see or talk to

72

any of my friends, and Christ I can't do that. For in the first place I like them and do want to see them, and in the second place I'd be put down, and correctly, as a horse's ass if I started that. So what the hell to do I don't know. I'm amazed that I've been able to keep the column going at all."[47]

He was always tired, and he complained of being sick so often that the reader of his letters can only conclude that drinking, anxiety, fatigue and stress were sapping his body of its strength. He nursed colds for weeks at a time. When he was too hot he got tiny water blisters on his hands. When he felt too much stress his eyes went "out of focus." His chronic illnesses became a running gag between him and his readers — "Puny Pyle's Perpetual Pains" — but they were real enough to keep him in bed on a regular basis. A list of ailments he reported to friends early in 1938 was not at all unusual: "cold, cough, nervous tension in neck; an aching tooth; fingers split open from chapping; worst sinus I've had since 1923; drunkenness; and general mental confusion."[48] Drunkenness was a common state for Ernie. If he spoke of cutting back, he meant cutting back to two full glasses of "hard stuff" every evening before dinner. With friends, he often would get drunk nearly every night for days at a time, sometimes consuming so much he could remember nothing of the episodes the next day.

At times pressure and fear drove him down

into outright depression. One summer, on a solitary trip through the Midwest, he got so low he holed up in a hotel room in Chillicothe, Ohio, for three days, frozen by "anguish and lonesomeness."[49] "I've been so damn homesick and melancholy, clear down to the depths," he wrote Jerry, who was recovering from an illness in Washington. "I just don't see how we can go on with this ogre that the job has become. I wish we had the nerve to quit before it completely destroys us. The pleasure in the freedom of the job has become only occasional little flashes, and the pressure of day-after-day writing and all the correlary [sic] distractions that have come with it, have become a specter to me; and I know to you too. But what the hell is a guy to do? I don't know."[50] Hoping exotic scenes might revive his yen for the job, he booked passage for an extended tour of South America in the fall. But the trip had just the opposite effect, sending Ernie into "the mental doldrums and [a] melancholic dungeon for damn near three months. . . ."[51]

About this time, a photographer friend captured Ernie in a revealing study in Scripps-Howard's Washington office. Silhouetted against a window, his red hair is graying at the temples, his long neck thin in an unbuttoned collar. His shirtsleeves billow on bony arms. Veins stand out in his tense hands. The tendons in his neck are taut. Ernie's worried face peers back over his shoulder, the brow creased. It is

74

the face of a man in the vise of midlife, discontented in the present and uneasy about the future. Yet he was only thirty-seven.

Some time in 1937 the notion of selling Pyle's work to papers beyond the chain — through United Feature Syndicate, owned by Scripps-Howard — was discussed among the concern's top editors. Roy Howard quickly quashed the idea, insisting that writers he paid should appear only in newspapers he owned. ("The little dog in the manger," Ernie remarked privately.)[52] Hearing that Deac Parker was still advancing the idea, Ernie hinted of his interest, though he had little confidence the brass would make haste, telling friends, "probably by the time I'm all written out and never want to see another new town or write another column, they'll have it all fixed."[53]

When the prospect of syndication suddenly became quite real the next year, the struggle between ambition and self-doubt rose to the surface.

In February 1938, the death of the popular columnist O. O. McIntyre revived the issue. McIntyre wrote light feature material in a "down-home" style, so Pyle was seen as a natural successor who might take over McIntyre's syndicated slot in several hundred newspapers. "As a writer McIntyre was not in Ernie's class in my judgment," John Sorrells, Scripps-Howard's executive editor, told a colleague. "But the writings of both are characterized by a gentle whole-someness and wide-eyed country boy absorption with homely but essential trivia. It seems to me that the time is ripe to make more capital out of Pyle's column."[54] The major obstacle tumbled when Roy Howard dropped his objections. So, at a high-level Scripps-Howard gathering at Miramar, the California ranch of Robert P. Scripps, Deac Parker broached the idea with Ernie. His first instinct was to throw cold water on the idea. The column's unspectacular char-acter would make it hard to sell, he said, and it would take months to catch on with new readers. They left it at that, with Parker saying no action would be taken immediately.[55]

Ernie stewed. Contrary to what he had told Parker, his real fear was not that syndication would fail, but that it would succeed. Syndication would mean more money and wider influence, both of which appealed to him, however seldom he allowed himself to admit it. What "scared the hell out of me," he admitted to Lee Miller, was the threat syndication posed to his freedom to cut and run. Sitting in a hotel room in Hollywood, working on columns about a topic he detested — the movie industry — he pondered the implica-tions of syndication with mounting dread.

I don't know what the hell to do [he wrote Miller]. I told Deac I wasn't ambitious to be a great name or make a preposterous amount of money; that all I wanted was to make enough to build up some security for myself. The thing that frightens me worst is that if the thing should go over and get to running in a lot of papers, then a fellow would feel like he couldn't quit if he wanted to (or I'm afraid I couldn't). And that's always been part of my happiness in a job, that I felt the independence to quit a job anytime I felt like it. . . .

Aw to hell with it, I wish nobody had ever thought of it in the first place. I want it and I don't want it.[56]

That night he and Jerry discussed the matter at length. Both of them, Ernie told Miller the next day, were

afraid of stepping into the big-time stuff, if that should come about.

I don't mean that I'm afraid I can't do good enough columns; but we're afraid of the responsibility and harassments and lack of any private life that is bound to come with it; in fact, has come enough already to show us what might lie ahead. . . .

I'm afraid of being built into a position where I can't quit. It's all sort of a muddle in my brain right now; we love the traveling and it would be awfully hard for us to quit. But it has built itself into such a complicated thing; and writing has become so terribly difficult for me (I spend more time trying to write than I do in reporting); there's hardly a moment in our lives, except when we're actually driving down the road, where we have time or composure to be ourselves with each other or to enjoy life at all. I love to write, as you know, but I'm afraid that a column a day of this type, especially of the standard I try to keep up, is too much for a human being. It becomes an ogre and you fight it day and night. . . . As Jerry said, probably what I need most is a six-months mental vacation — but if a column is dropped for six months, it has sunk. So I don't know.[57]

But as he drove slowly eastward from California over the next several weeks, Ernie realized that he and his "ogre" were lashed together tightly indeed. "Although I'm afraid of the consequences . . . ," he told Miller, "I know also that I don't want to quit and go back on the rim somewhere, and a guy has to eat. So I suppose the thing to do is try to get syndication. And I suppose the sooner the better."[58] In May, the Pyles reached Washington. Ernie conferred with Miller, then the two flew to New York for a chilly meeting with George Carlin, head of United Feature. Carlin, accustomed to selling rights to the biggest names in American journalism, hinted that a small fry like Pyle would make a hard sell in the recession then afflicting the industry. Perhaps he would try to peddle the column in the autumn, he said. In the meantime, could Miller and Pyle collect some promotional materials to explain why an editor might want to take Pyle on?[59]

Early in 1939, Ernie and Jerry were wandering north through the South from Florida. Ernie was writing about poor sharecroppers and tenant farmers. In a bleak backwater of Louisiana, Ernie stopped to look for a relative, his uncle Clarence Pyle, one of Will's brothers, whom Ernie hadn't seen for many years. Knowing only that Clarence and his wife lived in the vicinity, Ernie and Jerry searched from farm to farm. Up one dirt lane he knocked on the door of a rude, unpainted shack, squalid and dirty. An old man appeared.

Did he know where Clarence Pyle could be found, Ernie asked.

"Right here," his uncle replied.

Ernie knew Clarence had fallen on hard times, but this scene was far worse than he had imagined — "two old people, cooking, eating, sleeping all in one room," he told friends. "They have one mule; 12 stumpy acres. They haven't a rocking chair. Uncle Clarence has no clothes but overalls." Ernie could judge a farm's value and he knew this one was "at the bottom." Clarence and Aunt Axie's things could have fit "in one wagon bed." What pained him most was the way Clarence, at the end of their visit, said good-bye, standing at his old gate and saying what an honor it had been to receive "a visit from Ernie Pyle." That "almost broke my heart," he told his parents, "for I am nothing especially and it's no 'honor' to have me visit them. I think he hated for me to see how they are living, but I was glad that he didn't apologize for anything . . . except . . . he said it seemed the older you got the harder you had to work. . . . It seemed so pitiful, after 40 years of hard work, to wind up living just as bad as the most poverty-stricken farmers of the deep south that I've just been writing about."[60]

He could not shake the experience. "[H]onest to Christ I've hardly been able to swallow for two days for thinking about him," Ernie wrote to Cavanaugh, and to the Shaffers he said: "I have never been so heart-broken in my life, and I just can't get over it." He would never end his days as a broken-down old farmer, he knew. But what he had just seen must have seemed only too similar to his nightmare image of a washed-up, rummy old newspaperman.[61]

In the spring of 1939, the wind seemed to shift, stirring hope in Ernie's aching mind. First came news that several large papers had picked up the column. Then came the invigorating Four Corners trip, which persuaded Ernie temporarily that he had not lost his writing touch.

"I believe things will pick up now . . . ," he told Jerry in a letter that summer. "I feel pretty good. . . ."[62]

"Too much war blab . . ."

When the Nazi-Soviet Non-Aggression Pact

was signed in Moscow on August 23, 1939, sounding the death knell of Poland and awakening England and France to their peril, Ernie lay under layers of sheets and blankets in his favorite Seattle hotel, nursing yet another cold. He and Jerry seized all the newspapers they could find, scanning the columns for war news. "Things are so black in Europe we can't think of anything else," Ernie wrote his parents.[63] The Pyles were worried about Lee Miller and his new wife, who were aboard a ship bound for England. But they felt a broader foreboding, too. "All these crises over the past couple of years we've never paid much attention to," Ernie wrote the Millers, "but something got in us about this one, and we've felt right from the first day . . . that this one was going to be war — not a war to end war, but a war to end everything. I've even been dreaming about it, and couldn't half sleep at night."[64]

Yet his dread quickly turned to an itch to see the action for himself, an old newspaperman's instinct that seized him whenever a really big story raised its head. First he kidded about his impulse to get abroad, telling Miller to meet him in Europe "and we'll become famous war correspondents. Dr. Miller can go to the front and be a hero and I will write 'homey' stuff from Wales or Denmark."[65] As war began and Hitler's Panzer divisions moved across western Poland in the first weeks of September, he could hardly keep his mind on his writing. Ernie's old disappointment of the spring of 1918, when Thad Hooker went to war and he stayed behind, gnawed at him. "Personally, I'm just about to bust I want to get over there as a war correspondent or something so bad . . . ," he told Cavanaugh. "Pacifism is fine as long as there ain't no war around. But when they start shooting I want to get close enough just a couple of times to get good and scared. For the last two weeks I've been so goddam bored writing silly dull columns about Mt. Hood . . . that I think I'm going nuts."[66]

As Ernie pondered how to sell his editors on a European trip, Jerry resisted fiercely. Then, just as she relented, Ernie began to change his mind. By the end of September he was telling friends the war bored him — though at night he still lay awake, "trying not to think of what it is going to do to all of us in the next few years."[67] In the first rush of events he had imagined people might like to read "my kind of war stuff," but then thought better of the idea. Censorship would make his approach impossible, he believed, and besides, he told Miller, "readers really do want a relief from war-writing. At least until and if we should get into it ourselves, when of course everything would go by the boards."[68] If this was worry-prone Pyle talking, he would eventually give way before the energetic patriot. But not until America itself joined the war.

From Seattle, the Pyles wandered south through Portland and along the Pacific coast into California. Ernie watched a car race in Oakland, covered a bedmaking contest in San Francisco, toured a chinchilla farm. In the East, friends told him, the war seemed real and urgent, but here he sensed a curious placidity among the people he met — not indifference to the war, but a fatalistic belief that U.S. involvement was inevitable, and at the same time, an unsettling naïveté about what that involvement might mean.

Just before Christmas 1939, the Pyles reached New Orleans, where Ernie made plans for a trip to Central America that would include a visit to the Panama Canal. With Hitler's submarine "wolf packs" prowling the Atlantic, and German fifth columnists suspected in Latin America, the canal loomed larger than ever in the fortress of American strategy, and the issue of the Army's readiness for an attack on the Canal Zone was attracting comment in the United States. This made Panama a "serious" story, and thus anathema to Ernie. He said as much to Lee Miller, who had returned from Europe and was planning his own reporting tour of defense installations throughout the western hemisphere.

"As for Panama she's all yours brother," Ernie told his friend. "I hope the office won't even suggest that I do any military columns down there. . . .

"If there's one thing in this world I hate and detest, it is writing about the Army."[69]

3

★★★★

"A Slightly Used Secondhand Man..."

MAY 1940–JANUARY 1943

Ernie stayed healthy throughout the Pyles' two-month tour of Central America. But soon after they flew to Florida in February 1940 and began to motor northward, physical aches and mental depression gradually slowed his pace to a crawl. "I have been lower . . . than I've ever been in my life," he told Cavanaugh. "I guess maybe I've got a psychosis of some kind, and better have myself looked into."[1] Three days of tests in a Memphis clinic revealed no psychosis but certainly a bad case of nerves — specifically, a stomach spasm brought on by tension and exhaustion, plus low blood pressure and anemia.

Ordered to rest, he and Jerry drove south to the Mississippi Gulf Coast, where Fred and Ann Moreton, old friends from aviation days, owned a home near the water in Biloxi. For three columnless weeks Ernie rode a bicycle, read books and played three hundred and fifty hands of Solitaire. This left plenty of time for reading the newspapers, which was why, in spite of the enforced regimen of rest and warmth, he was

84

still sniffling from a cold and nursing a painful knot in the back of his head when the three weeks were up.

For on May 10, a week after the Pyles arrived on the coast, the papers brought news that German divisions had crossed the borders of Holland, Belgium and Luxembourg. On the 15th, Ernie read of the devastation of Rotterdam from the air; on the 16th that German tanks had penetrated the French frontier; and on the 20th that the French army was in flight and that the Germans were harrying the British Expeditionary Force toward the Channel port of Dunkirk.

It was a time when crawling panic seemed a logical response to events. When Ernie suggested that he might like to cross the Atlantic to get a look at the war, the normally unflappable Lee Miller shot back: "Europe is OUT. Good God, there won't be any Europe in a week or two."[2] So Ernie glumly dealt his Solitaire hands and tuned in the radio news. "Can't think of anything else" but the war, he told Miller, though "half of these dopes down here don't even know there is one."[3] He slept well and didn't drink, yet his strength remained at low ebb. "I think, if I must be a self-analyst, that the war has considerable to do with my slow picking up . . . ," he told friends. "I've been so saturated with horror and despondency over it that I couldn't see much point in living. The slaughter has been so terrible and the Allied efforts so discouraging."[4]

He and his friend Fred Moreton spent hours on the beach, discussing the distant battle as they watched the smooth surface of the Gulf. Resuming the column, Ernie wrote: "The birds sing all night down here, and sometimes I waken deep in the night, and the birds are gay out there in the dark stillness, and I can picture the lovely magnolia tree in the back yard, and everything is so hushed and gentle and sweet, and I wonder if ever again in this world there can be such peace as this."[5]

"Hopeless both ways"

For Ernie there would be no peace. From now on, the world crisis and the disintegration of his personal life would swirl about him ever more swiftly. In the end he would have no choice but to surrender and allow himself to be sucked into the maelstrom.

By this point Ernie knew that his efforts to rescue Jerry from emotional oblivion through constant travel had only put off an inevitable crisis. While he went about talking with people and seeing sights, sometimes for several days at a time, Jerry sat alone in an endless series of hotel rooms, working puzzles, reading and drinking. Her routine on the road, Ernie later concluded, had been essentially "empty and meaningless."[6] Others who knew her well agreed. "It didn't matter to Jerry whether the room was in a hotel in Rio de Janeiro or Kansas City," Paige

Cavanaugh recalled. "She never looked out anyway."[7] To many who met her, Jerry continued to seem spritely and engaging in these years. Her wit was sharp. She read widely and seriously. At parties she could join in uproarious fun. But in private her energies were consumed in self-loathing. As the years passed, the depressions were compounded by alcoholism and abuse of amphetamines to the point of suicidal despair. Self-mocking remarks in her few surviving letters offer glimpses of her ordeal. She was a "worm," she said, or "a wash-out in so many . . . respects," or a member of "The Society of the Contributors of Nothing to Posterity."[8]

One collapse had followed another. During the Pyles' trip to Hawaii in 1937, she suffered an alcohol-related breakdown. In the spring of 1938 she entered a sanitarium for several days after a prolonged drinking siege with Ernie and friends. She suffered a more dangerous collapse in December of that year, at the end of a tour of South America. Frightened, she appeared to rally so strongly that Ernie could tell Miller a year later that "Jerry has had her battle out, and she's won it."[9] But within weeks it became obvious that she had been fooling him, and was drinking as much as ever.

The effects on her marriage were devastating. What had begun as a companionship of unusual mutual devotion became a tortured dance of partners who could neither find contentment nor break free of the bonds that locked them together. Ernie was at a loss. He knew little about mental illness and believed alcoholism could be tempered simply by "cutting down." He doubted that Jerry would submit to a psychiatric evaluation — a fear that later proved well founded, at least for a time. And she was so often her old self, vibrant and companionable, that he could justifiably believe her miseries to be temporary and remediable. If only she would decide once and for all to become well, he believed, she could do so. When she did not, slipping again and again into drinking and depression, his hopes dissolved in bewilderment and frustration. He continued to be tied to her by strong bonds of affection and history, but the relationship had less and less of the reality of a marriage.

By the summer of 1940 he felt detached enough from Jerry to allow himself a brief but intense affair with a young woman he met while traveling alone in Indiana. This represented a long stride away from Jerry, a betrayal of the mutual trust and devotion they had always shared. Yet he no sooner had left Indiana than he became absorbed in the idea of building a house in New Mexico, hoping this anchor might restore Jerry to stability, perhaps even provide their marriage with a new sense of purpose. "I have a feeling it is gravely important for us," Ernie told Cavanaugh. "Somehow this past cut-up summer has sort of curdled our companionship and Jerry, desperate within herself since the day she was born, has seemed to become more so. I have a feeling that the only possible peace for her, even though it may be temporary, is a new interest and then a possibility for solitude out there. . . . I am terribly afraid of our future as we're going now; if the business in New Mexico can offer her a minute of contentment, I'll jump at it. It isn't this job as such that's doing it; it's people and harrassment [sic] and no time to think. We've thrashed it over a good many times, and I've been ready to quit, but we both realize we're in a trap where I can't quit. . . . [A] step-back into financial worry would throw us into a more helpless despond than we're now in. In other words it seems hopeless both ways."[10]

Ernie bought a corner lot in an Albuquerque subdivision and hired a contractor to build "a regular little boxed-up mass production shack" — a two-bedroom, green and white ranch house whose chief attraction would be a spectacular view across the Rio Grande and the immense flatlands stretching to the west. For a time Jerry seemed to take an interest. Yet she soon confided to friends that "the situation seems to me as diabolically ironical as any ever devised."[11]

The irony was obvious. There would be no settling down. Ernie was leaving again.

"A small voice said, 'Go' "

With France in ruins by the end of June 1940, Hitler had swung his gaze across the English

Channel. By August the planes of the German Luftwaffe were pounding the English countryside. In September, bombs began to fall on London. Americans looked on with rising fear as isolationists and interventionists waged a great battle for public opinion. The crucial question was whether Britain was beyond the point of saving. Each day, in American farmhouses and city apartments and suburban kitchens, radios were switched on and dials carefully adjusted to catch the sober baritone of a CBS reporter named Edward R. Murrow saying, "*This* is London," with the noise of raining bombs and antiaircraft guns in the background.

Traveling through the East, Ernie listened as avidly as anyone. "The war is beginning to get me down," he wrote Cavanaugh. "Reading about London actually makes me sick at my stomach."[12] In Washington he sat for a long time with W. P. Simms, Scripps-Howard's courtly old European correspondent, who spoke "in most intimate detail" of his experiences during the fall of France, and Ernie came away "greatly moved."[13] Near the end of October he chatted with Deac Parker in Washington, and a decision was quickly made. The pull of the world beyond his personal sphere had once again proven irresistible. As he explained his feelings later, "It seemed to me that in London there was occurring a spiritual holocaust — a trial of souls — that never again in our day could be re-enacted. I felt that to live your span in this time of ours, and to detour around an opportunity of sharing in the most momentous happening of that time, was simply to be disinterested in living. It seemed to me somehow that anyone who went through the immersion into fear and horror of the London bombings, could not help but be made fuller by it."[14]

Ernie stepped onto English soil in a small coastal town on December 9, 1940. He walked to the Customs office among British soldiers carrying gas masks and women in khaki uniforms. Despite the cold drizzle he was charmed by "the gabled buildings, the language of the signs, the many smoking chimney pots." It was "a picture from a Dickens novel . . . the England of fiction, so peaceful, neat and secure. I had not been ashore three minutes before I was in love with England" and its "lovely, courteous people."[15]

Ernie took little more than a newspaper reader's interest in the strategic aspects of the Battle of Britain. He was tone-deaf to high politics, even to the point of uncertainty whether England was wholly in the right and Germany wholly wrong. What he sought was the personal experience of war. He was eager to immerse himself in its sights and sounds, he told Lee Miller, then "put the whole picture into columns — not at all for propaganda or because I think a 'message' needs to be got over, but because of the same old basis the column has always been written on, of making people at home see what I

91

see."[16] And especially he wondered how he would respond to the experience of hearing whistling bombs overhead.

He set out exploring, taking long walks through the West End, past the Houses of Parliament and Westminster Abbey, through Piccadilly and Leicester Square, and among the great shopping districts of Regent and Oxford Streets. He ventured with policemen into the destitute East End, spending Christmas Eve in the Underground shelters there. He saw how a factory could appear normal from the street though its rear sections lay in a charred heap. Yet two weeks went by without a bomb coming anywhere near him. Apart from distant rumbles of planes, bombs and antiaircraft guns, danger approached only in the form of a chunk of shrapnel that flashed by the window of his room at the Savoy one night with a "ghostly 'whooo-isshhh' " and "damn near scared me to death. My heart stopped a few seconds waiting for the explosion, but it never came."[17]

Despite his fascination with London, he feared his early columns were suffering from a want of feeling. "As for myself I couldn't be better . . . ," he told Miller in a letter dated December 28, 1940. "My only worry is that I haven't been able to get emotional about anything I've seen — for that reason I fear the columns are dull. . . . I am enjoying it over here; but may change my tune as soon as the first bomb goes off outside my window."[18]

He did not have long to wait — for emotion or for bombs.

On the night of December 29, 1940, one hundred and thirty German bombers attacked London in one of the largest incendiary raids of the war. Working in his hotel room, Ernie heard them coming, heard "the quick, bitter firing of the guns" and "the boom, crump, crump, crump, of heavy bombs at their work of tearing buildings apart." The Savoy had a fine basement bomb shelter. But Ernie, sensing an opportunity, gathered a couple of friends and went to a high balcony affording a view of a third of London's skyline. He stayed there for hours, watching as nearly two thousand separate fires roared throughout the city, the worst of them in the neighborhoods around the historic dome of St. Paul's Cathedral. Ernie's description of the scene, written the next day and sent by cable for publication just before New Year's, 1941, combined stunning imagery with an appreciation of war's aesthetic rewards.

For on that night this old, old city — even though I must bite my tongue in shame for saying it — was the most beautiful sight I have ever seen. . . . [T]he thing I shall always remember above all the other things in my life is the monstrous loveliness of that one single view of London on a holiday night — London stabbed with great fires, shaken by explosions, its dark regions along the

Thames sparkling with the pin points of white-hot bombs, all of it roofed over with a ceiling of pink that held bursting shells, balloons, flares.

Amid the din of airplane engines, Ernie and his friends gazed from their high perch into dark spaces where

whole batches of incendiary bombs fell.

We saw two dozen go off in two seconds. They flashed terrifically, then quickly simmered down to pin points of dazzling white, burning ferociously.

These white pin points would go out one by one, as the unseen heroes of the moment smothered them with sand. But also, while we watched, other pin points would burn on, and soon a yellow flame would leap up from the white center. They had done their work — another building was on fire.

Directly in front of Ernie, the largest of all the fires sent flames hundreds of feet high.

Pinkish-white smoke ballooned upward in a great cloud, and out of this cloud there gradually took shape — so faintly at first that we weren't sure we saw correctly — the gigantic dome of St. Paul's Cathedral.

St. Paul's was surrounded by fire, but it

came through. It stood there in its enormous proportions — growing slowly clearer and clearer, the way objects take shape at dawn. It was like a picture of some miraculous figure that appears before peace-hungry soldiers on a battlefield.

The streets below us were semi-illuminated from the glow. Immediately above the fires the sky was red and angry, and overhead, making a ceiling in the vast heavens, there was a cloud of smoke all in pink. Up in that pink shrouding there were tiny, brilliant specks of flashing light — anti-aircraft shells bursting. After the flash you could hear the sound.

Up there, too, the barrage balloons were standing out as clearly as if it were daytime, but now they were pink instead of silver. And now and then through a hole in that pink shroud there twinkled incongruously a permanent, genuine star — the old-fashioned kind that has always been there.[19]

Ernie had been sincere when he told Lee Miller he only wanted to tell readers how things looked and felt. Yet he could no more write an objective description of London under the Blitz than he could have concealed his personal reactions to the subjects of his travel column. He may have been willfully ignorant of high politics, but his street-level images were saturated with meaning. His word portrait of the great London fires communicated profound sympathy for the British cause. In this he joined Murrow in building a structure of solidarity between Americans and British, providing the emotional struts and beams upon which Franklin Roosevelt would soon erect the policy of Lend-Lease, by which the United States extended aid to Britain. Day after day, Ernie described the particulars of British fortitude. Repeatedly he addressed two questions that loomed large in American minds that winter: Would the British cave in under pressure, like the French? If not, had the Blitz done so much damage that Britain was already all but beaten? His answer to both was an emphatic no. "True, the destruction has been immense," he wrote.

But these ghastly blows actually have hurt London less than it is possible to imagine or believe without seeing for yourself.

Believe it or not, London as a living, enduring institution is not gravely injured. Not in its architecture, or in its mode of existence, or its utilities, or its transportion, or its health. And above all, not in its spirit.

So far, the blitz on London is a failure. London is no more knocked out than the man who smashes a finger is dead.[20]

He told readers he would not dwell on "London's amazing ability to take it," as they had heard it all before, but at least he would confirm it: "You get it in the attitude of people, you get it in the casual way common folks talk, you get it just by looking around and seeing people going about their business." For proof he offered small details: the remark of his hotel maid — "I'll never forgive that old Hitler if he gives us a blitz on Christmas Day" — and the unrelenting voluntary drills that antiaircraft gunners put themselves through. " 'Is that because they like guns,' I asked their officer, 'or is it because they want to get ahead?' 'It's literally because they're that determined to win this war,' the officer said."[21] He recorded the polite persistence of an air-raid warden investigating the traces of light that leaked from under Ernie's blackout curtains.[22] He captured Londoners' ingenuity in the image of the sandbags placed by every lamppost so that any passing pedestrian might douse the flames from an incendiary bomb.[23] He assured Americans that whatever their own fears of a British defeat, "Such an ending is inconceivable to the British."[24]

Hints came that his copy was stirring remarkable reactions at home. First Miller wired Ernie that his "marvelous stuff" was getting "terrific play" in the newspapers, and that a Scripps-Howard editor in Ohio was begging the brass to extend Pyle's stay in Britain, as he was "building [a] tremendous following."[25] A British correspondent in New York wired a portion of Pyle's fire column back to London for reprinting. *Time* also reprinted the column, saying: "Until last week Ernie Pyle, an inconspicuous little man with thinning reddish hair and a shy, pixy face, was not celebrated as a straight news reporter . . . [but] from a hotel room high above Britain's blazing capital . . . Pyle last week sent one of the most vivid, sorrowful dispatches of the war."[26] Then, on January 10, 1941, a bombshell arrived in Ernie's mailbox. "YOUR STUFF NOT ONLY GREATEST YOUR CAREER," wired Roy Howard himself, "BUT MOST ILLUMINATING HUMAN AND APPEALING DESCRIPTIVE MATTER PRINTED AMERICA SINCE OUTBREAK BATTLE BRITAIN . . . YOUR STUFF TALK OF NEW YORK."[27] Simultaneously pleased and unnerved, Ernie quoted Howard's cable to Jerry in full and asked: "Isn't that the damndest thing you ever read? It gives me stage fright so bad I've hardly been able to write a line since."[28]

From his January peak Ernie descended to more pedestrian stuff, leaving London for a tour of Scotland and the Midlands, then returned to the city for most of February and March. In New York, Howard began to worry the series was running too long and complained to Lee Miller, who agreed to cut back on Ernie's London coverage. But Miller defended Ernie in a cogent analysis of his appeal. "It is perfectly true that Ernie's copy lost considerable altitude, compared to his early weeks in London," Miller said. But the typical Pyle reader did not expect "something sensational every day. He looks on

Ernie's column as a sort of cross between a travelogue, a highly personalized and humanized diary, and a reporting job." Howard was mistaken, Miller argued, if he regarded "a leisurely, 'trivial,' 'unimportant' piece by Ernie as a mistake or a failure. Some of his most unpretentious pieces have evoked more interest and reaction than columns that have been really newsworthy. The fact is, in my judgment, that the great mass of Ernie's readers are a sight more interested in Ernie Pyle himself, and his reaction to things and people both large and small, than in the strictly objective reporting that Ernie does."[29]

Ernie returned to Albuquerque in March 1941, depleted by his trip and grieving the death of his mother earlier that month. He hoped to spend a few quiet weeks in his new home, writing his final columns on England at a leisurely pace while savoring the novelties of home ownership. But no such respite was in store. Fans ranging "from grocery boys to the city rabbi" wanted to see him, shake his hand, have their pictures taken with him.[30] "The damn place is like a museum. People drive around and around, and park out front and stare, and even come look in the window."[31] He had to buy a new car and go through a flood of mail — "all kinds of wires and letters from lecture bureaus and all that crap."[32] This left no time for "any renewal of acquaintanceship at all with Jerry."[33] In "the most ironic touch of the year," he had to flee the house in order to write. "After spending millions building this retreat out here, and Jerry working all winter on it, I . . . had to come downtown to a hotel this morning to write," he told Miller, "and here I sit . . . in the only real solitude available in this world — a hotel room!"[34] Sniffling from the cold he had been nursing since England, he had no choice but to make plans to leave town in search of new columns. After London, the prospect of dredging up domestic copy seemed more dismal than ever. A friend recalled that after "the beauty, the terror" of London, "he found roving around pretty tame."[35]

He had not quite left the war behind. A New York publisher, Robert M. McBride & Co., wanted to collect Pyle's British columns in a small volume to be entitled *Ernie Pyle in England*. Though unable to "work up much blood pressure" about the idea, Ernie believed a book sold through Scripps-Howard and his subscribing newspapers might help to promote the column.[36] The publisher wanted Ernie to write two short, new pieces to bracket the book. For the epilogue he constructed a small piece of master craftsmanship about the illusory distance between peace and war. Perhaps it was meant as a quiet call to the American conscience, resting uneasily in its continental fortress as Europe burned. Certainly it testified to Ernie's new emotional bond to the British, even to the war itself.

The long trip home is done. The wars are far distant, and over the desert there hangs an infinity of space and time that seems put here to prohibit any contemplation of giant struggles far away.

It is so quiet out here just at dawn. I don't know what, but something awakens us — the silence or the gentleness — something awakens us just at daybreak. And we get up, and watch the light come softly over the bare Sandias to the east, and it is a perfect hour. The little birds hop from the sage-filled mesa at daylight, and they come over into our yard and they peck in the fresh earth. . . .

He described "the friendly hot sun" passing overhead, reaching the distant western horizon, and turning "the unearthly long line of the mesa rim . . . into a silhouette" at sunset. He watched it every night, he said, drinking in "the gentle rolling vastness of the desert," a scene that was "finer than any words."

All this is here for us to relish, so lovely and beautiful and serene. But when we sit in our west window at sundown it is past midnight in London, and the guns are going and the bombers are raising hell and my friends of yesterday are tense and full of a distracting excitement — peering, listening, alert to death and the sounds of death.

Out here, so remote from turmoil, the ghostly rustle of a falling bomb can surely be only something you dreamed once in a nightmare. There can be no truth in it. And yet you know. Day and night, always in your heart, you are still in London. You have never really left. For when you have shared even a little in the mighty experience of a compassionless destruction, you have taken your partnership in something that is eternal. And amidst it or far away, it is never far out of your mind.[37]

"There must be a drastic change . . ."

Upon Ernie's arrival from Britain, Jerry told him she had been "soul-searching" and that she wanted to have a child. Numb to the idea, he could respond only with bewilderment, and several weeks later Jerry made an ineffectual gesture toward suicide by turning on the gas in her new kitchen. A year after the "cut-up summer" of 1940, they were back precisely where they had been then — Jerry tottering at the edge of a precipice, Ernie physically and emotionally spent yet chained to a job that pulled him relentlessly forward. "Trying to get the columns started again is about to drive me insane," he wrote to Rosamond Goodman, the Scripps-Howard secretary and friend who helped him with his mail. "If you run onto anybody in the market for a slightly used secondhand man, who weighs a hundred pounds, has gray hair and a tired look, let me know."[38]

He dragged himself through a grim, hot summer alone in the Midwest. Then Jerry suffered her worst episode yet — a colossal drinking spree that left her close to death from a gastric hemmorhage. Doctors warned Ernie that if she continued to drink, she would certainly die soon. She now needed constant care, yet she refused to enter a sanitarium. So Ernie asked his superiors at Scripps-Howard for a three-month leave of absence — from early September to early December 1941 — and they agreed. Like his previous efforts, this one failed to bring about a change. The leave became "a time of constant worry and bewilderment," with Jerry suffering one relapse after another.[39] "Nobody can help but her," he concluded as his furlough dragged to an end, "and she can't, or won't. Everything looks blue."[40] Again he dreaded resuming the column. Yet he had no choice but to make travel plans for the winter of 1941–42.

For some months he had been contemplating a trip to the Far East, and now, given Jerry's apparently hopeless state, an escape of that magnitude tempted him beyond resistance. He envisioned his longest trip ever — the Philippines, China, Rangoon, Singapore, the Dutch East Indies, Australia, perhaps even a round-the-world swing through England in the spring. Though the newspapers that fall brimmed with stories of impending war between Japan and the

United States, he imagined there could be little danger in a tour of places so distant from Japan. In November, Ernie visited Washington to arrange for visas, permits and inoculations. He brought back a little Shetland sheepdog for Jerry and then added a Great Dane, hoping the dogs would keep her company and spark her interest in living while he was away.

Jerry said she wanted Ernie to go, and he convinced himself that he could do little more for her by staying in Albuquerque. All was in order for him to board a plane in San Francisco in early December and fly to Honolulu, where he would catch an ocean liner bound for Manila. At the eleventh hour, however, the State Department bumped him from the airplane, leaving him to cool his heels in Albuquerque as December began. He suspected the cancellation was a piece of State Department retaliation against Scripps-Howard, whose editorial pages had been railing against Roosevelt's foreign policy. "IF CAN'T GET TO ORIENT DONT KNOW WHAT TO DO THIS WINTER . . . ," he cabled Miller. "CANNOT STAND THOUGHT OF PACKING UP CAR . . . AND TOURING IN SNOW."[41] Getting more "bitter and disgusted" by the day and "ready to drop [the] whole thing," he waited for something to happen.[42]

A week later, of course, something did.

Ernie, like everyone else, knew only that the Japanese attack on Pearl Harbor on December 7 would transform the life of the nation. He could

104

not guess how thoroughly his own life would be caught up in the events set in motion that Sunday.

All that day and the next he huddled in the little house, ear to the radio, getting "jitterier and gloomier by the moment." Obviously the Far East trip was impossible. Twitchy with anxiety and curiosity, he cabled Miller to propose a month of California columns, "since feeling of war intimacy probably highest there."[43] On the 9th, his newsman's instincts seized control. "When the rumor came there were two Japanese carriers off San Francisco," he told Cavanaugh, "I just said fuck it, and went to the phone and got a seat on the first plane out."[44]

Yet when Japanese ships failed to materialize at the Golden Gate, war fever relaxed its grip on Ernie's mind, just as it had in the autumn of 1939. In its place came an ill mood of lethargy and fatalism. For weeks he wandered the West Coast from San Diego to Seattle and back again, struggling to write lackluster columns, drinking heavily, and feeling a "tight, swollen up feeling in my face and head . . . and a general all around debilitation and disinterest in everything."[45] The future looked foggier than ever. Government rationing of rubber for domestic automobile tires threatened to curtail the long-distance motoring his paycheck depended on, and the draft loomed. "[I]nstead of being grim and deadly about the war, I already feel a what-the-hell attitude about personal things," he confessed in a letter to the Shaffers, "and find myself wanting to play and ignore responsibilities rather than buckle down to years of hard serious work with little fun."[46]

Certainly his "what-the-hell attitude" applied to his marriage. Perhaps he believed he had walked the extra mile for Jerry during his leave of absence, and that when this final effort to restore her stability failed, his duty to her finally had expired. More likely his sense of marital loyalty simply buckled under the weight of depression and loneliness. In any case, these tense months found Ernie pining for companionship with other women. One of these women was Lucy Livingstone, known to family and friends by the nickname "Moran," a vivacious and attractive woman whose husband, her second, was chief of the Associated Press bureau in Albuquerque. In the autumn of 1941 the Livingstones and Pyles had fallen into the same social circle, and a warm attraction had grown up between Moran and Ernie. In California, Ernie fell hard for yet another "other woman." The affair was intense — so intense, in fact, that it moved Ernie to seek medical treatments for the impotence that had plagued him for several years — but he soon despaired of finding any way of making the relationship work permanently. Wherever he turned — his work, his love life, his future — all seemed hopeless, and he slid downward in confusion and depression. In fact, the first months of 1942 were the lowest of Ernie's life. Writing was "a torture."[47] He was "shrivelled up . . . mentally."[48] "I had a nice letter from Deac [Parker] this morning, telling me to follow my nose," Ernie wrote Lee Miller from Seattle. "But if I do, I'll probably just follow it to the bottom of a lake somewhere."[49]

The last shreds of his dedication to Jerry began to give way. Holed up to write at the Desert Inn in Palm Springs, he typed a plaintive plea for advice to the Shaffers, saying he could no longer carry on "under the present set-up; it's all too pointless, either from Jerry's standpoint or mine. . . . I believe what affection there is left between us is only one that comes in bursts of sentimentalism about old times and long years of wearing the same shoe. . . . I've got to do something soon, other than just go on for the next half century in our present unendurable state."[50]

For two more days he waited in vain for letters Jerry had promised, growing ever more bitter and angry. Then he began a letter of his own — the only one he ever began simply with "Jerry:" rather than his customary "Darling." They had broached the topic of divorce before, only to veer away. Now he bored in upon it with a will.

I can't attempt any longer to know what motivates you in any certain direction, or what you really want from life. We've done everything as you wished it done, and apparently all in vain.

You've always said you needed to have

107

me in your background, but now obviously you no longer do. So I'm ready to call the whole thing off if you are. Maybe a drastic change or a fresh start would give you strength and interest. . . . I know you are lonely, but so am I, often desperately so.

Even as he sat typing, a cable arrived from Jerry. But he pressed on to present his grim proposal, beginning, with some disingenuousness, "I suppose neither of us could likely form a new companionship."

For physical reasons alone a new one is forever denied me. But our old companionship is gone. . . . [W]e might both be less burdened if we ceased to carry the empty carcass. . . . [W]e have contributed nothing to each other in two years. All I can suggest is that you think this possibility over, as I have tried to do. There must be some solution soon for both of us, or we'll both collapse completely.[51]

Ernie drove home to have the issue out with Jerry, but she insisted she could make another try. He left quickly and drove across the bland immensity of West Texas. In Amarillo he turned the car around and retraced the three hundred miles to Albuquerque. On April 14, the wire services carried a small item: "Ernie Pyle, well-known travel reporter for a newspaper chain, and his wife were divorced today. . . ."[52] Over the next few days, readers showered Scripps-Howard newspapers with questioning, hurt letters.[53] But no public explanation was given.

Ernie told friends that Jerry, finally, had been the one to propose divorce; he called it "a necessary and last-hope form of psychological surgery" to shock her into self-help, with the understanding that they might remarry later.[54] Perhaps Ernie was sincere about this, but according to Moran Livingstone, he drunkenly proposed marriage to her several days after the divorce. If these details remained murky, the essential truth was obvious: Ernie's life now lay in shards around him.

The day after the divorce Ernie took a second radical step by trying to enlist in the Navy, but he was rejected as too small. Expecting that the Army, with its lower weight standards, would draft him soon as a private, he began to consider enlisting. But his Scripps-Howard superiors, "under the impression that I've gone all to pieces," called him to Washington.[55] Deac Parker wanted him to resume the column in the United States. With Japan advancing in huge leaps across the Pacific and Germany seemingly on the verge of conquering the Soviet Union, American nerves were raw. In this atmosphere, Parker argued, Pyle could play a crucial role by offering people a diversion from the war.

The worth of what you are doing is some-

thing you can't fully sense [Parker wrote]. But at a time like this when people are strained and worried . . . the human quality of your writing holds many a reader down to earth; acts as balm to sore souls.

With most everything you read it's war and slaughter and tragedy and fear of what may come. Those writers who can do what you are doing are rare. In fact, there is no other that I know of who brings the same result — a consciousness or a subconsciousness that this is still the America we know, and that, after all, there are other things than war. . . . [Y]ou are a comfort to many thousands of readers in a time of turmoil and mental misery. . . .

You have done and will do everything that can be done about Jerry. Beyond that you can't go. Don't let the problem get you down and wreck your life. If you were just one person — a nonentity — it wouldn't make any considerable difference in the large scheme of things whether your life was wrecked or not. But you are not just one person. . . . [Y]ou have a job to do that transcends Ernie Pyle and affects the lives and happiness of many more people that you or I ever will fully realize.[56]

It is a measure of Ernie's anomie that Parker's persuasive plea left him cold, as did a proposal from Walker Stone, editor of the Scripps-

110

Howard Newspaper Alliance, that he do straight news reporting on the war. When Ernie startled everyone by passing the Army physical, Stone waxed enthusiastic about the notion of a twice-weekly Pyle column written from inside the Army. But Ernie's interest in enlisting now shriveled as quickly as it had arisen. He was thinking instead about a second trip to Britain, where he might write about American soldiers gathering for action against the Axis. "I got to thinking how I'd probably hate the damned Army after a couple of weeks," he told Cavanaugh, and talked Parker and Stone into approving the trip to Britain.[57] Even this failed to get him very excited, but the editors insisted he return to work. He continued to agonize about Jerry and felt the same dark foreboding about his future as ever, especially in view of the war. Of these few weeks in Washington Ernie said later simply that he had "wanted to die."[58]

At the insistence of her sister, Jerry entered a sanitarium early in June. Two weeks afterward Ernie found a seat on a Pan American Clipper bound for Ireland. A six-month tour of the war zones was planned, with the expectation that upon his return to the United States he would enlist as an officer in Air Corps intelligence. For now, he would make an extended tour of U.S. encampments in Great Britain. "And there is just a possibility," he told Jerry, "I might go to Africa or someplace in the fall."[59]

"I really feel that I can never be successful with the columns again. . . ."[60]

"Just marking time"

Ireland and England again, but with none of the glamour of the Blitz. He spent four months there. He envied the soldiers and reporters who seemed to be absorbed in the war, but he couldn't feel the same. It took him two weeks just to summon the energy to do any columns at all. Instead, he sat alone in a Dublin hotel room, playing Solitaire. In London he found "a silly little pool-table game" in the club at the Savoy, and he got into a routine of playing a few games every night — "the one thing over here that I actually enjoy."[61] Sometimes he would stroll through Hyde Park and Kensington Gardens, stopping at the little statue of J. M. Barrie's Peter Pan, "which to me is just dainty and whimsical enough to be one of the most lovely things I've ever seen in the world."[62] "Today is my birthday," he wrote Lee Miller on August 3, 1942. "Just an old broken-down, washed-up 42-year-old sonovabitch. . . . Wonder if I'll ever be 43, and if so why?"[63] There was no American war to cover yet, just thousands of soldiers, sailors and fliers, training and waiting under sodden skies. Going about his everyday business, moving from camp to camp and office to office, Ernie met many of them. He made lots of contacts in the bureaucracies that supported them, too — Army intelligence, the Red Cross, the British and American information agencies. Everyone wondered when and where Allied leaders would send troops into battle against Germany, but no one knew. Feeling the need for some sort of plan, Ernie thought he might do well to specialize in the Air Corps, becoming "sort of an adopted unofficial biographer to them," as he wrote Miller. "In a way I could revive the old aviation column, with all the broader aspects of war and human interest in it."[64] In the meantime he wrote soldier-boy stuff — column after column after column.

He described "homey touches" in the U.S. Marine barracks in Londonderry — beer cans made into bed lamps, and stars painted on a ceiling to resemble a night sky.[65] He wrote about soldiers' eating habits (they were grousing about the monotony of British food, and they generally lost weight for the first few weeks in camp); about their health (the rate of venereal disease was only two-thirds what it had been at home); and about relations with the Brits, who were "a little taken aback by . . . our loud boisterousness [and] our speed both in driving cars and in getting an arm around a girl," but who "seem to enjoy it and to be getting used to it and it's only the snobbish minority who turn up their noses."[66]

It was low-altitude stuff, but John Sorrells, Scripps-Howard's executive editor, thought Ernie was hitting just the right note. "Folks with 'boys' over there are a damned sight more interested in reading the homely, every day, what do they eat and how do they live sort of stuff, than they are in reading the heavy strategic, as-I-predicted-in-my-analysis-back-in-1920 sort of stuff," he told a colleague.[67] Ernie was getting the same idea. Soldier after soldier pulled out clipped copies of his column sent to them by relatives in the United States. Still, the word from United Feature in New York was that editors weren't much interested. There was a war on, after all. "Every new arrival over here reports that the column is just what the people want to know and nobody else is doing it," Ernie told Jerry, "but it's the old story of not being able to get it past the editors."[68] But he felt encouraged enough to believe he was better off abroad than at home. Using the argument that he "could do more good over here keeping the parents informed than by being a 104-pound typist-soldier at Ft. Bragg or someplace," he won his draft board's permission to stay overseas as a reporter for at least six more months.[69]

The news of Jerry was surprisingly encouraging. She had left the sanitarium in Denver and returned to Albuquerque, where she was taking classes to prepare for a Civil Service job. She was living in a cottage on the grounds of St. Joseph's Hospital and spending much of her time among the nuns there. Despite Jerry's atheism, these women succeeded in brightening her outlook where all others had failed. A long letter from her left Ernie feeling sparks of their old intimacy, and he unburdened himself to her:

> Somehow I feel that my character and my mind have deteriorated so terribly; I don't have any spiritual stability within myself at all. . . . I'm no tragic hang-dog figure or anything like that, but all purpose seems to have gone out of life for me (except the one of hope) and I've no interest in anything. I'm getting to feel about people much as you did. I don't like to be alone and yet I don't enjoy being with anybody, and don't hear what they say. . . . I really am concerned about my mind. It's as though extreme old age had overtaken me. I don't think straight any more, I get things confused, it's an absolutely literal and real feeling of my mind being solid so that nothing can penetrate it. I can't remember like I used to, and my mind doesn't seem to focus.[70]

He had painful daydreams of a simple life he could not have. "I told somebody the other day I felt I never wanted to do a thing again in this world but 'keep house' in Albuquerque — run the dog and water the lawn and make benches and wash the dishes and clean the house. . . ." Both of them, he thought, might now be ready for such a life. "Somehow I feel we have both matured into something new — you up to a new eagerness and interest in life, me down to a view of contentment that doesn't need excitement nor ambition nor change in it. Just peacefulness, and simplicity."[71]

Late in September Ernie received a highly improper tip, prompting him to write Miller a highly improper letter. "It isn't impossible that I might shoot off to Africa very suddenly along about November," he said. "It depends on events. . . . I don't know much and can't tell you what I do know, so you'll just have to trust my judgment on the proper time to go, if at all. . . ."[72] On November 8, American invasion forces landed in Morocco and Algeria. Ernie followed two days later, sailing in a convoy that reached Oran, Algeria, on November 23, 1942.

Operation TORCH was the first Allied assault against Hitler from the West and the baptism of American troops on the Atlantic side of the war. The invasion had two military purposes: to convert French North African troops heretofore loyal to the collaborationist government in Vichy; and to seize the key Tunisian ports of Tunis and Bizerte in cooperation with the British Eighth Army, fresh from its great victory at El Alamein in Libya. TORCH had two political purposes as well. It would allow Franklin Roosevelt to boast of an early American strike at Hitler, and satisfy Prime Minister Winston Churchill's desire to wear down the Axis on its periphery rather than striking an all-out blow at its heart. Conceived in this murky stew of motives, manned by inexperienced commanders and soldiers, TORCH would proceed in slow agony. Though French forces quickly came over to the Allied banner, German commanders directed a massive reinforcement from Europe that denied Tunis to the Allies. By December, hopes for a painless success in North Africa had been dashed. Both sides prepared for a protracted winter campaign.

At first, North Africa represented simply another assignment to Ernie — more exotic and dangerous than usual, but otherwise not much different from one of his trips to Central or South America. Oran had been pacified days before he arrived, and the fighting had quickly moved eastward toward Tunisia. Most of the war correspondents, several dozen in all, had followed. Ernie, learning that these reporters were having terrible trouble transmitting their dispatches from the front, stayed put in Oran. If he went to the front before he could build up a large cushion, he risked creating a gap between columns. Besides, people arriving in Africa direct from the United States were telling him that "what readers want most of all is to know how the boys are being taken care of."[73] He could tell them that from Oran, where thousands of troops remained. So he planned an itinerary: a few weeks in Oran to build a cushion, including a visit to nearby Sidi bel Abbes, home of the fabled French Foreign Legion; then a visit to the new American air bases in eastern Algeria; then a month-long stay at the front to picture soldiers in action. Then, if all went well, he would venture farther east to India, China and Australia, picking up the thread of the global tour he had abandoned a year earlier at the time of the Pearl Harbor attack.

His decision to go slow and follow his familiar reporting techniques — still "just marking time" — soon paid unexpected dividends. By passing time with rear-echelon Army bureaucrats and getting comfortably acquainted with Army censors, Ernie broke the first significant news story of the North African campaign.

In the early weeks of the Allied occupation of French Algeria, one of the Army's trickier tasks was to maintain civil authority. For expediency's sake, control was ceded to former officials of the Vichy administration, who were generally understood to be collaborators with the Germans at best and proto-Nazis at worst. This unseemly business was obvious to American reporters, but any who tried to write about it were rebuffed by censors, who judged the material too embarrassing for disclosure in the United States. Certainly it was not Ernie's sort of story. But at dinner one night in Oran, some acquaintances in the Army Counter-Intelligence Corps, unhappy with the coddling of French fascists, dumped the whole tale on him and nudged him to write about it.[74] At about the same time, he heard from some newly arrived sailors that "people at home think the North African campaign is a walkaway . . . that our losses have been practically nil; that the French here love us to death, and that all German influence has been cleaned out."[75] Seized by an uncharacteristic spasm of indignation, Ernie pounded out two pointed columns. To puncture overconfidence at home, he stated flatly that America's green, undersupplied troops would need months, not weeks, to match the fighting capacity of their German opponents. As for the disciplining of French collaborators, "our fundamental policy still is one of soft-gloving snakes in our midst. . . . The loyal French see this and wonder what manner of people we are. They are used to force, and expect us to use it against the common enemy, which includes the French Nazis. Our enemies see it, laugh, and call us soft. Both sides are puzzled by a country at war which still lets enemies run loose to work against it."[76]

It was one thing to type up such copy in an Algerian hotel room but quite another to ship it intact to American newsrooms. Every dispatch was checked once by Army censors in Africa and again in the United States. Yet somehow Ernie's column penetrated both screens and was published as written, causing a minor uproar at home. If Pyle knew how this feat was managed, he never said. Possibly some in the Army, frustrated by U.S. policy, pulled strings to have the story exposed. Certainly Ernie enjoyed chummy relations with the local censors. After the main body of correspondents left Oran, only Pyle and one or two other reporters were left to provide work for the phalanx of Army censors. "The censors are so bored that when I bring my column in the entire office staff grabs for it and reads it hungrily, everybody makes flattering remarks, and then we all go out and have a bite to eat."[77] Still, it seems doubtful that a censor would have risked his rank to give Ernie a break. More probable is an unattributed account: the censor responsible, accustomed to Ernie's innocuous fare, had noted "By Ernie Pyle" at the top of the page, yawned, and affixed his stamp of approval without reading the piece.[78]

Ernie was pining for Jerry. Long absence and distance allowed him once again to idealize her. One night he had a vivid dream that she had married someone else, and he wrote to broach the possibility of remarriage. "It wouldn't bring me home any quicker but somehow I know I'd feel happier about things."[79] In mid-December he conferred with an Army lawyer to arrange a remarriage by proxy. He sent the proxy to Sister Margaret Jane, the Mother Superior of St Joseph's Hospital, asking her to present it to Jerry when she seemed ready.[80] Then he waited for mail that failed to materialize week after week. Certainly there was little else to raise his spirits in Oran. Miller cabled that several major papers had picked up the column, but Ernie could no longer kindle ambitions for big-time success. "I have no feeling at all about that any more," he wrote Jerry. "My only professional interest is to keep on doing the best I can till the war is over, and then a long rest and then 'take up some other line of work.' "[81]

Early in January 1943, Ernie's column carried a deliciously exotic dateline: "A Forward Airdrome in French North Africa." (Censorship prevented him from naming it, though as he noted, "the Germans obviously know where it is since they call on us frequently.")[82] It was the great American airfield at Biskra, the base for American bombers flying daily missions north over the Mediterranean ports of Bizerte, Tunis and Tripoli. Biskra was an oasis town called "the Garden of Allah." It was hot under a brilliant sky during the day, cold at night. To Ernie's homesick eyes, the land bore a striking resemblance to the landscape around Albuquerque. The purple mass of the Atlas Mountains blocked the horizon. Soldiers wore goggles against the blowing sand, which drifted around the dry shrubs and penetrated the gears of trucks and planes. For the first time he found himself in real danger. Just three hours after he arrived, German planes bombed the field. In spare moments soldiers swung picks and axes to deepen their slit trenches, intermittently scanning the sky for parachutists. After England and Oran, this was a sizable step closer to war as Ernie had imagined it.

Just as he had done a dozen years earlier, Ernie sat talking with pilots and mechanics and and tracked the daily departure and arrival of planes.

And just as good stories had come to him at Bolling Field on the Potomac, one came to him now at Biskra. It was the story of an American bomber given up for lost.

While dropping its load of bombs over Tripoli with the other bombers of its squadron, the Flying Fortress, nicknamed "Thunderbird," had lost two engines on the same wing, usually a fatal blow. Falling fast and left for lost by the other Americans, the ten-man crew managed to keep the plane aloft despite attacks by German fighters. When the Germans gave up for lack of fuel, they flew on alone, scraping through a mountain pass and creeping toward the airfield just at dusk.

Any competent newsman could have woven these facts into a readable tale of skill, courage and luck. Pyle's version, which he told in three columns, accomplished something larger. In the second and third columns he told the story as most reporters would have, reconstructing the day's events as the crew of the missing Fortress had experienced them: the crippling of the plane, the loss of altitude and gasoline, the perilous flight through the mountains, and so on. But the first column of the series was different. It was the story of Ernie's day, of the one who waited. It was the story not of the crew's deeds, but of an observer's first encounter with the mixed emotions of war.

He began by setting the scene: "It was late afternoon at our desert airdrome. The sun was lazy, the air was warm, and a faint haze of propeller dust hung over the field, giving it softness." Their missions complete, Fortresses were landing, all but one. "The last report said the Fortress couldn't stay in the air more than five minutes. Hours had passed since then. So it was gone."

Next came an image other reporters might have left out as a taint on a heroic story. In Ernie's tale it provided an essential counterpoint. "We had already seen death that afternoon," he said.

> For one of the returning Fortresses had released a red flare over the field, and I had stood with others beneath the great plane as they handed its dead pilot, head downward, through the escape hatch onto a stretcher.
>
> The faces of his crew were grave, and nobody talked very loud. One man clutched a leather cap with blood on it. The pilot's hands were very white.
>
> Everybody knew the pilot. He was so young, a couple of hours ago. The war came inside us then, and we felt it deeply.

It was Pyle's first report of a combat death and probably the first he had seen.

After the dead pilot was brought down from the plane, Ernie and others ascended the control tower to watch the desert sunset and to learn if

German bombers were approaching. "[T]he day began folding itself up. . . . All the soldiers in the tent camps had finished supper. That noiseless peace that sometimes comes just before dusk hung over the airdrome. Men talked in low tones about the dead pilot and the lost Fortress."

Then "an electric thing happened" — a red flare arched across the northern horizon. An officer fired a green flare in response. Ernie and his companions saw the plane — "just a tiny black speck" — on the horizon. "It seemed almost on the ground, it was so low, and in the first glance we could sense that it was barely moving, barely staying in the air. Crippled and alone, two hours behind all the rest, it was dragging itself home.

"I am a layman," Ernie said, "and no longer of the fraternity that flies, but I can feel. And at that moment I felt something close to human love for that faithful, battered machine, that far dark speck struggling toward us with such pathetic slowness." Ernie narrated the bomber down — over parked planes, over the runway, onto the tarmac — whereupon "the thousands of men around that vast field suddenly realized that they were weak and that they could hear their hearts pounding. . . . Our ten dead men were miraculously back from the grave."[83]

Lee Miller pronounced the column "a proper son-of-a-bitch" — a verdict seconded in many quarters.[84] Madison Avenue converted the story into a goodwill advertisement. In Hollywood, a scene uncannily like the Thunderbird column became the climax of *Memphis Belle*, one of the war's great movies. The column was a harbinger. It showed that for all Ernie's fears that his mind had grown foggy from the effects of depression, clarity could return instantly when he witnessed compelling events. It showed that he had not lost touch with his strongest method — to report his own feelings. And it was significant that his first notable war story dealt not with heroic blows against the enemy but with servicemen accomplishing the feat that matters most to the individual at war: sheer survival. Like many columns to come, a reassuring spirit flowed through it. The pilot's bloody cap and death-white hands were balanced by the "miraculous" flare in the distance; death "came inside," but life persisted and triumphed.

4

★★★★

"In It to the Hilt . . ."

TUNISIA: JANUARY–MAY 1943

On the evening of January 19, 1943, Captain Patrick Riddleberger, an Army regular with the 601st Tank Destroyer Battalion, was doing what a soldier usually does. He was waiting. His unit was in bivouac in a farmyard near the ancient Arab town of Sbeitla in central Tunisia, a cold place where stone-and-plaster houses mingled with Roman ruins. The winter light was fading. Someone had told Riddleberger the battalion would move a long distance in convoy that night — where, he didn't know. His jeep was assigned to the convoy's tail. He had been overseas for many weeks. With a wife and child at home, he hoped to enter graduate school after the war and become a professor of history. His companions had been limited to soldiers for so long that he welcomed the sight of a small, older man, obviously a civilian, who approached, introduced himself, and asked if he could ride along in the convoy.

Riddleberger had heard the name before — correspondent, he thought. The two men went into a little shed to wait for their turn in the convoy, and soon they fell into conversation — hometowns, the war, families, former lives. "He was very easy to talk to, and one felt at ease with him immediately," Riddleberger recalled long afterward. "There was nothing threatening about him — just the opposite, in fact. He didn't probe me with questions. We didn't talk about the operations and what was going to happen next. It was just a kind of nice, quiet conversation two strangers who found a certain affinity would carry on." Riddleberger especially remembered "his natural modesty, and a feeling that you wanted to help this guy along somehow."[1]

Outside, trucks, jeeps and half-tracks rumbled by. Shortly after midnight it was their turn to join the convoy. They drove without headlights to avoid detection by the Germans; only the tail lights of the five or six trucks ahead of them reminded them of the train of vehicles many miles long. They climbed steep mountain roads in the dark, sometimes stopping to wait as traffic jams were unsnarled far ahead. They passed a column of French soldiers on foot. When morning came, false alarms about German fighter planes sent them tumbling out of the jeep on the run, looking for ditches. About noon they came to their destination. The reporter picked up his gear, thanked Riddleberger, and said good-bye.

Though Riddleberger enjoyed the company, the night for him had been merely another miserable and monotonous passage in a long succession. But for Ernie Pyle this night had been a magic loom where a picture emerged of ordinary men transformed into figures in an awesome pageant, terrible yet magnificent. In war he had found, in F. Scott Fitzgerald's words, "something commensurate to his capacity for wonder."

We would shut off our motors and the night would be deathly silent except for a subdued undertone of grinding motors far ahead. At times we could hear great trucks groaning in low gear on steep grades far below, or the angry clanking of tanks as they took sharp turns behind us.

Finally the road straightened out on a high plateau. There we met a big contingent of French troops moving silently toward the front we had just vacated. The marching soldiers seemed like dark ghosts in the night. Hundreds of horses were carrying their artillery, ammunition and supplies.

I couldn't help feeling the immensity of the catastrophe that has put men all over the world, millions of us, to moving in machinelike precision throughout long foreign nights — men who should be comfortably asleep in their own warm beds at home.

War makes strange giant creatures out of us little routine men who inhabit the earth.[2]

In the last week of January 1943, Ernie left the airfield at Biskra and went out among the shifting olive green mass of the United States Army's II Corps — some eighty thousand riflemen, engineers, artillerymen, tankers, quartermasters and cooks. He went more out of a sense of obligation than eagerness. "I'm sorry to leave the Air Corps, as they were so grand," he told Jerry, "but I can't stay with them all the time and will have to do my stint with the ground forces. . . ."[3]

Over the next month, Ernie drove hundreds of miles around the area of the American front, sometimes alone, sometimes with a companion, usually Will Lang, a Time-Life writer, or Don Coe of United Press. He especially liked Lang, who often sat in silence for long stretches, allowing Ernie to gaze out at the landscape without interruption. Central Tunisia was starkly different from the sunny palm groves of the Biskra airfield. Cold wind drove against the abrupt, mountainous *djebels* that rose from the brush-covered plains. In some places soldiers had to etch their slit trenches into rocky grit; elsewhere the soil was a yellow, glutinous sand. It rained a lot that winter, and mud clung to Army fenders and tires. The scattered towns looked dirty and uninviting. It was anything but the hot desert imagined by many Americans at home. "The goddam weather is no better than

England's," Ernie said, "dark, wet, cold and disgusting."[4] To fight the cold he piled on layer after layer of clothing. He wore rough Army coveralls over sweaters and shirts, no tie, a long-billed cap, and heavy overshoes. In the back of the jeep — or whatever vehicle he happened to climb into — he stowed a pistol belt with a quart canteen of water (but no pistol, as correspondents were unarmed), gas mask, helmet, dispatch case with writing materials, a musette bag filled with personal gear, his typewriter, plus a seventy-five-pound bedroll containing four blankets, a tent and extra clothes.[5]

Coming into a camp or command post, he would set up a tidy bivouac, then find a group of soldiers or fall into a mess line and introduce himself. Being a reporter hardly guaranteed Ernie a warm welcome. Loud and brash men gave the correspondents' corps a reputation as blowhards among the G.I.'s, who greeted them with the same mixture of condescension and contempt they reserved for untested officers assigned to headquarters far in the rear. Headquarters, in fact, was where most correspondents spent most of their time. In the morning, intelligence officers would tell them where the day's action was. There the reporters would rush, riding shotgun next to Army drivers. Once near the action, if they could find it, they would look around and ask a few hurried questions: what happened here? what time? anyone hurt? what's your name? who's your commander? They would scribble a few service-able quotations, then hurry back to headquarters to attend press conferences, type their stories and submit them to press relations officers for censoring and sending. The next day would be the same. To the correspondent writing for a daily deadline, the routine was a matter of simple necessity. He might wish to spend more time in the field, but his editor needed today's news today. To the G.I., the correspondent was a fly-by-night.

But they encountered a different species in Ernie Pyle. Not only was he not so rushed, but he seemed "really a swell apple," one soldier wrote his father at home, "a pleasant talker, easy-going and with a faculty for becoming 'one of the boys' in two seconds flat."[6] Ernie's intro-ductions and hellos became small conversations. Where was the soldier from? Anybody here from Indiana or New Mexico? Ernie's extraordinary knowledge of the United States was a wonderful aid. Was the man from Seattle? Ernie had been there not long ago. Did he know so-and-so? What part of town did he live in? He might jot down a name and address in the little notebook he kept in his pocket, but he took few other notes. "Ernie never seemed to be trying 'to get a story,'" recalled Horace Miner, an officer who saw Pyle many times in Africa. "Men were nat-ural with him because of this. . . . When [the] banter contained something Ernie could use, he would write it. He never tried to guide the conversation into channels which would be useful to him." Miner recalled seeing Ernie slouched in the grimy, four-room mud house that served as press headquarters at the village of Tebessa, where II Corps was based. "It was cold as the devil. Candles and flashlights were the only light except for a smudgy fire which burned in a corner fireplace. . . . A lot of reporters were in other rooms writing stories. We were talking about some experiences around Gafsa. Ernie was just a tired little fellow who sat huddled at the side of the room and finally collapsed into his blankets and sleep. But it was a story for him."[7]

Ernie had always been the outsider with people he covered, the casual observer alighting briefly, then moving on. Now, with the Army, he was possessed by a "feeling . . . of being in the heart of everything, of being a part of it — no mere onlooker, but a member of the team."[8] He got on friendly terms with every American general in Tunisia, from the ill-fated Lloyd Fredendall to the irrepressible Terry Allen, commander of the Army's First Division, a warlike and "wonderfully profane" Texan who not only commanded Ernie to join him in his tent but directed him to call him by his first name. The generals spoke frankly with Ernie as well as other correspondents, knowing that censors would screen their dispatches for breaches of military security, and they took it for granted that reporters were "on the team." "There was no hedging" from officers, Ernie said. "I've never known an instance where correspondents were not told, with complete frankness, what was going on."[9]

Though comfortable with the brass, he spent most of his time with enlisted men and junior officers. He dug slit trenches with them, ate meals with them, kibbitzed with them, dove for cover with them when German planes appeared overhead. Some became friends whom Ernie saw repeatedly. He observed G.I.'s' feats of improvisation and followed suit. He learned to brew a cup of coffee over a fist-sized hole in the sand filled with gasoline. The Army's ubiquitous gasoline cans became skillets and stewpots. "I don't believe there's a thing in the world that can't be made out of a five-gallon gasoline tin."[10] He learned that a mess kit could be kept clean with sand and toilet paper, "the best dishrag I've ever found." A quiet cheer welled in him as he performed small acts of self-reliance, perhaps because he had felt powerless in his personal life for so many months. He slept on the ground, often waking in the morning to find his bedroll dusted with snow. Arriving at a farmyard command post one evening, Jack Thompson, the *Chicago Tribune*'s black-bearded correspondent, watched Ernie prepare an overnight nest for himself under a decrepit wooden wagon. "From one corner of the farmyard he took a few sheets of corrugated iron which he erected as a wind break. Then with all his clothes on he crawled into his sack, pulled his old cap down tighter around his head, snuggled down and grinned."[11] Ernie told readers he had laughed over the inordinate pleasure he had taken in constructing his little shelter that night. "It was the coziest place I'd slept in for a week. It had two magnificent features — the ground was dry, and the wind was cut off. I was so pleased at finding such a wonderful place that I could feel my general spirits go up like an elevator."[12]

This hard outdoor life fascinated Ernie. It was challenging, disorienting, yet strangely liberating. Hal Boyle, an AP reporter who soon became a close friend of Ernie's, remarked one day that in war, physical discomfort overshadowed danger. Ernie agreed. "The danger comes in spurts; discomfort is perpetual. Dirt and cold are almost constant. Outside of food and cigarettes there are none of the little things that make life normal back home. There are no chairs, lights, floors or tables. There isn't any place to set anything, or any store to buy things. There are no newspapers, milk, beds, sheets, radiators, beer, ice cream or hot water. A man just sort of exists, either standing up working or lying down sleeping. There is no pleasant in-between. The velvet is all gone from living."[13] Yet he reveled in the "magnificent simplicity" of the front, where normal life's rules and responsibilities evaporated, leaving a state of freedom limited only by the hovering menace of the enemy. His eyes sparked with a curiosity he had not felt since the best days of the column at home. Eating ravenously, he gained weight. The African wind burned his face a ruddy, healthy red. The perennial symptoms of stress faded — the "tight feeling" in the back of his head, the blurred vision, the aches and pains in his head and neck. "You don't have appointments to keep," he reflected. "Nobody cares how you look. Red tape is at a minimum. You have no desk; no designated hours. You don't wash your hands before you eat, nor afterwards either. It would be a heaven for small boys with dirty ears."[14]

At home, Scripps-Howard editors were a bit dumbfounded at the extent of Ernie's immersion in front-line life, but delighted. "Some of this stuff out of Tunisia by wireless is really terrific," Lee Miller told a colleague. "Ernie is right up there with the combat elements, sleeping in his clothes on the ground, freezing to death, going bathless for a month, and so on. His account of the life of our troops . . . is in my opinion really great newspaper copy."[15]

"Is war dramatic, or isn't it?"

Captain Riddleberger's jeep arrived in the Ousseltia Valley of central Tunisia in the middle of February 1943. Foreshadowings of a German offensive had rattled nerves there for at least a day, but no one knew where it would come. Then, at noon on February 14, word came that German Panzers had pushed through the mountain pass at the town of Faid, about a hundred miles to the south of Ousseltia, then flooded across the plain around the village of Sidi Bou Zid. Now they were speeding westward toward the outfits that Ernie had just left at Sbeitla. He repacked his jeep and hurried back alone, arriving just before sunset in the sprawling cactus grove where the First Armored Division had its command post. He had just begun to dig a nest for his pup tent when a soldier shouted, "Here they come!" His trench was only four inches deep, but he sprawled into it, "torn between getting under cover and staying out to see what was going on."

He watched, terrified and fascinated, as plummeting Stukas took aim at the Americans. When it was over, Ernie found two other correspondents — Graham Hovey of International News Service and Noland "Boots" Norgaard of AP — who were telling of their narrow escape from the bombers. A jeep carrying three soldiers fifty feet ahead of theirs had suffered a direct hit. Hovey had just arrived at the front; the bomber that nearly killed him was the first German plane he had ever seen. Ernie walked back with the two reporters to the site of the bombing. "It was then," Norgaard recalled later, "I began to get some idea of the strong personal feeling the little guy . . . had for the men and boys who did the fighting. We walked around picking up bits of paper and envelopes in hopes of getting the identity of the three men who had been blown to bits, carefully trying to avoid stepping on the occasional tiny fragments of flesh that were scattered over a radius of perhaps a hundred yards." Ernie went about the work in silence — looking, pausing, stooping.[16]

The next morning, he listened for hours as enlisted men and officers told their stories of the day before, drawing lines on the ground with shoes and sticks to show him the path of the Germans' push out of Faid Pass, the collision of armor at Sidi Bou Zid, where many American tanks were disabled or destroyed, and the U.S. retreat. He spoke with officers who explained the counterattack planned for the afternoon. Eager to be in on the operation, Ernie bummed a ride in a lieutenant's jeep; they drove into the flat, treeless valley around Sidi Bou Zid, carpeted now with "American equipment — tanks, half tracks, artillery, infantry — hundreds, yes, thousands of vehicles extending miles and miles and everything standing still." Motors roared; tanks and trucks clanked and moved in a great procession, Ernie's jeep snaking among them. From a small rise they got a view of "little streaks of dust, like plumes" on the horizon: German Panzers. Ernie judged them to be ten miles distant.

He turned to the lieutenant.

"Let's get up there."

The American tanks on the plain before Sidi Bou Zid were clanking forward into disaster. Their counterattack that day was quickly shattered in the largest tank battle of the war to date. The Americans staggered backward through what Ernie called "awful nights of fleeing, crawling and hiding from death."[17] Ernie fled through the mountains of Tunisia's Western Dorsal at Kasserine Pass.

Back in Algiers, Ernie found a fine hotel room with a balcony overlooking a street crowded with Arabs, Frenchmen and Americans. He had found little time to write during his frenetic weeks in Tunisia, and he had not much wanted to. "You get so interested and become so much a part of the constantly changing war machine at the front, that you resent ever taking time off to be a newspaperman and do any writing," he wrote Jerry.[18] So his cushion was perilously thin. As he sifted through his memories of the front, he pictured Americans at home reading the disillusioning news reports about the string of defeats culminating in the Kasserine disaster. He felt an urge to explain. He didn't whitewash the defeat, which he called "damned humiliating" and "a complete melee."[19] But he also felt a powerful paternal instinct to defend the young soldiers. "You need feel no shame nor concern about their ability," he told readers. "I have seen them in battle and afterwards, and there is nothing wrong with the common American soldier. His fighting spirit is good. His morale is okay. The deeper he gets into a fight the more of a fighting man he becomes." Pyle was shaping a motif he would use again and again throughout the war. It was an emotional triangle with the soldier at one point, the reader at home at the second, and himself at the apex. At one moment he reassured home-front readers; at the next he chastised them. It was not a want of courage on the battlefield that lay at the root of defeat, he hinted, but an insufficiency of war production at home: "We had too little to work with, as usual. . . ."[20] He had joined the Army team as surely as if he had enlisted. Though he was in the field on the reader's behalf, he had begun to act at least as much on behalf of the soldiers, explaining their needs and testifying to their hardships.

He felt the sense of having survived a harrowing passage — not through danger, though the danger had been real enough, but from one phase of his life to another. He now understood the behavior of the soldiers who had so enthusiastically welcomed him back to their cactus command post on the day after the Faid breakout; he had left them only four days earlier, yet they had greeted him like a long-lost comrade, pumping his hand. "I thought this was odd, at first," he wrote, "but now I know how they felt. They had been far away — far along on the road that doesn't come back — and now that they were still miraculously alive it was like returning from a voyage of many years, and naturally you shook hands."[21] He wanted to explain what it had felt like to venture down that road, but he worried that "the subject was too big for me. . . . I'm terribly disappointed in the columns I've written since returning from Tunisea [sic]," he wrote Jerry. "They were ones I wanted to do especially good on, but they are especially bad."[22]

He had seen deeds that a copy desk man would have called "heroic," but the reality fell short of the word. Extremes jumbled together: boredom and action, disastrous luck and miraculous deliverance; frightened men doing one bold thing. Waiting around one day at an airfield, his musings had bubbled up into conversation. He had been leafing through a stack of American magazines. As he told readers, one magazine in particular had caught his attention.

It was full of photos and stories of the war; dramatic tales from the Solomons, from Russia, and right from our own African front. The magazine fascinated me and, when I had finished, I felt an animation about the war I hadn't felt in weeks.

For in the magazine the war seemed romantic and exciting, full of heroics and vitality. I know it really is, and yet I don't seem capable of feeling it. Only in the magazine from America can I catch the real spirit of the war over here.

One of the pictures was the long concrete quay where we landed in Africa. It gave me a little tingle to look at it. For some perverse reason it was more thrilling to look at the picture than it was to march along the dock itself that first day.

140

He wondered aloud if something was wrong with his powers of perception.

"Here we are right at the front," he had said aloud, "and yet the war isn't dramatic to me at all." One of the pilots had said he felt the same way, that the war was "just hard work, and all I want is to finish it and get back home."

So I don't know. Is war dramatic, or isn't it? Certainly there are great tragedies, unbelievable heroics, even a constant undertone of comedy. It is the job of us writers to transfer all that drama back to you folks at home. Most of the other correspondents have the ability to do it. But when I sit down to write, here is what I see instead:

Men at the front suffering and wishing they were somewhere else, men in routine jobs just behind the lines bellyaching because they can't get to the front, all of them desperately hungry for somebody to talk to besides themselves, no women to be heroes in front of, damn little wine to drink, precious little song, cold and fairly dirty, just toiling from day to day in a world full of insecurity, discomfort, homesickness and a dulled sense of danger.

The drama and romance are here, of course, but they're like the famous falling tree in the forest — they're no good unless there's somebody around to hear.[23]

Of course, he would be the one who was "around to hear" for the American G.I. What he would hear was not the old romance of Victorian wars, not the gallant heroism of the Rough Riders' charge, but a new heroism of "little routine men."

"The only writer who brings the war home to us . . ."

Within days, Algiers began to rub Ernie's nerves raw, especially when he saw reporters covering the war between cocktail hours, fighting for scraps of official news from Eisenhower's headquarters. "It's a minor Washington only not so minor," he confided to Miller. "It's overcrowded, the correspondents' corps here is just as greedy and back-biting as in Washington, everything is devious. Thank goodness my work isn't along this line and I don't have to play this game. . . ."[24] He felt nostalgic for the front and began immediately to make plans to return. He also began to sniffle with a cold, though at the front he had "never felt so good in my life." In Algiers there were cloying public relations officers and ringing telephones and red tape, while "the closer you get to the front the simpler, more direct, more genuine everything and everybody seems to become."[25] At the front life became "so wonderfully simple," he told Paige Cavanaugh. "There are only four essentials — clothes, food, cigarets, and whatever portion of safety you can manage to arrange for yourself. . . . No letters, no obligations, no worries — what more could a man ask?"[26]

"You are in the heart of everything," he told readers, "and you are a part of it. . . . I've written . . . that war is not romantic when you're in the midst of it. Nothing has happened to change my feeling about that. But I will have to admit there is an exhilaration in it; an inner excitement that builds up into a buoyant tenseness which is seldom achieved in peacetime."[27]

After ten days in Algiers he had written himself out and restored his cushion. The front remained quiet as Allies and Axis alike recalibrated their options in the wake of the debacle at Kasserine. With his own options open once again, Ernie decided on the spur of the moment to take a month-long trip by air to remote U.S. bases in the storied regions of Africa — the Sahara, the equatorial jungles, the Valley of the Nile. At the front he had withstood Tunisia's winter cold surprisingly well, but now, shivering in his hotel room, he wanted to be warm at all costs. He could return to Tunisia in time for the climactic battles that everyone expected in the spring; to go back to the front sooner would risk repetition.[28]

Beyond Tunisia, he couldn't see. Several weeks earlier Jerry had refused to sign the marriage proxy, and little other news was reaching him — until, while traveling in equatorial Africa, he received a cable from United Press in London: "NEW YORK REPORTS YOU MARRIED

FORMER WIFE BY PROXY. HOW ABOUT GIVING US YARN. . . ."[29]

"I can't tell you how relieved and glad . . . I am," he wrote Jerry. "I know it means you are well and your old self again, and for me it fills up again the mere shell that living had become . . . I think one of the reasons I wanted this is that if anything should happen to me before this war is over, I wanted to go out that way — as we were. Not that I'm counting on anything happening, but in war as all encompassing as this one, anything can happen, of course. At any rate, what I'm trying to say is that now I feel some peace with the world again; life was incomplete and purposeless before. . . .

"I'm convinced that especially in these times nobody can step aside and just let the world pass by without achieving a feeling of utter defeat for himself," he told her. "I . . . hate and detest the war and the tragedy and insanity of it, but I know I can't escape and I truly believe the only thing left to do is be in it to the hilt."[30]

One day that spring, the city editor of the *Washington Daily News* tore open a bulky envelope to find a stack of green bills, $52 in all, and a letter from three anonymous denizens of the capital press corps. As the letter explained, the three reporters had been kibbitzing about war correspondents one night at the National Press Club and disagreeing violently about every issue raised, "except Ernie Pyle." They concurred that "he is the only writer who grips us every day and who brings the war home to us." Their wives, office associates, and teenage children were grabbing each day's copy of the *News* to read Ernie's column. Thinking about all this, they had decided to take up a collection for Pyle, and now, sending in the proceeds, they asked the *News* "to ship Pyle a box of something" as a token of appreciation.[31]

The city editor published the letter; declared his intention to send Pyle two $25 cases of cigarettes to hand out to soldiers in Africa; and challenged readers to contribute enough for a third case. This was quickly done, and more money was solicited. "Come on, boys; let's bury this city editor in money," wrote a "friend of Ernie." "A buck for Ernie Pyle, the best reporter of the human side of the war," said a soldier's wife. "One of Ernie's columns could do more toward making us want to do 'something extra' than all the pleas to buy bonds," said another reader.[32] Papers in other cities published the appeal, and more donations arrived. In Indianapolis, $11,395.43 was raised in twelve days. Before the impromptu campaign dwindled some weeks later, several million cigarettes had been purchased for soldiers who did not need them in the name of a reporter who was baffled by the entire episode.

"How come they do that?" Ernie wrote Miller when he heard about it. "I don't understand it."[33]

The answer was that readers on the home front realized before Ernie did that he had found a mission. In Ernie's columns they found glimmers of comfort. He had the reassuring quality of an old song. As big things changed, he spoke of the continuity of small things. Some Scripps-Howard editors may have wanted more action from Ernie — more London firestorms, more returning bombers, more tank battles — but readers treasured the small, homely topics that occupied many more of his column inches day by day. At home Ernie had said, "I'm really a letter writer." Before television, and with no telephone contact, there was only the mail, and it was a vulnerable strand made all the dearer by frequent snafus, delays, and the poignant staccato of telegrams. One could not hear a loved one's voice for months or even years at a time. All one had were letters, and soldiers were not always reliable or satisfying correspondents. Yet here was Ernie Pyle to stand in for them six days a week, in comforting and colorful detail. And the illusion that he was writing letters on behalf of the soldiers fostered a second illusion: that he was acting as their *paterfamilias,* a wise and omnipresent uncle looking after the boys in their time of peril.

His readers were multiplying at an astonishing rate. When Ernie arrived in North Africa in November 1942, his column was appearing in forty-two newspapers (twenty-two Scripps-Howard papers plus twenty United Feature clients) with a combined circulation of 3.3 million. By January 1, 1943, the number of papers had risen to sixty-five; by the end of March to eighty-two; and in April alone forty new papers signed on, bringing the total to one hundred and twenty-two with a combined circulation of nearly 9 million. Extrapolating from that figure, based on the average number of readers per household, would put the number of actual readers much higher.[34] Scripps-Howard executives were staggered and delighted. From the *Cleveland Press*, editor Louis Seltzer wrote to headquarters: "In all of my newspaper experience I have not heard anyone so widely discussed and such extravagant praise heaped upon a man or woman for an outstanding journalistic job." Ernie's was "the best column now being written by *anybody*," John Sorrells said.[35] The London press printed Pyle excerpts, calling him the most popular war correspondent in America.[36] Three prominent publishing houses approached Lee Miller with proposals to publish a book of Pyle's Africa dispatches.[37] News of all this reached Ernie only in fragments. In the Gold Coast capital of Accra he ran into the writer Quentin Reynolds, fresh from the United States, who bubbled with news of Ernie's reception there. If Ernie went home, Reynolds declared, he could spin book and radio deals into $50,000 in three months.

"I'm not coming home," Ernie told Lee Miller, "and who wants $50,000 anyway?"[38]

On April 22, 1943, the Allies launched their spring campaign against the Germans, now wedged in a quarter circle around the ports of Tunis and Bizerte with the Mediterranean at their backs. While the British Eighth Army aimed at Tunis, the Americans of II Corps, hoping to redeem their humiliation at Kasserine, were assigned to take the lesser prize of Bizerte. Ernie hooked up with the First Division, calculating that these troops, the most experienced of the American units, would see intense action. Ernie felt bonds of kinship tugging him toward these men, "my old friends." But he perceived a change in them that he had not undergone. Before Kasserine they had been merely civilians thrust into Army green. Now they were soldiers. He heard the transformation in "the casual and workshop manner in which they now talk about killing. They have made the psychological transition from the normal belief that taking human life is sinful, over to a new professional outlook where killing is a craft. To them now there is nothing morally wrong about killing. In fact it is an admirable thing." He didn't hear this sort of talk in the rear echelons, only among the rifle companies at the tip of the spear. The front-line soldier "wants to kill individually or in vast numbers. He wants to see the Germans overrun, mangled, butchered. . . ." It was a profound difference, shocking yet necessary. "All the rest of us — you and me and even the thousands of soldiers behind the lines in Africa — we want terribly yet only academically for the war to get over. The front-line soldier wants it to be got over by the physical process of his destroying enough Germans to end it. He is truly at war. The rest of us, no matter now hard we work, are not."[39]

Ernie realized that he had undergone an emotional transformation of his own — not as profound as the soldiers', but significant nonetheless — an inner hardening that protected him from emotional breakdown in the face of pain and death. When he was alone and quiet, the shield would soften and collapse, leaving him vulnerable. "When I sit alone away from it all," he told readers, "or lie at night in my bedroll re-creating with closed eyes what I have seen, thinking and thinking and thinking . . . at last the enormity of all these newly dead strikes like a living nightmare. And there are times when I feel that I can't stand it and will have to leave."[40] These demons closed in on him one night in a gum-tree grove behind the American lines, where he and another correspondent pitched their tent one night before the offensive. Sounds crowded in on them — antiaircraft fire; a German dive bomber; and "the steady boom of big guns in the mountains ahead of us . . . like the lonely roll of an approaching thunderstorm — a sound which since childhood has always made me sad with a kind of portent of inevitable doom." Sleep was impossible. A dog raced through the camp, barking crazily, and suddenly realities turned to phantoms.

> My mind seemed to lose all sense of proportion. . . . Concussion ghosts, traveling in waves, touched our tent walls and made them quiver. Ghosts were shaking the ground ever so lightly. Ghosts were stirring the dogs to hysteria. Ghosts were wandering in the sky peering for us in our cringing hideout. Ghosts were everywhere, and their hordes were multiplying as every hour added its production of new battlefield dead. . . .
>
> Next morning we spoke around among ourselves and found one by one that all of us had tossed away all night. It was an unexplainable thing. For all of us had been through dangers greater than this. On another night the roll of the guns would have lulled us to sleep.
>
> It's just that on some nights the air becomes sick and there is an unspoken contagion of spiritual dread, and you are little boys again, lost in the dark.[41]

The advance to Bizerte was to be the First Division's hardest fighting in North Africa. The path before them ran over range after range of treeless hills studded with German fortifications. The only cover for the advancing Americans was knee-high wheat. In daytime the G.I.'s lay motionless amid the wheat so as not to attract artillery fire. When it grew dark they would stumble or crawl forward, trying to outflank each German emplacement, hill by hill. They tripped on rocks and ruts. Exhaustion spread. Ernie knew a man who fell asleep while speaking into a field telephone.

It was Pyle's first time with an infantry unit advancing into combat. For four days he followed them, "an awed semi-participant," as they trudged in single-file lines over endless mountain paths; fought in head-to-head ferocity with the Germans; fell back briefly to rest; then walked and fought again. For three days of the four-day advance Ernie's unit was under fire nearly continuously.[42] Dueling artillery roared ahead and behind like a hurricane, filling the air with "the intermixed rustle and whine of traveling shells." One day was particularly dangerous — "one of those days when you sit down on a rock about once an hour, put your chin in your hand, and think to yourself: 'What the hell am I doing here, anyway?' . . . I don't believe there was a whole minute in fourteen hours of daylight when the air above us was silent." Machine-gun bullets danced off the ground within ten feet of Ernie's hole, and shells pummeled the ground within a hundred yards, producing "a special kind of horror inside you . . . a confused form of acute desperation."[43] Then came more marching, more attacking, sometimes with wave after wave assaulting the same battered hill position until the Germans fell back, only to reinforce the next bastion. For probably the only time during the entire war, Ernie, traveling without his typewriter, did what he was endlessly but erroneously credited with doing: he actually jotted drafts of columns in his foxhole as snakes, lizards and scorpions crawled nearby, and soldiers peered over his shoulder to see what he was writing.[44]

On May 7 and 8 the Allies broke through to the ports; the next day Germans began to surrender *en masse*. Behind on his columns, Ernie settled into a tent camp set up by Army public relations near Bizerte. He warmed up for his writing with a letter to Miller. It had been "an incredible week right in the lines," he said. "This is a totally different type of warfare up here. . . . Was under constant fire for three days and nights, and it ain't no play."[45] He began to craft a series of columns, choosing his words with deep seriousness, as if testifying in a trial about some terrible event that he alone had witnessed. As usual he wrote with a simple purpose — "to make the reader see what I see" — but now what he had seen seemed so important that he must etch each image with exacting care. He had written about fliers, gunners, cooks, MPs, doctors, nurses and tankers. Now he turned finally to the American foot soldier — "the God-damned infantry, as they like to call themselves," "the mud-rain-frost-and-wind boys . . .

that wars can't be won without."

Correspondents in World War II operated within a new consensus about the proper role of war news. In earlier conflicts, only the exceptional military establishment had viewed reporters as anything more than a necessary evil; they were to be monitored closely to prevent unhelpful disclosures. But now, thanks to a new appreciation of propaganda in its various forms, high American officials regarded reporters' words as powerful weapons of war. As a result, reporters gained greater status and access, but they also faced the pervasive expectation that they would help win the war. Few if any rebelled at this expectation; they took for granted the need to fight the Axis and assumed they could do their jobs while wholeheartedly supporting the Allied cause. No generals had to tell a reporter to "get on the team," as generals would in Vietnam two decades later, but they did seek to use reporters to advance their own interests — or the interests of their own service branches — in the name of patriotism.[46]

Such was the case with Captain Harry Butcher, naval aide to General Dwight D. Eisenhower and Ike's informal liaison to the press, who threw a press party shortly after Ernie returned to Algiers from Tunisia. Butcher, who was acutely sensitive to the role of public opinion in the war, had just returned to Africa from the United States, where he had become convinced the Navy was besting the Army in the interservice rivalry for public support. Critics of "Atlantic First" — Roosevelt's strategy to concentrate Allied efforts against Germany while fighting a holding pattern against Japan — were saying victory in Africa was already a foregone conclusion. "The American public seems more interested in activities in the Pacific," Butcher confided to his diary, "perhaps because hardships [there] have been dramatized and victories, no matter how small or large, thoroughly exploited in newspapers, magazines, and radio. . . . Unless we . . . make the public more intimately aware of our difficulties [in North Africa], public opinion is likely to succumb to the wooing of the salesmanship of the Pacific."[47] Butcher told the reporters about his fear of complacency on the home front, and Ernie was disturbed. "It was a pretty disheartening picture he gave . . . of the people's mental attitude," he wrote Miller, "their apparently distorted views of the European end of the war, their greed and so on."[48] Butcher's views were no surprise to Ernie — he had gained similar impressions of the public mood during the first months of the war — but they reinforced his instinct to give his home-front readers hell by pointing out the travail of the men whom he had adopted as his own. He spoke directly to "you" on the home front, shaming the reader into working harder for the war, because "no matter how hard people work back home they are not keeping pace with these infantrymen in Tunisia."[49]

Yet the bond that now wedded Pyle with the American infantryman drew upon sources much deeper than Ernie's desire to do his bit for the war. The writing transcended propaganda; it was richer, more heartfelt. Indeed, Pyle's columns on the First Division in northern Tunisia represent a historic match between writer and subject. For he saw himself in the infantry. Describing their long-suffering and underappreciated travail, he might have been describing the terrain of his own emotional journey. Just as he had created the larger-than-life Everyman named "Ernie Pyle," he now shaped the slogging, anonymous infantryman into a larger-than-life hero, all the more admirable because he persevered through mud and cold and the absence of glamour and glory.

In his account of the few hundred riflemen at the edge of the American advance, Pyle did not describe any of them firing so much as a single shot, nor did he describe any stealthy flanking of the enemy, or an ambush or a heroic seizure of an enemy position. As he sat in the press camp, staring at his typewriter, the image that dominated his memory — "just one of the ineradicable pictures I have in my mind today" — was of nothing more heroic than a line of walking men. As Ernie explained it to his readers, he had stepped off the trail to rest. He sat on the rocky ground facing "a vast rolling country to the rear." A heavy-weapons platoon was passing, loaded down with equipment.

A narrow path comes like a ribbon over a hill miles away, down a long slope, across a creek, up a slope and over another hill.

All along the length of this ribbon there is now a thin line of men. For four days and nights they have fought hard, eaten little, washed none, and slept hardly at all. Their nights have been violent with attack, fright, butchery, and their days sleepless and miserable with the crash of artillery.

The men are walking. They are fifty feet apart, for dispersal. Their walk is slow, for they are dead weary, as you can tell even when looking at them from behind. Every line and sag of their bodies speaks their inhuman exhaustion.

On their shoulders and backs they carry heavy steel tripods, machine-gun barrels, leaden boxes of ammunition. Their feet seem to sink into the ground from the overload they are bearing.

They don't slouch. It is the terrible deliberation of each step that spells out their appalling tiredness. Their faces are black and unshaven. They are young men, but the grime and whiskers and exhaustion make them look middle-aged.

These phantoms were not soldiers as Americans knew them — not the storybook characters of wars long past, certainly not the sons and brothers who had left home only months before.

156

These were actors in a Stygian drama, dark angels on whom history had foisted some unconscionable burden.

In their eyes as they pass is not hatred, not excitement, not despair, not the tonic of their victory — there is just the simple expression of being here as though they had been here doing this forever, and nothing else.

The line moves on, but it never ends. All afternoon men keep coming round the hill and vanishing eventually over the horizon. It is one long tired line of antlike men.

There is an agony in your heart and you almost feel ashamed to look at them. They are just guys from Broadway and Main Street, but you wouldn't remember them. They are too far away now. They are too tired. Their world can never be known to you. . . .[50]

That evening the men were ordered to stop and dig in on a ridge offering protection from German shells. They rested for two days, surprising Ernie with evidence of "how quickly the human body can recuperate from critical exhaustion, how rapidly the human mind snaps back to the normal state of laughing, grousing, yarn-spinning, and yearning for home." The soldiers slumbered in their holes, then ate hot food brought from the rear in jeeps. Mail arrived.

They washed. On the second day they cleaned their rifles, kibbitzed in groups, asked Ernie what he was writing. "They are all disappointed when they learn I am not permitted to name the outfit they're in, for they are all proud of it and would like the folks at home to know what they've done." As darkness came they received orders to prepare to move further forward. Half the battalion was to attack at 3:00 A.M.; the second half, which Ernie went with, was to leave later, dig in by dawn, and await orders. Again, the image of men in motion haunted Ernie's memory.

There is no excitement, no grouching, no eagerness either. They had expected it.

Quietly they roll their packs, strap them on, lift their rifles and fall into line.

There is not a sound as they move like wraiths in single file down tortuous goat paths, walking slowly, feeling the ground with their toes, stumbling and hushfully cussing. They will walk all night and attack before dawn.

They move like ghosts. You don't hear or see them three feet away. Now and then a light flashes lividly from a blast by our big guns, and then for just an instant you see a long slow line of dark-helmeted forms silhouetted in the flash.

Then darkness and silence consume them again, and somehow you are terribly moved.

Simple sensory images filled Pyle's account of this second march — feeling for bomb craters with one's feet in the dark; the scuffle and thud of a man stumbling and falling; the lonely voice of a radio operator trying over and over all night to raise a distant comrade. Then came an order to cease all talking, and they "marched in silence except for the splitting crash of German artillery ahead and of ours behind. . . . There would be the heavy blast of the guns, then an eerie rustle from each shell as it sped unseen across the sky far above our heads. It gave the night a strange sense of greatness. As a first-timer I couldn't help but feel a sort of exaltation from this tense, stumbling march through foreign darkness up into the unknown."[51]

With this series of columns Pyle gave his countrymen a new breed of war hero. His sketch of "the god-damned infantry," colored in and rendered in fine detail through the larger campaigns to come, stamped the American war with its distinctive symbol. Ordinary men from ordinary places, his subjects had been transformed into "strange giant creatures." They were straw spun into gold.

5

★★★★

"I'll Just Drift with the War . . ."

SICILY: MAY–AUGUST 1943

As the victory celebrations in North Africa dwindled, Ernie surrendered to "utter exhaustion such as I had never known before. . . . My mind [was] as blank as my body was lifeless."[1] Still feeling depleted after four days of slumber and bleary-eyed inactivity, he packed his jeep for a leisurely drive to Algiers, where he could catch up with his columns and mail, bathe, collect his thoughts and make plans. But his drive along the Mediterranean coast was studded with disturbing delays. First he struck and injured an Arab boy who ran in front of the jeep. Then, at an American base, dozens of Air Corps acquaintances besieged him, wanting to catch up with the news and reminisce. Within an hour the knot twisting in his stomach forced him to find a doctor.[2]

Algiers was more hectic still. "Always a place of strange mixtures," John Steinbeck wrote about this time, "it has been brought to a nightmarish mess by the influx of British and American troops and their equipment. Now jeeps and staff cars nudge their way among camels and horse-drawn cars. The sunshine is blindingly white on the white city, and when there is no breeze from the sea the heat is intense."[3] For the man who had found himself contented and purposeful in the midst of thunderous battle, the chattering city felt unbearable. Ernie's old complaints of "tightness in the back of the head and . . . 'eyes out of focus' " crept back within hours of his arrival. "Back here," he told Jerry, "with crowds and street noise and too many people you know and correspondence and obligations, I have that old panicky swamped feeling again. . . . I guess my time at the front has completely spoiled me for 'civilization.' "[4]

He fled.

"Laughter . . . and wine and lovely flowers"

A half-hour from the city he found a small Army camp at the seaside village of Zeralda. Here, with a couple of correspondent friends, he pitched his tent by a tree and set up a new cot and a German folding table. The nearby surf rustled under a brilliant blue sky. The only other sounds rose from "the birds singing in the scrub bushes that grow out of the sand and lean precisely away the sea." The breeze and the sunlight created a mood of such peace that Ernie could hardly escape "a sense of infidelity" to the men in Tunisia, "whose final awareness was a bedlam of fire and noise and uproar."[5]

A thick pack of mail had been waiting for him

161

in Algiers. Scripps-Howard's executives were beside themselves. "RECENT COPY BEEN ABSOLUTELY TERRIFIC EVERYBODY PROUD OF YOU," Miller cabled. The *New York World-Telegram*, the Scripps-Howard flagship that had customarily snipped the column to ribbons, was now blazoning it on its front page. Newspapers outside the chain ran entire articles about soldiers whom Pyle had merely mentioned in the column. *Time* magazine pronounced him "America's most widely read war correspondent." More papers were calling United Feature each week to sign up for the column.[6]

As the delightful particulars of his new fortunes began to penetrate his tired mind, Ernie was alternately perplexed, pleased, irritated, proud. In a letter to his father and aunt he assumed his country-boy tone. "It looks from all the reports that I'm the No. 1 correspondent of the war," he said. "That's nice, but I'm glad I'm not at home and have to go through all the fuss that goes with it."[7] Of course, he was more than shrewd enough to realize this new fame — even if it was, as he believed, a kind of benign freak of nature — might erase the financial worries of many years. In Washington, Lee Miller was spending much of his time fielding inquiries about Pyle's availability for various money-making schemes. Four publishers were asking to put out a book of Ernie's Africa columns. After some dickering, Miller reached a deal with Henry Holt for a book to be titled — at Ernie's suggestion, though he continued to prefer something else — *Here Is Your War,* an exclamation to the reader that drove home the propaganda value of the book's contents. Ernie's advance was to be $5,000, more than a third of his 1942 income, with sales predicted to exceed 50,000 copies. Hollywood, too, was sniffing at Miller's door.[8]

Reviewing his income tax returns, Ernie calculated that he was now earning money at nearly twice the rate of the previous year, with perhaps far more in store. "Christ," he wrote Miller, "if something doesn't happen to stop all this nonsense, we're gonna get rich."[9] In a letter to Dana he sounded almost apologetic. "Sometimes it seems wrong to be making big money during the war when so many are dying and getting nothing," he told Will Pyle and his aunt, "but after all I'm not profiteering and I'm doing it the hard way by being right here myself where it's far from safe, and I feel I am contributing some good through the column."[10] There was no more talk of leaving the Army behind to circle the globe. "I guess I'll just drift with the war."[11]

The swelling tide of letters from readers — from "generals' wives, from aircraft workers, from old schoolmates, shipyard presidents, school kids, Pacific heroes, and hundreds of . . . mothers and fathers of soldiers" — confirmed the transformation in his prestige. The normal transaction between a newspaper reader and a reporter was commercial and impersonal — a nickel casually dispensed in return for a few columns of war news. But the bond between Pyle and his readers was far more intimate. Strangers sent him family photos, clippings, drawings, life histories. They offered him home remedies. They shipped packages of soap, books and cookies. Some wrote him as many as twenty times. One letter writer in three begged Ernie to look up a particular soldier, either just to say hello or to check on his safety or to find out why he had not written a letter home in so long. To the writers of these letters, Ernie seemed a ubiquitous spirit in North Africa, always within a stone's throw of their beloved soldiers, always able to peek in their tents to see they were safe.

So many letters arrived at Algiers he couldn't possibly respond individually. So he did so collectively, in two warm columns expressing his gratitude and his explanation of why he could not do what many asked. "Many of you write long letters about how things and people are in your home town, just as though that were my home town too. I like that. Your letters have kept me pretty well informed on the progress of rationing, shortages, and public spirit at home. Most of you write from your own goodness just to tell me you enjoy the column." Some few letters, painful to read, came from families who had received "the dreaded telegram from the War Department. Those telegrams are stark, blank things — they deal you the blow and leave you hanging in thin air. Your letters ask me to try to find out all the little details of how it happened and let you know. How I wish that it were possible. Those are the letters I would give anything to comply with. Those of you who have lost close ones seem to write so beautifully, so resignedly, and so patiently, that it is doubly hard on me to be forced to do nothing about your letters." At first he had tried to comply with these wishes, but the mounting numbers made it impossible to do so any longer.

I know how you feel — you think to yourself, "But surely he could find time to answer just this one little request." That's true. I could find time to do one. But it isn't just one. There are scores of them. If I were to obey my impulse and carry out these touching requests I would have to stop writing the column altogether. . . . And so this column is addressed to all of you readers who have written me, and even to a large percentage of my personal friends back home, to tell you why I can't answer your letters individually, and yet to thank you from the bottom of my heart for writing them.[12]

Zeralda's breezes were "a mean temptation, a beckoning to somnolence," for he had much work to do. In addition to columns and letters, he agreed to write a guest column for *Stars and Stripes,* the Army newspaper published in every war theater. It was a rough mark of honor that the editors asked him to address the troops directly, and he responded with relish as a wise-cracking comrade-in-arms. *Stripes* had asked him to write *about* the G.I.'s, he said, but "I don't know why [I] should be telling you about yourselves. If you don't know where you're at and how you feel by this time, you must be too dumb to read anyhow." So he told them about himself: "I've traveled 20,000 miles in Africa, got myself shot at once or twice, and died a thousand deaths from freezing. I know three generals by their first names, and have almost been court-martialed once. I've stolen one jeep and had two stolen from me. Since leaving home I've sent back nearly 300,000 words about you and your current careers, to coin a phrase. You didn't suspect you were that interesting, did you? Well maybe you aren't, but brother I've got a living to make."[13]

Ernie's most notable piece of writing at Zeralda was an epilogue for *Here Is Your War*. It was a meditation on the passage marked by the African campaign — passages of the country, the soldiers, himself. After "letting loose of life as it was . . . the new war life finally became the normal life to us." Early in the campaign there had been "days when I sat in my tent alone and gloomed with the desperate belief that it was actually possible for us to lose this war," but now he no longer feared defeat. Soldiers who might have accepted a negotiated peace six months

166

earlier just to get home now worked with "a vague but growing individual acceptance of the bitter fact that we must win the war or else. . . . We have washed out the bulk of our miscomprehensions, have abandoned most of our fallacies, and have hardened down into a work-weary and battle-dirtied machine. . . ."

Toughening came at a price. "Our men can't make this change from normal civilians into warriors and remain the same people." Their language had turned from "mere profanity to obscenity." They put little stock in the norms of property, wasting or stealing it with abandon, figuring "what's wrong with a small case of 'requisitioning' when murder is the classic goal?" And what of himself after half a year at war? "It may be that the war has changed me, along with the rest," but the changes were subtler. He groped to name them. He sensed small redemptions, for instance, "a new patience with humanity that I've never had before. When you've lived with the unnatural mass cruelty that mankind is capable of inflicting upon itself, you find yourself dispossessed of the faculty for blaming one poor man for the triviality of his faults. I don't see how any survivor of war can ever be cruel to anything, ever again."

His early "miscomprehensions" and "fallacies" about war had given way to a broader vision. It encompassed laughter and exhilaration, the intoxicating "wine of danger-emotion," but not the romance of Hollywood or boys' books. Nor did his vision sweep beyond the horizon, encompassing the strategies of distant leaders. It was a vision of the particular and the concrete, of one line of men, one man, one face. "I haven't wrtten anything about the 'Big Picture,' " he wrote in a passage often quoted later,

> because I don't know anything about it. I only know what we see from our worm's-eye view, and our segment of the picture consists only of tired and dirty soldiers who are alive and don't want to die; of long darkened convoys in the middle of the night; of shocked silent men wandering back down the hill from battle; of chow lines and atabrine tablets and foxholes and burning tanks and Arabs holding up eggs and the rustle of high-flown shells; of jeeps and petrol dumps and smelly bedding rolls and C rations and cactus patches and blown bridges and dead mules and hospital tents and shirt collars greasy-black from months of wearing; and of laughter too, and anger and wine and lovely flowers and constant cussing. All these it is composed of; and of graves and graves and graves.[14]

With his extra writing tasks out of the way, Ernie allowed himself to relax. He scrounged for an assortment of books — *Great English Short Stories, Beau Geste,* Henry James's *Turn of the*

Screw, a Joseph Conrad novella, a volume of Somerset Maugham stories and Sinclair Lewis's *Arrowsmith* — and he sat reading for several hours each day. One morning the war artist George Biddle, who had been assigned by the Army to direct a small group of professional artists in making visual records of the war, sketched Ernie's portrait. The sketch became the cover illustration for *Here Is Your War*. It portrays a sad, saintlike Pyle. In his war diary, Biddle, the scion of an aristocratic Philadelphia family, offered a word picture of his subject that explained his visual theme:

June 15. This morning I did a drawing in red sanguine of Ernie Pyle. I only put into it, I am afraid, a small part of his rare personality. He seems Yankee to the core, though hailing from Indiana farm stock. Ascetic, gentle, whimsical, shy. Frugal in his habits. Like so many Americans, his expression is fundamentally sad, yet full of tenderness. Of course a stubborn, thin-lipped individualist, and probably hard as granite under his timid manner. I like to think of him as he sits on the beach toward sundown, a white and slender Gandhi, swathed in towels and wrappers, for he hates the cold as much as he fears the sun. He does not swim and dislikes bathing. So he spends his week's holiday as follows: He sleeps three hours each day; reads for three hours; and then, being at his wits' end what to do, he sits down and writes a column. He puts his whole life into his column: his shy love of human beings, his tenderness, and his hard, salty, Indiana-farmer humor.[15]

"Men of new professions"

"I think I ought to do something on the Navy, don't you?" Ernie asked Miller at the close of the Tunisian campaign. "You might sound them out and see if they have any ideas. I don't want to go begging around for any Navy trip for I don't give a damn, but if they have something come up sometime they think would make good copy . . . I'd like to do it."[16]

The Navy certainly had "something coming up." The invasion of Sicily, mounted simultaneously from North Africa, England and the United States via some two thousand British and American ships in three massive fleets — destroyers and transports, minesweepers and minelayers, sub-chasers and self-propelled barges — was to be the largest seaborne assault ever undertaken to that time. The great Italian island lay only a hundred miles over the northern horizon from Tunisia. But invading Sicily meant invading Europe, the homeland of the Axis. It was the logical strategic stepping stone, yet to cross that narrow boundary of water was to take a vast step from the periphery of the war into its heart. The invasion was scheduled for July 10,

1943. A few days beforehand, Ernie was secretly whisked away from Algiers and driven back to Bizerte Harbor, where he boarded the headquarters ship USS *Biscayne.*

Days passed as stevedores and sailors rushed about, cramming ships' holds with supplies. Ernie, resting on a fat cushion of North Africa columns, had little to do but edit the ship's mimeographed daily newspaper, a small, volunteer chore that left him many hours to lounge on deck listening as men speculated about what their target would be and traded declarations about how they would meet the test. In Britain and North Africa Pyle had written little about the motives of men entering battle; but now he got to speculating on what actually propelled soldiers toward the attack.

The question was critical for a war correspondent, for it lay at the heart of a larger if unspoken one: What sort of heroes were these Americans? Were they gallant warriors in the old Victorian style — latter-day Teddy Roosevelts charging up a new San Juan Hill for country and glory? Or were they democratic heroes, fighting against fascist tyranny to protect President Roosevelt's Four Freedoms? Or was there some other explanation? Over the next ten days Pyle addressed his readers four times on the subject. He seemed to be sorting out his own confusion: at first he seemed to *want* to detect patriotic motives; then, just as suddenly, he stopped looking for them.

In his *Stars and Stripes* guest column, which was reprinted in Scripps-Howard papers, he gently chided his soldier friends for their perpetual talk of going home. "If you were suddenly offered the chance of going home for good — I don't mean a few select ones to be used for training, I mean everybody just up and quit and go home merely because you want to go home — I'll bet not one in 100 of you would vote to go until the war is won."[17] He returned to the topic in an account of men listening to the propaganda broadcasts of "Olga," a Nazi propagandist claiming to be an American turncoat. "As usual," Ernie wrote, "they laughed with amusement and scorn at her childishly treasonish talk. In a vague and indirect way, I suppose, the privilege of listening to your enemy trying to undermine you the very night before you go out to face him expresses what we are fighting for."[18] The next day, readers read his report of the *Biscayne*'s last night before leaving for Sicily, and again he detected purposes in men's minds that doubtless pleased Allied propagandists writing similar messages in Washington.

I never heard anybody say anything patriotic like the storybooks have people saying. There was philosophizing but it was simple and undramatic. I'm sure no man would have stayed ashore if given the chance. There was something bigger than the awful dread that would have kept them there. . . . It was, I think, just the application of plain, ordinary, unspoken, even unrecognized, patriotism.[19]

Pyle seemed to be groping for something he wasn't sure existed. Did a love of country really propel this monstrous assault force? When a man risked his life on a bullet-swept beach, did he take each step in the name of liberty? Certainly other correspondents weren't afraid to say so. But Pyle couldn't quite bring himself to agree. Examining his own urge to accompany the invasion, he found none of that "unspoken . . . patriotism," but rather "an irresistible egoism in seeing myself part of an historic naval movement."[20] As the *Biscayne* moved toward the misty horizon on the evening of July 9, he saw what "resembled a distant city . . . a solid formation of uncountable structures blending together." It was "our invasion fleet formed there far out at sea, waiting for us." His awe expanded as the evening turned to night. From the deck he watched the sharp outlines of hundreds of ships fade to blurry shadow, then disappear altogether. "Nearby ships were only heavier spots against the heavy background of the night. Now you thought you saw something and now there was nothing." Then a messenger from the ghostly armada broke into Ernie's consciousness.

Out of nowhere, a rolling little subchaser took on a dim shape alongside us and with

173

its motors held itself steady about 30 yards away. You could not see the speaker but a megaphoned voice came loudly across the water. . . .

Out in the darkness the voice was young. You could picture a boyish skipper over there in his blown hair and his life jacket and binoculars, rolling to the sea in the Mediterranean dusk. Some young man who had so recently been so normally unaware of any sea at all — the bookkeeper in your bank, perhaps, and now here he was a strange new man in command of a ship, suddenly transformed into a person with awful responsibilities carrying out with great intentness his special small part of the enormous aggregate that is our war on all the lands and seas of the globe.

In his unnatural presence there in the rolling darkness of the Mediterranean you realized vividly how everybody in America has changed, how every life suddenly stopped and suddenly began again on a different course. Everything in this world has stopped except war and we are all men of new professions out in some strange night caring for each other.

That's the way you felt as you heard this kid, this pleasant kid, bawling across the dark waters. . . .

Then, with half a sentence, Pyle departed for

good from the patriotic school of war correspondents:

> Not a pinpoint of light showed from those hundreds of ships as they surged on through the night toward their destiny, carrying across this ageless and indifferent sea tens of thousands of young men of new professions, fighting for . . . for . . . well, at least for each other.[21]

Conventional wisdom said Americans fought for flag and freedom. For a time Pyle mouthed it with the rest of the correspondents. But suddenly it strained his credulity beyond the breaking point. Abstractions shrank to insignificance on the "ageless and indifferent sea"; he no longer could believe they were "bigger than dread." But something else was, something hard to name. He had yearned for it since youth and now had found it in war. In fleeting moments war offered a sense of transcendence, of communion with a realm vastly larger than the self. In this seaborne immensity of machines and men, he absorbed the experience with every sense.

Such moments of awe were not to be had without a price, and Pyle now began to pay. As he prepared to go ashore at Sicily late in July 1943, Ernie was telling Jerry and his superiors at Scripps-Howard that he planned to stay with the Army through the end of this campaign and on

175

through the expected autumn battle for the Italian mainland. Yet before another month had passed, he had decided with a suddenness born of desperation that he must get away from the war.

Ernie had become unusually fatigued even before leaving North Africa. While still in port he stayed up late every night, jawboning with sailors and soldiers, then rose early to work on the ship's newspaper. This was followed by the wide-eyed tension of the invasion convoy and the landings. By D-plus-one he was complaining to Jerry of "the worst exhaustion I've ever experienced."[22] To fulfill his sense of obligation to the Navy he bunked aboard the *Biscayne* for a week and a half after the landings, but he itched to get ashore. As soon as he could, he fled the Navy's dry berths and hot showers, "a world that is orderly and civilized by comparison with the animal-like existence of living in the field."[23] It had been "a strange delight," he told readers, "and yet for some perverse reason I seemed to look forward to going back to the old soldier's way of sleeping on the ground and not washing before breakfast and fighting off fleas."[24]

Ashore, he resumed a grueling pace, though he no longer felt the electric thrill of Tunisia. "I find myself more and more reluctant to repeat and repeat the old process of getting shot at," he told Jerry. "I don't know whether it's cowardice on my part or experience or what, but the other correspondents who have been with it a long time say they are having the same reaction. When you get shells whining and falling around you . . . you sort of cringe and say 'Oh God do I have to go through this all over again?' "[25] Nonetheless, Ernie raced to catch General Patton's Seventh Army, which had broken out of the beachhead and surged a hundred miles across Sicily to take the port of Palermo on the island's northern coast. Near Palermo Ernie hooked up with an old friend, Raymond Clapper, a political columnist for Scripps-Howard who was making a brief tour of the European theater. Together they drove east along the coast, chasing the American advance toward Messina, Patton's key strategic goal. Twice they had to navigate around gaping holes in the road blasted by the retreating Germans. Elsewhere they waited as U.S. engineers dynamited obstacles. There was only one peaceful interlude. It came in an olive grove where Pyle, Clapper and Jack Thompson of the *Chicago Tribune* stumbled upon the makeshift command post of General Matthew Ridgway, commander of the 82nd Airborne Division.

The reporters found Ridgway seated at a table under a tree. A colonel sitting beside him dealt a hand of cards. All around them exhausted paratroopers slept on the ground, their boots protruding from dirty blankets. The men discussed the campaign for a while, then drifted to the topic of books and poetry. Ridgway, a soldier-intellectual like Patton but with none of Patton's pomposity, had been reading a work of the poet Stephen Vincent Benét. But his favorite poet, he said, was Kipling, who, because he had lived with soldiers in the Indian campaigns of his day, had been able to capture the universalities of the soldier's life. As Ernie and his friends listened, Ridgway recited a favorite passage from memory. It was Kipling's tribute to war reporters:

> *I have eaten your bread and salt.*
> *And I've drunk your water and wine.*
> *The deaths ye died I watched beside,*
> *And the lives ye led were mine.*[26]

The next day, Ernie and Clapper moved on toward the front. When they came within a half-mile of exploding shells, Clapper let Ernie off and went back. Pyle was the only reporter at the end of the line. "It seemed sad to leave him there," Clapper wrote later, "a frail little fellow in Army fatigue coveralls, carrying a bedroll. It seemed as if he was being left all alone with the whole war."[27]

Privately Clapper wrote to Lee Miller, urging that Pyle be ordered home for a rest. Clapper had glimpsed Ernie near the end of his rope; within forty-eight hours Ernie presented himself at a medical clearing station of the 45th Division, complaining of a burning fever and aching limbs. First the doctors diagnosed malaria, then dysentery, then, finally if vaguely, "battlefield fever," which they said was the result of "too much dust, bad eating, not enough sleep, exhaustion, and the unconscious nerve tension that comes to everybody in a front-line area."[28] He convalesced at the little tent hospital for less than a week, then joined the divisions of II Corps as they slogged through Sicily's mountainous midsection. Here the Americans' rapid advance slowed to a crawl, for in these redoubts the Germans waged intense and bloody defensive warfare. Ernie spent three days accompanying General Omar Bradley, commander of II Corps, as the Americans struggled to reduce the German stronghold at the town of Troina. Then Ernie shifted back to the coast road, where he came down with "the famous military disease known as 'the G.I.s' " — diarrhea. One day he walked four miles with a group of combat engineers and spent half the next day unable to rise from his bedroll.

In the middle of August, he entered Messina. The battle for Sicily was over. Three days later, he cabled Washington to say he was coming home. "I've reached a state of mental dullness . . . ," he told Miller. "It's absolutely necessary for me to get freshened up before bogging down completely."[29]

Five weeks may seem a short time for a man to shift from eagerness to utter depletion. But infantry combat compresses time. Scenes and experiences of a type few people see over a lifetime are jammed into weeks, even days. And few realize this who have not been through it; the non-veteran has experienced the war through discreet filters and euphemisms — "retrograde movement" to designate the panicky rout at Kasserine Pass; "mopping up" and "cleaning out" to designate brutally difficult engagements with small but lethal groups of the enemy.[30] Neither the war correspondents of World War II nor historians of the war have lingered long over the destruction of human beings that was the principal business of combat units on either side of the front lines. But we know what Pyle saw.

In North Africa he had seen dead and wounded men but not in such concentrations as in Sicily. Here he seldom if ever ventured into the narrow band of territory where front-line combat actually took place. But the intensity of the warfare in Sicily and the speed of the advance meant there often was more to see just to the rear of that band than there had been in Tunisia. One day, for example, Ernie came to a place where someone had piled the bodies of some two hundred German and Italian soldiers. In *rigor mortis* the penises of many of the dead had become hugely erect, some of them protruding through the buttons of their soiled trousers. The bulk of Pyle's Sicilian education came in the medical clearing station, where trucks backed up to the tents all day and night to discharge their burdens of wounded. Outside the surgical tent there was a shallow pit filled with bloody sleeves and trouser legs, cut away from wounds to ease the surgeons' tasks. Ernie spent an entire day standing by the operating table, and for many more hours he lay on his own litter, talking with those who could talk, watching and listening. The power of the armories struck his consciousness directly, through no filter of euphemism or camera lens.

Bullets were among the least of the infantryman's worries; they accounted for perhaps ten percent of non-fatal wounds and were more easily treated than injuries caused by mortars, grenades, and especially artillery shells: exploding in trees or smashing into brittle rocks, shells shattered into jagged fragments, often piercing men's bodies in many places at once, tearing twisting paths through tissue and bone. Some men were decapitated or cut in two. Hot flying metal tore off limbs, ears, jaws and occasionally genitals. A soldier standing in a tank hit by a shell might find his legs compressed into a single shapeless mass.[31] The damage done to a smaller group of men whom Pyle saw in the clearing station did not appear on their bodies. Their affliction carried an assortment of understated labels — shell shock, anxiety neurosis, neuropsychiatric casualties, combat exhaustion, battle fatigue. All such terms represented the efforts of Army doctors to create an accurate label for the various states of emotional disintegration that came eventually to nearly every man who survived long enough in the front lines.

Among the casualties of war, battle fatigue

cases were — and remain — perhaps the least publicized and the most poorly understood. They emerged in large numbers only in wars of the latter half of the nineteenth century, when soldiers were first exposed to sustained periods of intense, long-range artillery bombardment. Doctors and generals have fought bitterly over the causes and treatment of battle fatigue, probably because it raises questions of such profound moral and practical consequence. Is it wholly a matter of personal will — of bravery — for a soldier to remain for many weeks at the front amid the horrific stresses of modern battle? Is the combat fatigue victim merely a coward dressed in psychological jargon? Or is battle ultimately and literally unbearable? If so, how can any army prevail once it makes this admission? No culture wants to acknowledge that its warriors flinch. And though people know their loved ones have a good chance of escaping death or injury on the battlefield, few know, as one authority has said, that "battle . . . if it is sufficiently severe, intense, and long in duration . . . will ultimately break everyone committed to it."[32]

Symptoms often began with relatively mild physical complaints, such as headache, backache, lightheadedness, gastric problems and heart palpitations. Other victims showed signs of extreme emotional tension: irritability, sleeplessness, tremors, feelings of insecurity or inadequacy. As the case worsened, the mind's basic powers faltered. The soldier answered questions slowly, could not respond to orders, forgot things, could not perform routine tasks. He lost interest "in comrades, military activity, food, even letters from home," and he withdrew into himself. The death or maiming of a close friend or a respected leader could cast him into a profound depression.[33] Combat medics quickly became accustomed to what one psychiatric report called "the shrunken apathetic faces" of men who came "stumbling into the medical station, sobbing, trembling, referring shudderingly to 'them shells' and to buddies mutilated or dead . . ."[34]

Battle fatigue in World War II has been closely associated in the American public mind with the Sicily campaign, for it was in Sicily that George Patton gained notoriety for publicly slapping and humiliating two privates who admitted to suffering from attacks of "nerves." Both incidents occurred at medical stations, the first during and the second just after the American assault on Troina, where the exchange of artillery fire was particularly intense. It happened close to where Ernie spent several days with the headquarters staff of II Corps. Word of the incidents quickly spread, and three correspondents became so incensed that they went to Eisenhower and threatened to publish the story unless Patton were fired. Eisenhower prevailed on the reporters to stay mum, saying Patton would be disciplined. The episode reached home-front ears only after an interval of several months; in late November 1943, the columnist Drew Pearson told a version of the story on his radio program.

Pyle knew of the Patton slappings but wrote nothing about them. "Ernie . . . hated Patton's guts," his friend Don Whitehead of the Associated Press said later. "Patton's bluster, show and complete disregard for the dignity of the individual was the direct antithesis of Ernie's gentle character."[35] But rather than criticize Patton, Ernie preferred to lionize the modest and plain-spoken Omar Bradley. This was in part the result of clever public relations by the Army. Eisenhower himself had urged Ernie to "go and discover Bradley."[36] When Pyle did so, approaching Bradley through his aide, Captain Chester Hansen, the general resisted. But Hansen, whose public relations acumen would later carry him to a high PR post at IBM, saw that contact with Pyle could pay off for his boss. "General," Hansen told Bradley, "for those 80,000 troops [in II Corps] you've got better than a quarter-million fathers, mothers, wives, and what-have-you in the United States, all of them worrying about these men. A good many of them are probably asking themselves: What sort of a guy is this Omar Bradley? Is he good enough to take care of my man? [T]hey've got a right to an answer. And believe me, Pyle is just the bird to give them a good one."[37] When Bradley agreed, the result was a laudatory series that helped "the G.I. general" on his way to the pinnacle of the Army. Plenty of U.S. generals scrambled for publicity; committed grave errors of bravado, timidity or incompetence; or, like Patton, terrorized their subordinates. But not in Pyle's column.

Ernie saw soldiers maimed and wrote about it, but his accounts stopped only just short of sugar-coating. In his columns about the tent hospital, even men with the ugliest wounds somehow were going to turn out all right. There was the soldier hit by a machine-gun bullet that gouged a tunnel along his nose, through his cheek, and out beneath his ear. "It gave you the willies to look at it, yet the doctors said it wasn't serious at all and would heal with no bad effects." Another man had two great holes in his back — "You could have put your whole hand in either one of them" — yet in surgery the patient gaily "talked a blue streak" about how hungry he was and how he had just killed five of the enemy with a single grenade. A third G.I. had been hit by some two hundred shards of shrapnel, "yet none of them made a vital hit, and the soldier will live." Three shocking wounds; three game survivors — better odds, certainly, than a soldier could actually expect. Ernie also declared himself "flabber-gasted" to hear "a tentful of wounded soldiers . . . beg to be sent right back into the fight." Or perhaps not "a tentful," he admitted, but "at least a third of the moderately wounded." One can guess what he heard the other soldiers say — but did not report — about hurrying back to the front.[38] Thus Ernie's readers learned that many wounds were worse than Hollywood's discreet bullet holes to the chest. Yet they lay down their newspapers with the image of hearty recovery foremost in their minds, especially because of "the thoughtful and attentive attitude of the doctors and ward-boys toward the wounded men. . . . It couldn't help but be a moving and depressing experience," he wrote, "and yet there was something good about it, too."[39]

As for cases of battle fatigue, Ernie mentioned them only in passing. He had tried to do more. At a press camp in North Africa a couple of months earlier, Ralph Martin, an Army sergeant serving as a correspondent for *Stars and Stripes*, had come upon Ernie, morose and drunk. Pyle asked Martin to sit down, then read the typescript of a column aloud. It was about shell-shocked U.S. soldiers. "He read it with a great deal of feeling," Martin remembered. Then Ernie said: "They won't let me send it." The censors had kicked it back to him.

"He was bitter," Martin recalled. "He was angry. He was almost in tears."[40]

Thus the war that appeared in Ernie's columns did not square with the war he was seeing and feeling. The symptoms he mentioned in private letters — intestinal trouble, dullmindedness, depression — were surely signs of his own mild case of battle fatigue. The fear that had carried a little electric thrill in North Africa was growing, and the thrill had left. "I know the longer we stay with this the smaller our chances are of getting out," he told Don Whitehead one night. "It's the inevitability of death in war that finally gets you down.[41] And he was deeply tired. He talked to friends in the First Division who had been in the front lines for twenty-eight days, "walking and fighting all that time," men who had "pass[ed] the point of known human weariness."[42] He didn't dare compare his exhaustion to theirs, but he plaintively told his readers that war correspondents, too, could wear out. "It is true we don't fight on and on like the infantry, that we are usually under fire only briefly. . . . Yet our lives are strangely consuming in that we do live primitively and at the same time must delve into ourselves and do creative writing. That statement may lay me open to wise cracks, but however it may seem to you, writing is an exhausting and tearing thing. . . . We travel continuously, move camp every few days, eat out, sleep out, write wherever we can and just never catch up on sleep, rest, cleanliness, or anything else normal." Reporters who had begun in the earlier days of North Africa had:

grown befogged. We are grimy, mentally as well as physically. We've drained our emotions until they cringe from being called out from hiding. We look at bravery and death and battlefield waste and new countries almost as blind men, seeing only faintly and not really wanting to see at all.

It's the ceaselessness, the endlessness of everything that finally worms its way through you and gradually starts to devour you.

It's the perpetual dust choking you, the hard ground wracking your muscles, the snatched food sitting ill on your stomach, the heat and the flies and dirty feet and the constant roar of engines and the perpetual moving and the never settling down and the go, go, go, night and day, and on through the night again. Eventually it all works itself into an emotional tapestry of one dull, dead pattern — yesterday is tomorrow and Troina is Randazzo and when will we ever stop and, god, I'm so tired.[43]

Private questions about his role, even about the war itself, resurfaced in his mind. "The war gets so complicated and confused in my mind," he told Jerry. "On especially sad days it's almost impossible for me to believe that anything is worth such mass slaughter and misery. . . ."[44]

So, on August 20, he decided to go home.

His explanation to readers bordered on apology. Perhaps, he said, they would wonder how he could leave Europe at such an important moment. If he had kept writing without a rest, he would have let them down. "Battles differ one from another only in their physical environment — the emotions of fear and exhaustion and exaltation and hatred are about the same in all of them. Through repetition, I had worn clear down to the nub of my ability to weigh and describe. You can't do a painting when your oils have turned to water. . . .

"I had come to despise and be revolted by war clear out of any logical proportion. I couldn't find the Four Freedoms among the dead men."[45]

He had been overseas for four hundred and twenty-eight days. He could think of little but the prospect of easing into a chair in Albuquerque. For a time, at least, he could try to forget incoming artillery and cold K-rations and bloody flaps of skin hanging oddly from men's bodies. He had to write a handful of columns more on Sicily; but then, he believed, he would have several weeks of blissful rest.

Waiting in Algiers for his flight to the United States, Ernie talked and drank with old friends and new acquaintances in the correspondent corps. Among the greenhorns was his literary hero, John Steinbeck, sent overseas by the *New York Herald Tribune* to cover the coming campaign in Italy. "I'm glad that Steinbeck is at last with the wars," Ernie wrote in his column. "For he carries to them a delicate sympathy for mortal man's transient nobilities and beastlinesses that I believe no other writer possesses. Surely we have no other writer so likely to catch on paper the inner things that most people don't know

189

about war — the pitiableness of bravery, the vulgarity, the grotesquely warped values, the childlike tenderness in all of us." He did not say, but might have, that this expressed his own ideals as a war correspondent. Nor did he say if he thought he was meeting them.[46]

In Algiers, Ernie also ran into Graham Hovey, the young Hearst reporter whom he had befriended in Tunisia a few months earlier. Hovey had just returned to Africa after a furlough at home.

"Ernie," Hovey said, "you don't have any idea what's going to hit you when you get to New York."[47]

6

★★★★

"The Number-One Correspondent..."

HOME FRONT:
SEPTEMBER–DECEMBER 1943

Lee Miller came up from Washington to meet his friend at LaGuardia Field. The Clipper landed before dawn on September 7, 1943.[1] By 8:00 A.M. they were in their rooms at the Algonquin Hotel in Manhattan. The telephone rang at ten minutes after eight. Miller answered.

Would Mr. Pyle be willing to speak on a radio program? Miller said no. How about for $1,500? Still no.

The phone rang again. Would Mr. Pyle be interested in making a lecture tour for a guaranteed minimum fee of $25,000? Again, no.

A third call: Mr. Marshall Field, of the Chicago department store, would be pleased to have Mr. Pyle dine with him on his way west. Sorry, thanks.

More calls: Could Mr. Pyle meet with Army intelligence? Would he join the Secretary of the Treasury in a radio pitch for War Bonds? Could he pose for a picture? Would he endorse a cigarette? Did he have news of a certain major in

Sicily? Could he meet with his book publisher?

A knock on the door: the Associated Press. How about a quote on the soldiers in Europe? Another knock: *Editor and Publisher*, the magazine of the trade. A wire from Oklahoma. Denver calling. Washington calling. Indianapolis calling. CBS, NBC. It continued all day and into the next. Close friends were enlisted to fend off "strangers, cranks . . . people who want a piece of Ernie for this cause or that." Indiana University wanted a speech. The Office of War Information wanted a recording for the troops. People on the street wanted handshakes. Girls at the United Feature office went "ga-ga." Pyle and Miller rushed for a taxi to Penn Station, where at last anonymity could be found: a redcap turned his back on Ernie's sixty-pound duffle bag. The train began to move; Pyle hoisted the bag on his shoulder, ran, leaped aboard.[2]

"No statesman . . . or general or admiral or movie star," an editorialist wrote a few days later, "ever got a quicker or more complete bath of fame than has this thin man from Indiana."[3]

"You couldn't really tell it in words"

Look magazine offered the standard explanation for the overnight transformation in Ernie's status: "Eight months ago, Ernie Pyle's column was published in 42 newspapers and nobody much gave a hoot. Today it appears in 149 papers (at last count) and is, to anyone who wants to be informed about the war, a 'must.' " Before the war, the article went on, "he wrote about unimportant, inconspicuous people, what they thought and said. . . . But when war broke out, his little people were transported from Omaha and Tucumcari to the slit trenches and foxholes of North Africa. What they said and thought suddenly became very important."[4] That overlooked Pyle's genuine prewar popularity — readers of his forty-two papers *did* give a hoot — and it failed to explain why he alone was gaining a reputation as *the* correspondent of the war. But it did capture an important truth about Pyle's new fame. He and the G.I. were now fused in the public mind — the apotheosis of the Common Man in a single heroic image.

This can only be understood in the context of the American home front during World War II — a context that has been blurred nearly beyond recognition under a half-century-old gloss of nostalgia. It is hard to remember now, when the war stands in public memory as a monument to national righteousness, that Americans tiptoed toward entry into World War II with the greatest reluctance, and indeed might have stayed out altogether had it not been for two catastrophic blunders by the Axis powers: Japan's attack on Pearl Harbor and Hitler's declaration of war on the United States. Once these acts occurred, Americans supported the war effort with something approaching absolute unanimity. But hidden beneath the newsreel images of waving flags and marching columns were dark eddies and swirls in public opinion. Polls showing full support for the war also revealed that one in four citizens worried that the chief threat to the nation was neither Germany nor Japan but "people in the U.S. who are not taking the war seriously enough."[5] A California woman expressed these forebodings in a letter to the president: "In these crucial days, we feel that our people are not truly aware of the critical situation of our Nation. We have friends who laugh and vacation, drive their cars and do not buy war bonds just through pure inability to feel the urgency of the war."[6]

Pearl Harbor had united Americans, but it hadn't given them any sense of purpose larger than the instinctive drives for self-protection and vengeance. Even at the end of 1942, a full year after Pearl Harbor, the polltaker George Gallup had found that one in three Americans, when asked, "Do you feel you have a clear idea of what this war is all about?" would answer, "No."[7] In the White House, in congressional offices, in propaganda agencies, in the boardrooms of corporations and newspapers, people who felt responsible for guiding public opinion spoke in concerned tones about "the morale problem." In a total war — its outcome uncertain, its duration unpredictable — public support for unprecedented industrial production and economic dedication was essential. Watching people wasting gasoline, squandering fat war pay-checks, and lounging on country-club barstools, opinion-makers worried early in the war that if it dragged into a stalemate, some portion of the public might drift toward sympathy for a negotiated peace. As the war went on and Allied prospects improved, that fear changed to a fear of complacency — a lazy indifference or overconfidence that could sap the drive for war production.

These fears had an obvious cause. All the other Allies — France, Britain, Russia, China, Poland — had watched the war roll over their own soil. But to Americans, the battles could not help but seem remote. People knew, vaguely but with pangs of guilt, their soldiers were undergoing a sacrificial ordeal on their behalf. To understand that ordeal, and to convince themselves they were sharing in it, they read the war news avidly. And no writer was read more avidly than Ernie Pyle. What Pyle felt, the soldier was presumed to feel, and vice versa. The public possession known as "Ernie Pyle" was the emotional current running between the civilian and the war. He was the interpreter, the medium, the teacher who taught Americans what to think and how to feel about their boys overseas.

It soon began to dawn on Ernie that this new status meant money. In the spring of 1943, Holt had offered an advance of $2,500 for *Here Is Your War*. Miller had negotiated that sum upward to $4,000, then to $5,000 — nearly half of Ernie's annual salary. But as Ernie's popularity mounted during the late spring and summer, Holt began to predict a sale of some 50,000 to 60,000 copies; this would send the book toward the bestseller charts.[8] Next, the Book-of-the-Month Club bought the book. Then the Council on Books in Wartime ordered 50,000 copies for soldiers overseas.[9] All this promised a vast increase in Ernie's income. But Hollywood was offering even more.

The origins of the movie that became *The Story of G.I. Joe* — largely forgotten now but acclaimed as a classic of its genre in 1945 — lay in the Army's continuing fear of falling behind in its race against the Navy for public favor and congressional appropriations. There was much consternation in the Army's upper echelons about the trend of Hollywood's early war offerings. All the action movies seemed to feature dashing sailors among the waving palms of the Pacific, where the Navy was in charge of the war. The Army Air Corps was drawing the moviemakers' attention, but that, too, threatened the prestige of generals whose careers were rooted in the ground forces. So, early in 1943, the Pictorial Branch of the Army's Public Relations Division contacted Lester Cowan, a portly young Hollywood producer with "a grin like a cantaloupe slice."[10] Cowan had worked for the Academy of Motion Picture Arts and Sciences and made a movie called *Commandos Strike at Dawn*. The Army urged Cowan to "show the world something of the miserable, thankless life of the fighting GI."[11] Cowan had turned for advice to Ernie's old boss, Lowell Mellett, who was now head of the movie division in the Office of War Information (OWI). Mellett in turn spoke to Raymond Clapper, who told Cowan, "If you want to learn about the infantry, talk to a little guy named Ernie Pyle."[12]

Cowan read Pyle's columns and instantly conceived an irrepressible enthusiasm for the reporter and the project. Meeting with Ernie and Lee Miller in Washington, the producer won the rights to make a movie based on *Here Is Your War* with a solemn vow to break the mold of war films. He pledged to portray the lives of infantrymen with an absolute minimum of "hokum." Ernie agreed to let himself be played in the film, but only if other correspondents were represented, too, and he wanted the focus on the G.I.'s, not himself. Ernie insisted on the right to review the final script and to have Miller and Mellett do the same. Cowan said amen to all conditions, but Ernie remained skeptical. He had trouble believing any producer could resist the temptation to schmaltz up the film with love stories, phony heroics and misty-eyed patriotism. And he knew all too well that combat veterans literally laughed at the war movies they saw, a fate he was desperate to avoid. As the weeks passed and Ernie traveled from Washington to Dana to Albuquerque, Cowan continued to shower him with reassurances. But Ernie's main concern was the as-yet-unwritten script, and the unknown "boy-writer" whom Cowan had hired to create it.

This was none other than Arthur Miller, a Brooklyn-born playwright of only twenty-eight. In New York literary circles he was considered a writer of enormous promise — promise that would be fulfilled in *Death of a Salesman* and *The Crucible* — but in 1943 he was largely unknown. Twice rejected for military service, Miller had attracted Cowan's eye as a fresh talent who might write a script free of the usual war movie clichés. Cowan had dispatched Miller on a tour of domestic Army bases where he might find veterans of North Africa to tell him what war was really like. Miller had written an 85,000-word diary of this foray among the soldiers, in whom he was seeking confirmation of his own fervent beliefs about the war. Like many New Deal liberals and intellectuals, Miller scorned the idea that "Remember Pearl Harbor" was the sole rationale the war effort needed. To justify the nation's enormous sacrifices, many liberals were demanding a bolder, more affirmative sense of mission. To them, the war was — or ought to be — an idealistic, anti-fascist crusade to advance the cause of political and social democracy throughout the world. Miller was among these true believers, and he wanted his script to spread the faith.[13]

The young dramatist, tall and hawklike, arrived at Ernie's front door in Albuquerque in the middle of October. At first the two men were politely wary of each other. Miller feared that as an idealistic young New Yorker and a "serious" writer, he would find little common ground with the older, laconic midwesterner schooled in deadline journalism. To Pyle, Miller knew, "the very word 'Hollywood' meant fraud." And the playwright had no high regard for his host's talents. He thought Pyle's columns "too fragmentary, too letter-like," and lacking in the idealism Miller held dear. Yet he needed Pyle's approval if his script were ever to reach the screen. "It was true, after all, that I had merely brushed shoulders with the men who were going to fight this war, and he had lived with them and seen them die," Miller wrote later. "And the meanings I was seeking in their lives never seemed to penetrate his columns. The war, in his columns, was a series of essentially disconnected incidents involving millions of men who had few things in common that could be called ideas."[14]

That night Miller left the training camp diary for Ernie to read. When they met again the next day, Pyle pronounced himself much impressed. Over the next four days they talked at length, relaxing in the Pyles' tiny living room, walking the quiet streets at night, reviewing Miller's ideas for the script. He wanted to trace the actions of an imaginary group of infantrymen. In keeping with the democratic faith, no man would be featured above the others; through their relationships and actions, "the democratic ideals of the war" would be brought to life. Though he showed respect for the reporter's experience, Miller wanted to reach beyond the column, which he saw as morally neutral. He wanted to know what Pyle really believed; or more precisely, he hoped to learn that Pyle believed what he, Miller, believed about the war. Ernie, though patient with these probings, was an uncomfortable oracle. He was "chary of implanting any 'theme' upon the material," Miller wrote later.[15]

As Miller recalled a key exchange, he said: "The war is about something. What do you think it's about, Ernie?"

"Well . . . I don't know," Pyle replied. "I know what it could be about, but I don't know what it is about."

Miller asked about German prisoners. Weren't they fundamentally different from American boys — haughty, race-conscious, fascist? Some were haughty, Pyle conceded, but so were some American soldiers. "Soldiers are soldiers," he said. "When you take the German's gun away he's just a guy. . . . The war is between a lot of guys, millions of them."

Miller perceived that where he saw abstract ideals, Pyle saw only concrete "details about people." For Miller, this was not enough. A movie that realistically reported the facts of soldiers' daily existence might surpass most war pictures, he thought, but it would "not really be the truth," for "the truth is a larger thing than what man feels or knows at any particular time in his life. . . . It is about a lot of guys who are doing something which will have significance when their uniforms are moth eaten and don't fit anymore." Miller believed that "if the picture were to leave out the ideas being born in this war, and the ideas being destroyed in this war . . . what remained would be a meaningless pantomime of bloodshed, a weird witches' tale without sense or consequence."

But he couldn't say this to Ernie Pyle. "He was to me the psychological embodiment of all the soldiers I had seen," and "from the side-lines it is hard to tell such a man that you want to add to his observations." Whenever Miller began to discuss "the significance of the war in any terms approaching the political," Pyle "seemed a little uneasy."

But Miller kept trying. He described a scene he had in mind for the movie. Two infantrymen would be in a conquered village in Sicily. One is a no-goodnik Italian-American. Shaken by the deaths of several comrades, he sheds his uniform, goes AWOL, and hides out with a local family. The other soldier, a friend of the Italian-American who serves as his conscience, has joined the Army despite a bad ankle because of his anti-Fascist ideals. Thanks to the intervention of the Americans, particularly the idealistic soldier, the villagers are able to overthrow the local gang of Fascist officials. The villagers' joy at this turnabout spreads to the American G.I.'s, including the deserter, who recovers his lost self-respect by putting on his uniform again and rejoining his fellows. This act of liberation, Miller explained, would serve to justify the characters' existence as soldiers and to "give a piece of meaning to all the bloodshed we have shown on the screen."

> "I want to show that it is not meaningless, or at least that it need not be. What do you think?"
>
> He kept nodding. "Well, I'll be darned," he said. Then he nodded some more and patted the dog, and finally said, "Yup. That's all right." He was struggling with the facts. He was trying to find facts that would make the scene all right. . . . "It's pretty good. It could happen, I guess. Yeh, something like that will be all right."
>
> "Because I don't believe this war has no meaning."
>
> "Sure. You put that in," he said. It was as though, for a moment, he was happy to find himself carried along by my conviction that the war had political meaning, good ends, a certain justification even for the horrors he had seen.[16]

Miller "sensed a little fear in him that maybe it was going too far. I mean he wants to say the same thing and he wishes to hell the soldiers understood, but he's such a reporter man that any 'interpretation' such as a scene like this amounts to probably gives him a shade of feeling similar to that of a false dateline on a story."[17]

Try as he might, Miller could not dispel Ernie's uneasiness. The playwright's initial impression had been correct: he and Ernie had fundamentally different motives. Miller yearned to say what the war ought to be; Ernie aimed to say what it was. And even that aim, perhaps, beckoned from beyond his grasp. "The need to tell the truth seemed like an ache he was always feeling," Miller wrote. "Sometimes, listening to him, I confused it with worry over the fate of the soldiers, and I think he confused it with that too, but it was always the need for the truth. He was obsessed with it." What troubled Pyle, Miller believed, was that he had been "universally credited with having written the truth . . . . He had told as much of what he saw as people could read without vomiting. It was the part that would make them vomit that bothered him . . . . He tried to tell me that you couldn't really tell it in words. Not war, you couldn't. He tried in many ways to make it clear to me." [18]

Their conversations drifted to personal topics. Miller described his rocky marriage and a chance encounter he had recently had with another woman. As Miller recounts the story in his memoirs, he had been in Washington, where, through mutual friends, he had met and dined with a young woman whose husband, a sailor, had been reported lost on an Arctic convoy supplying war materiel to the besieged Soviets. She made regular inquiries still at naval offices, but it was plain that her husband was dead. On a dance floor with Miller, she told him all this, as well as the fact that she was now sleeping with other sailors, an admission he interpreted to mean that "through them she was reaching into the sea where her beloved lay dead." Miller found something deeply arousing in what the war had done to her. "I wanted to sleep with her myself, stimulated almost as much by the poetry of the idea as by her body. . . . [T]he brush of death had made her sensually attached to life, to sex, had given her a taste for the catastrophic."[19]

Ernie's emotional interruption caught Miller off guard.

"Don't, don't do anything like that ever," he told Miller. "The marriage is everything. That sex stuff is no good, it won't get you a thing. . . . You think you have to do it, but you don't. Your wife sounds like a wonderful woman. . . ."

"What amazed me suddenly," Miller recalled many years later, "was the depth and innocence of his caring. . . ."[20]

Ernie's four weeks in Albuquerque were not the respite he had envisioned. Movie discussions, other work and the pesterings of fans stole nearly all his time. And Jerry, though she had recovered a measure of stability and gotten a job at the air base outside Albuquerque, was not much better. For the first three weeks of Ernie's visit, she held herself steady. But when he resumed writing the column and prepared to leave for Washington, she lost her fragile composure, drank heavily and asked Ernie to take her to the hospital. "She just went to pieces from too much of the usual . . . ," Ernie told Lee Miller. "She says, and I believe her, that it isn't the result of too much chaos around here; actually it's . . . our time being so short and my getting ready to go and her working all the time I was here."[21] Overseas, he had nurtured fond hopes of a recovered Jerry. Now it was obvious she remained depressed and vulnerable to breakdown. Astonishingly, he persisted in finding reasons for optimism. "Her will to control herself is really so much [more] sincere than it used to be that I can't help but have hope in spite of the facts," he told Paige Cavanaugh.[22] When she came home from the hospital after three days, Ernie's departure was upon them. Between deadline-driven writing and pre-departure errands he had so much to do that he had to write out a daily schedule for himself. "I wake up and lie awhile before daylight every morning so fucking blue about leaving that I can hardly bear it."[23]

On his last day at home, Jerry gave him a going-away present, a wool-padded sleeping bag. She saw him off without incident. Aboard the train the next day he wrote to her: "I know my leaving was mighty tough for you yesterday, and it was for me too. I hope we'll never have to do it more than a time or two more in our lives. This trip may last anywhere from six months to another year and a half, but I have a feeling that when I come back this time it will be for good. I think I'll have had all the war I can take. Then maybe we can settle down and be sort of normal, war or no war."[24]

On his way east, on October 28, Ernie stopped in Dana, where Will Pyle was hospitalized with Bright's disease. Ernie feared — incorrectly, it turned out — that it might be the last time he would see his father. Ernie gave Will a little ivory kangaroo he had bought in Khartoum and a copy of *Here Is Your War*, which had been published that very day. Will set both on his bedside table. When visitors came in, he would point to the kangaroo and say, "See what Ernest brought me from Egypt?" Ernie did not draw Will's attention to the dedication on the book's flyleaf: "To My Father."[25]

"Sort of sparkly inside"

Whatever Ernie's private misgivings about his role as the war's truthteller, the fame it brought him was, for these few weeks, sweet indeed. Acclaim for *Here Is Your War* was reaching a peak just as he arrived in Washington. His publishers, who already had sold out most of their first run of 150,000 copies, were desperately seeking government approval to use more rationed paper on grounds that the book was good for the nation's morale.[26] At every newsstand Ernie could find glowing reviews. On the front page of the *New York Times Book Review*, the book was called "a graphic and absorbing picture of the fighting in Tunisia" as well as something "far more . . . important — a full length, deeply human portrait of the American soldier in action." The reviewer took a poke at silk-stocking writers who had composed war books from the safety of home after brief, safe tours of the Mediterranean or the Pacific. "There is no embellishment," he said, "no fine writing. This is not a book of memories, revived and polished on a sunny terrace in Connecticut. It was written behind rocks scarred by snipers' bullets, in pup tents, foxholes and dugouts, in freezing cold and cruel heat. . . ." (This last, of course, was not strictly true; Ernie's reputation as an "authentic" was outstripping authenticity.)[27] Eleanor Roosevelt praised the book in one of her own columns. *Saturday Review* spoke of "the sensitiveness of this man Pyle to the things that happen to a man's heart. . . . Seeing the war bit by bit, [he] succeeds in putting those bits together into an amazing whole. It took weeks of reading his daily dispatches to realize that he was assembling a magnificent mosaic right before our eyes."[28]

Demands upon his time were endless. *Life* called to ask for a special article. The Secretary of War wanted to chat. There were long meetings with Army generals and Hollywood executives about plans for the movie. Dozens of requests for radio spots had to be turned down, though Pyle agreed to one or two pleas for public service messages. ("If you could have been there for even an hour during the bitter fighting in Tunisia or Sicily," he told American housewives, "there would be no need . . . for anybody to ask you to save your used cooking grease. . . .")[29] At the Riggs National Bank he wrote a personal check for $30,000 in War Bonds — more money than he had made in any two previous years of his career put together. At Scripps-Howard's offices a cordon of secretaries and editors tried with only partial success to screen out callers wanting "just a minute" of Ernie's time. There was one visitor whom no one attempted to screen out: the glaring, smartly dressed Roy W. Howard, who promptly steered his most valuable property to a table at the Mayflower Hotel and ordered lunch. Why, the chairman of the board then asked, wasn't Pyle bound for the Pacific, where he might cast a favorable light on Howard's latest anti-Roosevelt idol, General Douglas A. MacArthur? Much to Pyle's relief, his explanation — that he felt he owed more time to the boys in Europe — "quite satisfied" the little titan, who was "perfectly nice" about it. Perhaps Howard had learned via the grapevine that two of Scripps-Howard's competitors were then offering Pyle handsome rewards to jump ship — offers he had rejected without second thoughts.[30]

Wherever he went, Ernie was recognized,

stopped, accosted for autographs. Seeing him coming, store clerks pulled out "shortage" items from under the counter. Restaurant maître-d's escorted him to the head of the line. Being with him in public in these halcyon days was like accompanying a movie star or a president, a friend remembered half a century later — "a mob scene!"[31] Dining out one evening at an Italian place near the White House, he was so distracted by autograph seekers that he finally stood and demanded a fee of one cigarette for every signature. By the time he fled, unable to eat his meal, he had collected several packs' worth.

He harbored one hurt. He continued to believe that his travel column — his own creation, a work of years, ingenuity and costly diligence — represented his best efforts. From 1935 to 1941, the column had owed nothing to the immense public attention accorded to the war. He could not ignore the fact that the times, not just his talent, were responsible for this leap to celebrity.

From his aunt Mary in Dana to bellhops at the Hay-Adams, everyone wanted to know how all this felt. "It feels pretty good," Pyle admitted as he returned to print. "When you hit a point where you're recognized every time you step out, you can't help but feel sort of sparkly inside. . . . I think anybody who tries as hard as I do to write a good column would be dishonest if he said the compliments of thousands of people meant nothing to him. The compliments of just one person mean a lot to me. When you finally get enough compliments to make you a celebrity, you feel hugely rewarded." He wondered aloud about the risks of being struck by "the bolt of fame." His family, his "real friends," his work — all could suffer, he knew, if he didn't keep his wits about him. To maintain a proper sense of balance, "apparently you just have to enlarge yourself inside, to make room for a little more than you've bargained for. It's a harder nut to crack than you might think."

. . . on the whole I'm fairly safe from the perils of celebrity. For one thing, it came a little too late. I'm 43, and it doesn't matter so much any more.

My life has been pretty full and pretty pleasant: I've got most everything I ever wanted, but I've had some blows too; I've contributed a little and received a great deal. Through the years I did my job the best I could, and this is what happened. I didn't plan it, and I didn't ask for this. I could have done without it, but now that it's here, I'm pretty sure I can take it.[32]

Of all these days, November 9, 1943, was the most remarkable.

Moran Livingstone's reporter husband had taken a leave from the Associated Press to do military work abroad. Moran had moved to Washington with her two children. When Ernie arrived in town, they arranged a lunch. Eighteen months earlier, at the time of the Pyles' divorce, Moran had spurned Ernie's erratic overtures. Since then they had exchanged a few affectionate letters. Now, in the midst of their faltering marriages and the rushing thrill of Ernie's fame, their friendship became intimate. Whatever the causes of Ernie's impotence, it is clear from later letters that he overcame them with Moran that afternoon at the Hay-Adams Hotel.

The affair was in part a simple lark, a holiday from two marital quagmires. Moran's son, John Cooper, who saw Ernie from time to time during the war, thought the two shared a hunger to escape their domestic problems into lightheartedness and fun. Their affair was no cheap fling but "an adoring relationship," Cooper recalled half a century later — an impression confirmed by the stream of tender love letters Ernie wrote to Moran throughout the rest of the war.[33] No doubt it was all the more exciting because it was fleeting, impractical and dangerous. This was the way of romance in wartime. After all, why would Ernie have responded so viscerally to the tale of Arthur Miller's sudden passion for the young widow — the woman "with a taste for the catastrophic" whom the war had made "sensually attached to life" — if he had not been wrestling with the same warborne emotions inside himself?

At three-thirty that afternoon, the ringing of Ernie's telephone interrupted the tryst. Ernie reached over, lifted the receiver to his ear, and listened with rising alarm to the female caller, who identified herself as Malvina Thompson, personal secretary to Eleanor Roosevelt.

Would Mr. Pyle care to join the First Lady for tea at five that afternoon? For an unaccustomed split second, Ernie mentally scanned the contents of his wardrobe. He recalled that his single suit was at that moment hanging in a London storage closet. Here in Washington he had only a shabby gray tweed jacket that was "out at the elbows — and I mean *out*," he told Miss Thompson. That didn't matter a bit, Miss Thompson assured him. If Mr. Pyle didn't care about his elbows, neither did Mrs. Roosevelt. So, ninety minutes later, Ernie presented himself at the wrought-iron front gate of the White House. He was led up the curving drive and through the front doors to a small waiting room. There, left alone, he lowered himself carefully into a red velvet chair. From an unseen corridor the high, aristocratic voice of the First Lady drifted to his ears, saying good-bye to the millionaire industrialist Henry Kaiser, her four-thirty guest.[34] Then she was in the doorway, extending a long hand and demanding with a smile to see her visitor's ragged elbows.[35]

"I sure wasn't fooling," Pyle replied, displaying the evidence. He had thought it "ridiculous" to buy new civilian clothes, he explained, knowing he must return to uniform in a war zone within a few weeks.

"Perfectly ridiculous," Mrs. Roosevelt reas-

212

sured him. "I agree with you."

Feeling, as he wrote later, "a little weakish, and sweaty around the upper lip," Pyle accompanied his hostess to the family quarters on the second floor, where she guided him to a comfortable sitting room at the mansion's west end. There Malvina Thompson joined them, saying this was one evening tea she did not intend to miss. Cups and saucers were distributed by the First Lady herself, who, Pyle recalled, maintained a soothing monologue over the silver tea set so that "I didn't need to think much until after I had calmed down a little." Mrs. Roosevelt spoke candidly of her husband's hopes for the postwar world and of recent letters from her four sons serving in the armed forces overseas. She spoke jovially, Pyle recalled, though whenever he said something, she peered at him "solemnly and intently, as though she were a little hard of hearing, though I don't think she is." Inevitably the talk turned to the writing of daily newspaper columns. After all, he and she were peers of a special sort, being arguably the two most famous newspaper columnists in the world.

Mrs. Roosevelt said she normally needed thirty minutes to dictate her daily column, "My Day." That was speedy, Pyle remarked. Normally one column took him at least half a day.

"Yes," Mrs. Roosevelt said. "But you write a much better column than I do."

She said she had wanted to meet Pyle for a

213

long time. (In fact they had been in the same room once before, in 1940, but Pyle then had been little more than a nondescript face in a crowd of anonymous newsmen, and they had not met.) Perhaps this was the only reason she had brought Pyle into the White House on this gray fall afternoon. But as a skilled politician, she must have known it could do her husband no harm to be associated with a figure whose vast popularity transcended the political struggles then consuming the capital. Or perhaps her intent had been to plant an idea about her guest's next assignment. In fact, he had no sooner taken his seat on the davenport and accepted his tea than she said, "I wish you would do for the boys in the South Pacific what you've done for those in Africa."

Actually, Pyle said, he had had the same notion. But after thinking it over, his editors and he had decided he ought to return to the fighting front in Europe instead, once this brief leave at home was over. She nodded. That was probably the right decision, she said, though she had learned from her own recent trip to the Pacific that soldiers and sailors there felt neglected. Pyle felt a twinge of regret. "You have such a sense of Mrs. Roosevelt's sincerity and genuine interest in people," he recalled later, "that I had to hold onto myself to keep from saying, 'Okay, I've changed my plans. I'm going to the Pacific.' "

Unsure how long he ought to stay, Pyle uncrossed his legs once or twice as if to rise, but

Mrs. Roosevelt talked on, seeming not to notice. After fifty minutes, he finally stood and declared he must let her proceed with her schedule. She acceded graciously. Downstairs he accepted his mackinaw from the butler. Letting out his breath at last, he walked back down the curving drive to Pennsylvania Avenue, where a White House policeman caught his eye and said hello.

How long until Ernie went back to the war, the cop asked.

Not long, he answered. Not long at all.

And then "I walked off across Lafayette Park alone, in the chill dusk air, feeling light as a feather."

Divided in his devotion to two women, divided between what he could and could not tell about the war, and torn by the war's twin forces of repulsion and attraction, he made his final preparations to embark on what would be the most eventful phase of his career.

"It is one of our popular heroic myths that anybody who comes back from the combat zone begins to itch after a few weeks, and finally gets so homesick for the front he can hardly stand it," Pyle told his readers on the eve of his departure. "In the movies, he starts back before his furlough is up." This was "pap," he said. "I've never hated to do anything as badly in my life as I hate to go back to the front. I dread it and I'm afraid of it. But what can a guy do? I know millions of others who are reluctant too, and they can't even get home. So here we go."[36]

On the long ferry route back to Algiers, Ernie was delayed three days in Miami, where a reporter buttonholed him. He had no stomach for returning to the front, he said. "But I am going back because that is the only contribution I can make to the war. I can't be a dollar-a-year man, or run a lathe. It's sort of like holding a tiger by the tail. I simply have to see it through."[37] At an air base in British Guiana there was another stop and another reporter, asking this time for a quote on how long the war would last. "I leave that sort of thing to the typewriter generals," he replied. And a word of inspiration for the G.I.'s stationed there? "I'm no good on messages to build up morale. Just tell 'em they're a lot better off being here than where I'm going."[38]

The trans-Atlantic crossing took ten hours in a converted bomber. Ernie slept the whole way on a pile of mail bags. After stops at more air bases in the African jungle and the Sahara, he arrived in Algiers. Everywhere he saw friends. He was flooded with questions about the home front, and an officer he had never met hailed him from across the street and shouted, "Welcome home!" At Army headquarters he dropped off a copy of *Here Is Your War* for General Eisenhower, and at the Aletti Hotel he unrolled his new sleeping bag on a balcony he had slept on a year earlier, before the campaign in Tunisia.[39] Then he wrote to the two women consuming his private thoughts. To Moran he wrote, "I'm still about half home and half here, very confused; desperately reluctant to give up the things. . . . I loved so briefly; yet anxious in a way to end my hurting by getting back to physical misery and to have the job completely fill up my time and demand most of my thoughts." To Jerry he wrote of "feeling sort of depressed and strange. . . . It's good in a way to get away from all that Washington . . . hullabaloo, but even here life isn't as simple as I'd like it. I miss you so much, and long so for a normal life with just us in it. . . ."[40]

Then came the final hop across the Mediterranean to Naples, grimy and demoralized in the wake of the Allied conquest. Ernie had planned to stay in the city for a week or two, readjusting himself to the war in relative safety before moving up to the front. But "something happened," he told his readers. "I hadn't been in Naples two hours before I felt I couldn't stand it, and by the next evening there I was — up in the mud again, sleeping on some straw and awakening throughout the night with the old familiar crash and thunder of the big guns in my reluctant ears."[41]

7

★★★★

"The Ghastly Brotherhood . . ."

ITALY: DECEMBER 1943–FEBRUARY 1944

The Americans' struggle to conquer the Italian mainland was a muddy and horrible mess. Infantrymen of the U.S. Fifth Army were mired in monstrous conditions — heavy rains, winter cold, and bitter German resistance. The terrain alternated between sodden valleys where the mud was knee-deep and mountains strewn with rocks that shattered into lethal shards under the perpetual rain of enemy shells. Ernie's five months of "this semi-barbarian life" were a "blue funk" of depression, homesickness and heavy drinking, all because of his "obsession with the misery of the infantry." He could think of little but "the kids up there."[1] "They live and die so miserably and they do it with such determined acceptance that your admiration for them blinds you to the rest of the war," he confessed to his readers. "To any individual the war is seldom any bigger than the space of a few hundred yards on each side of him. . . . To me all the war of the world has seemed to be borne by the few thousand front-line soldiers here, destined merely by chance to suffer and die for the rest of us."[2]

The downtrodden G.I. as suffering servant: this was the symbol of the new heroism of World War II. It was largely the creation of Ernie Pyle, and the key work was done during what he called "the long winter misery" of the Italian campaign.

"In the shadow of the low stone wall"

On December 13, 1943, elements of the U.S. 36th Infantry Division climbed to the summit of a rocky hump called Mount Sammucro, also known as Hill 1205, one of the endless series of German-held strongpoints that separated the Americans from Rome. The Germans had been dislodged from the hilltop a day or two earlier, but now they were counterattacking, firing shells and mortars from the other side of the ridge. Men crouched among boulders for cover. The gradient was too steep and the trails too narrow for trucks, so mules were enlisted to supply the soldiers on the summit. The mule trains moved only at night, when they could not be seen and shelled by German artillery across the valley. Near the summit the trails became too difficult even for the mules, so soldiers had to haul supplies the rest of the way on their backs, using ropes to pull themselves up the steepest stretches.

Ernie came to the foot of the mountain on December 14. He found a small clay mine dug into the slope where soldiers were huddling to keep dry. A clearing was being used as a staging area for the mule trains. Ernie joined the men in the mine, settling in to watch as the mules started off or returned from the four-hour trek up 1205. Near evening, a tall, thin soldier came into the clearing. A youngster of nineteen, he walked with the ginger tread of a trench-foot victim, and Ernie, approaching him, saw he was distressed. The youngster, a private named Riley Tidwell, said his company commander had been killed by a shell that morning near the top of the mountain. He had been the captain's messenger. At the sound of incoming shells the captain had pushed Tidwell to the ground, only to be fatally struck himself in the chest. To comfort the boy, Pyle said, "He must have been a fine man." Tidwell said yes, he had been like a father — "one of the finest people I ever met."

Tidwell had laid the body along the trail on the ridge, he said, where he expected it would be found that night and carried down on a mule.[3] But when Ernie inquired the next day, he was told the body had not been recovered, nor was it that night. On the third night, Tidwell, worried lest the body be forgotten when the regiment moved on, took a mule up the trail to fetch it. On the way down, he was struck by shrapnel but kept going. At the clearing by the mine, a couple of men lifted the body off the mule and lay it on the ground. Tidwell and a few other men, officers and non-coms, stood by the body for a few

220

minutes. Ernie looked on. Then they drifted away and slept.

A day or two later, Ernie returned to the press camp at Fifth Army headquarters. "I got back to base camp again last night after five days at the front with the infantry and mountain mule-packers . . . ," he wrote Jerry on December 19. "It wasn't an unpleasant trip at all physically, but rather depressing. I'm afraid I've grown inclined to get somber and touched too easily, as I was in Sicily. It's hard to see and be a part of all the misery and not be affected by it. I'm sure that in the papers at home the fighting over here now doesn't seem like much, but to the ones in it it's just as bitter and awful as though there were millions of men engaged."[4]

Ernie moved on to the U.S. air base outside Naples, where he befriended a flier named Edwin Bland, whose tent he shared for several days. One evening he pulled a sheet of paper from his typewriter, assembled it with two other sheets, and handed the sheaf to Bland. He said, "Ed, see what you think of this." A few moments later Bland handed it back and said, "Ernie, that's the finest thing I ever read."[5] It was Pyle's account of the men at the base of the mule trail.

AT THE FRONT LINES IN ITALY — In this war I have known a lot of officers who were loved and respected by the soldiers under them. But never have I crossed the trail of any man as beloved

221

as Capt. Henry T. Waskow, of Belton, Tex.

Captain Waskow was a company commander in the 36th division. He had been in this company since long before he left the States. He was very young, only in his middle 20s, but he carried in him a sincerity and gentleness that made people want to be guided by him.

"After my own father, he comes next," a sergeant told me.

"He always looked after us," a soldier said. "He'd go to bat for us every time."

"I've never known him to do anything unkind," another one said.

I was at the foot of the mule trail the night they brought Captain Waskow down. The moon was nearly full at the time, and you could see far up the trail, and even part way across the valley. Soldiers made shadows as they walked.

Dead men had been coming down the mountain all evening, lashed onto the backs of mules. They came lying belly down across the wooden packsaddle, the heads hanging down on the left side of the mule, their stiffened legs sticking awkwardly from the other side, bobbing up and down as the mule walked.

The Italian mule skinners were afraid to walk beside dead men, so Americans had to lead the mules down that night. Even the

Americans were reluctant to unlash and lift off the bodies, when they got to the bottom, so an officer had to do it himself and ask others to help.

The first one came early in the morning. They slid him down from the mule, and stood him on his feet for a moment. In the half light he might have been merely a sick man standing there leaning on the other. Then they laid him on the ground in the shadow of the stone wall alongside the road.

I don't know who that first one was. You feel small in the presence of dead men and ashamed of being alive, and you don't ask silly questions.

We left him there beside the road, that first one, and we all went back into the cow-shed and sat on watercans or lay on the straw, waiting for the next batch of mules.

Somebody said the dead soldier had been dead for four days, and then nobody said anything more about him. We talked for an hour or more; the dead man lay all alone, outside in the shadow of the wall.

Then a soldier came into the cowshed and said there were some more bodies outside. We went out into the road. Four mules stood there in the moonlight, in the road where the trail came down off the mountain. The soldiers who led them stood there waiting.

"This one is Captain Waskow," one of them said quickly.

Two men unlashed his body from the mule and lifted it off and laid it in the shadow beside the stone wall. Other men took the other bodies off. Finally, there were five lying end to end in a long row. You don't cover up dead men in the combat zones. They just lie there in the shadows until somebody else comes after them.

The uncertain mules moved off to their olive orchards. The men in the road seemed reluctant to leave. They stood around, and gradually I could sense them moving, one by one, close to Captain Waskow's body. Not so much to look, I think, as to say something in finality to him and to themselves. I stood close by and I could hear.

One soldier came and looked down, and he said out loud:

"God damn it!"

That's all he said, and then he walked away.

Another one came, and he said, "God damn it to hell anyway!" He looked down for a few last moments and then turned and left.

Another man came. I think he was an officer. It was hard to tell officers from men in the half light, for everybody was grimy and dirty. The man looked down into the dead captain's face and then spoke directly to him, as though he were alive:

"I'm sorry, old man."

Then a soldier came and stood beside the officer and bent over, and he too spoke to his dead captain, not in a whisper but awfully tenderly, and he said:

"I sure am sorry, sir."

Then the first man squatted down, and he reached down and took the captain's hand, and he sat there for a full five minutes holding the dead hand in his own and looking intently into the dead face. And he never uttered a sound all the time he sat there.

Finally he put the hand down. He reached up and gently straightened the points of the captain's shirt collar, and then he sort of rearranged the tattered edges of his uniform around the wound, and then he got up and walked away down the road in the moonlight, all alone.

The rest of us went back into the cowshed, leaving the five dead men lying in a line end to end in the shadow of the low stone wall. We lay down on the straw in the cowshed, and pretty soon we were all asleep.[6]

Much of the copy written by correspondents in Italy was sent home via the Army Signal Corps' voice-cast system, by which stories were read aloud over point-to-point short-wave radio and transmitted to United Press headquarters in New York for transcription and distribution. In December 1943, Fifth Army voice-casts originated in a run-down two-story building outside Naples. The building housed a tiny studio, little more than a microphone on a felt-covered table. The voice-cast man was Staff Sergeant Wallace Irwin, Jr. Among the dispatches before him one day at the end of December was Pyle's piece. Normally, voicecasting was a tedious business of reading article after article into the microphone at dictation speed, pausing to spell out proper names. But many years later, Irwin remembered, "I had to struggle through that piece to make my voice override my tears."[7]

In the United States, "The Death of Captain Waskow" was instantly acclaimed as Pyle's best effort to date and a classic account of men at war. Newspapers and magazines asked Scripps-Howard for permission to publish excerpts. Radio hosts read the column on the air. It was reprinted as a War Bond promotion. At Lee Miller's suggestion, the *Washington Daily News* paid tribute to its favorite son by displaying the article in large type across its entire front page without a headline, saying, "Page One is different today because we thought Ernie Pyle's story would tell you more about the war than headlines that Russians are 14 miles outside Poland. . . ." The comment of Grove Patterson, editor of the respected *Toledo Blade*, was typical. "When the war is over," Patterson said, "I predict it will be found that Ernie Pyle wrote the most beautiful lines that came out of the whole dark and bitter conflict. . . . His story . . . of the dead men coming down the hill is the most beautifully written newspaper story I have ever read, and that covers a lot of ground."[8]

Its meaning depended on the reader. A small-town editor in Colorado professed himself startled to learn American soldiers had said "hell" and "damn" in the presence of the dead; then he realized the soldiers actually had been "praying for a curse upon war."[9] Quite a different idea was obvious to the *Washington Post*; with their "reverent" cursing, the *Post* said, the soldiers bending over the captain's body had "silently dedicated themselves to fiercer opposition to oppression."[10] Others chose to read the column as Pyle's tribute to the young captain himself, ignoring the obvious fact that it says next to nothing about Waskow.

On the surface, the column is simply about some soldiers' affection for a colleague and commander. This has been called sugarcoating, even propaganda. In fact, Pyle's suggestion that many officers *were* held in high regard was well founded, at least in the front-line units he knew best. An Army survey of enlisted men's attitudes in the European theater revealed that privates in heavy-weapons and rifle companies believed well over half the officers in their own outfits took a personal interest in their men and were "willing to go through anything they [made]

227

their men go through."[11] Though Ernie chose, as usual, to accentuate the positive, the impression he left of soldier-officer relations was no fabrication. Veterans of Waskow's company attested long afterward that Pyle's report of their sentiments toward Waskow had been perfectly accurate. "He was a wonderful captain," said one. "He seemed to understand his men and he gave them every break he could. To me he was just a very good person."[12]

A closer look reveals a deeper theme: the sacred circle of comradeship among soldiers. The column is about "men of new professions out in some strange night caring for each other," like the soldiers and sailors of the fleet off Sicily. Even the dead share in the sacred circle. G.I.'s hold the first dead man upright as if he were "merely a sick man." He and the others "come down the mountain"; they frighten the mule skinners; they "lie all alone." Waskow himself is addressed "as though he were alive." Four different times Pyle tells us the dead are laid "in the shadow of the low stone wall." The phrase is not merely lyrical, for what are shadows but the region between darkness and light, between death and life, where the dead can linger with their living comrades? Finally, when we are shown the soldier "looking intently into the dead face" and fussing tenderly with the disordered uniform, we know the emotion Pyle wanted to convey is nothing less than love — not erotic or romantic love, but the love of comrades who share a kinship that excludes all others.

From the single phrase Lee Miller cut from Pyle's original version — "You feel small in the presence of dead men, *and ashamed of being alive*" — we know how deeply Ernie himself was feeling these bonds. Miller never explained the excision; perhaps the phrase revealed more of his friend's dark, depressive streak than he thought wise. But it suggested Ernie now regarded himself as a full-fledged member of the soldierly circle. A detached observer would have been more likely to feel a secret sense of relief. Guilt is the response of a comrade in arms.

"My personal hero"

"Beloved Captain," as Scripps-Howard titled the Waskow piece, was Pyle's signature column. Grove Patterson's prophecy was not far wrong; the column has enjoyed a vigorous afterlife for more than fifty years. It's a staple of war anthologies. It appears with predictable regularity in newspaper commemorations of war anniversaries. Still much admired for Pyle's graceful style, it nonetheless exemplifies a brand of war journalism that fell out of favor during the Vietnam War and has not recovered since. Seen from the perspective of the post-Vietnam consensus that governments are as a rule unreliable if not downright venal, the correspondents of World War II appear as little more than cheerleaders — hardworking and talented, perhaps, but essentially and irresponsibly uncritical of the things they covered. Caught up in the national cause, they allowed themselves to be coopted by military officialdom, and thus ignored errors and excesses that should have been brought to public attention. They were patriots first, observers second. The result was a half-reported war, with the nastiest truths neglected, censored, downplayed or discreetly screened from public view. "It is in the things not mentioned that the untruth lies," John Steinbeck wrote in the late 1950s, reflecting on his war pieces in the *New York Herald Tribune.* Steinbeck and other correspondents and critics charged themselves with a host of untruths: that "there were no cowards in the American Army"; that "we had no cruel or ambitious or ignorant commanders"; that combat was unpleasant but not unbearable; that men stationed in rear echelons longed to get into battle; that officers were universally admired by their men; "that the war was won without a single mistake, by a command consisting exclusively of geniuses"; and that "everyone on the Allied side was sort of nice." "It was crap — and I don't exclude the Ernie Pyles," a Canadian reporter for the Reuters news agency reflected long after the war. "We were a propaganda arm of our governments."[13]

There is much truth in this view. But journalists incline toward black or white versions of the world, no less when commenting on their own trade than when covering the news. This either-

or view of things often obscures more than it illuminates. There was more to the picture of World War II that emerged from the correspondents' typewriters than facts omitted and embarrassments papered over.

Military censors have come in for much of the blame. Their responsibility lay mostly in the realm of concrete facts omitted or lied about: numbers of ships sunk or planes downed; Allied errors and the names of officers responsible for them; misdeeds by American servicemen abroad, such as rioting and looting by members of the First Division after their victory in Tunisia. Still, considering the enormous amount of news reported in World War II, these factual deceptions were relatively few. Pyle, for instance, who had as much experience as any, was satisfied with the level of veracity he found among officers and censors.

A more powerful influence was not censorship itself but the threat of it, which in turn became self-censorship. Reporters were always mindful of what Steinbeck referred to as the "huge and gassy thing called the War Effort. Anything which interfered with or ran counter to the War Effort was automatically bad. To a large extent judgment about this was in the hands of the correspondent himself. . . . [H]e carried his rule book in his head and even invented restrictions for himself in the interest of the War Effort."[14] Was General Patton essential to the War Effort? More essential than the dignity of the soldiers he slapped? The answer was pretty obvious to most reporters in Sicily, so they stayed mum. Only three of them had to be asked to shut up by Eisenhower himself, and they did.

Reporters were carrying a notebook instead of a gun, and nearly all of them did so well behind the front lines. The contrast was not lost on them, and they considered it perfectly natural to want to make some contribution to the war. What else could be expected? After all, journalism is always written within some cultural context, and the unchallengeable context here was that the war needed to be won. Pro-American journalism wasn't necessarily bad journalism. Robert Sherrod's grim *Tarawa*, for instance, is considered one of the war's most realistic accounts of combat. Yet the motivation for Sherrod's stark realism, much like Pyle's motives, was his determination to shame civilians into working harder and sacrificing more. It was a little too easy, after the Axis powers were safely dispatched, to criticize reporters for their pro-American bias. While the war was still going on — while Hitler's Germany stood a reasonable chance of dominating the world — one should at least acknowledge the honest difficulty any journalist might have had in parsing out his professional and patriotic obligations.

The sanitized and superficial portrait of the war had as much to do with the demands of the news business as it did with censorship, self-imposed or otherwise. Every day, editors demanded an absolutely up-to-date answer to one central question: How's the war going? To answer it, their reporters needed concrete facts — miles gained or lost; signs of enemy weakness or strength; predictions about the next thing to come — and they needed them fast. Few writers enjoyed Pyle's freedom from breaking news or his mandate to wander at will among the troops. For nearly all reporters the premium was on sheer hustle: hustling to the morning intelligence briefing to learn where the day's action was; hustling out to the field; hustling up facts and quotes; hustling back to camp; and getting a creditable story back to New York before the competition.

Editors looked for one main theme, too: successful progress against the enemy. They wanted stories with action and good news. The result was coverage like Richard Tregaskis's *Guadalcanal Diary*, a series of tales of American valor and "lads . . . in high spirits as we shoved along the trail."[15] As for realistic accounts of wounds and suffering, that was the last thing reporters thought anyone wanted. "The tendency was to write what the people wanted to hear," recalled Ralph G. Martin, who worked alongside Pyle and many other reporters as a correspondent for *Stars and Stripes*. "They felt that nobody wanted to hear about the blood and the death. Most people wanted to hear about the successes and the heroes. Most papers urged their correspondents to do that. There was nothing like going into a town the day you took it and racing right back and putting that dateline on your story. That's what most of those daily paper fellows wanted to do. Very few people [among the reporters] cared deeply about all the horror and terror. . . . I don't think they thought about it much."[16]

Pyle was subject to all these pressures and concerns, even more than his colleagues, in a way, because by the time he reached Italy he was well aware of his influence at home. Certainly censorship, or at least the avoidance of it, influenced his work. His writing about battle fatigue was squelched in North Africa, and he knew but wrote nothing about instances of official bad behavior. Like the other reporters, Ernie was also acutely conscious of the need to "do his bit," and he deliberately tailored many pieces to instill a greater sense of urgency among his home-front readers. The tacit pressure to tell good news affected him, too; he was upbeat more often than downbeat.

But while Pyle labored against the same inhibitions that affected his colleagues, his interpretation of the war was far richer and more subtle than theirs. In short, he offered readers a modern myth, a way of seeing the chaos and misery that allowed them to make sense of it — even to feel that, as he'd written of the tent hospital in Sicily, "there was something good about it." If "we tell stories in order to live," as Joan Didion has said, then Pyle's stories allowed

American readers to live with a war that was boundless in its capacity to dehumanize and kill. His war, sad and poignant though it seemed, was what Americans remembered when they later spoke of "the Good War."

Surely the reporters were right in believing their readers had no taste for graphic accounts of killing, maiming and depravity. But they were wrong if they believed readers to be uninterested in the subject of death. Quite the contrary. Death, after all, was the undercurrent of all war coverage and all war debate, and it was made all the more alluring by the careful rationing of images of death in movies, advertisements and newsreels. It was the nearness of death that lent an electric intensity to the experience of reading about the war. In the realm of story, fictional or non-fictional, the issue of life and death is the only sure guarantee of drama. Most important, death was an ever present specter to those with loved ones overseas. With the nation's immediate security needs ensured after 1942, Americans dwelled on the personal safety of relatives abroad. Their personal wars largely came down to the question of whether a son or a husband or a brother or a friend would come home.

If most reporters didn't think much about all this, Pyle did. The key to his writing in Italy in the winter of 1943–44 is that he could not stop thinking about it. This was what accounted for what the poet Randall Jarrell called "the veneration and real love many millions of people felt for him, their unexplained certainty that he was *different* from all the rest." In Italy, where he sealed his reputation as the war's most influential correspondent, he completed construction on his mythical hero, the long-suffering G.I. who triumphed over death through dogged perseverance. The myth offered readers the sense that they were seeing a hard-bitten portrait of war as it really was, yet also a sense that life was affirmed and went on in the midst of death. This had been the theme of the Waskow column. But it was even more obvious and powerful in a series of columns that Ernie wrote several weeks later, when he returned to the mountains north of Naples and found the headquarters of the workhorse 34th Infantry Division.

The 34th enjoyed a reputation for reliability. Army analysts had found it to be "a division of particularly high morale whose psychiatric casualty rates were persistently below those of fellow units."[17] Many of its men had been fighting nearly every day since the American landings in Italy in September. Ernie was put with a rifle company — Company E of the 168th Infantry Regiment — that had just taken a town and was now awaiting its next orders. The company commander, a lieutenant from New York named John Sheehy, was summoned to regimental headquarters and introduced to Ernie.

Sheehy recalled a moment of surprise. "He looked so small [and] unassuming that if I had [seen] him around on the outside I would have called him 'sad sack G.I. Joe,' " he recalled later. Then, feeling "like a million dollars because my company had been . . . selected for Ernie to visit," Sheehy led Pyle back to company head- quarters about a thousand yards from the front, a stone farm house at the center of a grove of thousands of olive trees splintered by shells. The men were far enough away to be safe from German small-arms fire, close enough that most enemy shells passed over their head and fell well to the rear.[18] Here Ernie spent most of the next four days.

Of the two hundred men making up the com- pany when it arrived in the European theater, only eight remained. All the rest had been trans- ferred, rotated home, wounded or killed. To un- derstand the Army's progress in Europe, Pyle believed, one had to understand the small core of veterans in any infantry company, for "around a little group like them every company is built," and their attitude toward battle would ultimately determine the Army's success or failure. So he asked Sheehy to assemble the eight old-timers, several of whom Pyle featured in a series of col- umns.

The ones he chose were all of a certain heroic type familiar to Hollywood — the strong, ca- pable man whose tough hide conceals a tender heart. There was Sergeant Paul "Tag" Allumbaugh, "a great soldier, yet so quiet, kind and good-natured that you couldn't imagine him ever killing anybody." Another was an older sergeant named Jack Pierson, a pile-driver in civilian life, " 'really a rough man.' " But Pierson talked incessantly about his three children, especially a toddler named Junior whom Pierson had never seen.

> Well, one day in battle they were having it tough. . . . Tag Allumbaugh was lying within shouting distance of where Jack was pinned down, and he yelled over:
> "How you doin', Jack."
> And then this man who was hard in peacetime and is hard in war called back a resigned answer that expresses in a general way every combat soldier's pathetic reason for wanting to live and hating to die.
> He called back — and he wasn't joking — and he said:
> "It don't look like I'm gonna get to see Junior."[19]

One member of Company E drew Ernie's special interest. In the fullest character sketch that Pyle wrote during the war, this tired soldier became the quintessential Pyle hero. He was a platoon sergeant called Frank Eversole, nicknamed "Buck." He was twenty-eight, several years older than the average infantryman. He and Pyle met when Lieutenant Sheehy drew Ernie aside and said, "I want to introduce you to my personal hero." It took Ernie longer than usual to draw Eversole out, "but I didn't mind his reticence, for I know how Westerners like to size people up first." Soon the two established a deep rapport, talking at length over the next several days.

Eversole was an Iowa native who had moved on his own at age fifteen to Idaho, where he worked as a ranch hand until his Army induction early in the war. A quiet, uneducated man who kept to himself, Eversole impressed his longtime comrades — and Ernie, who seems to have sensed his special character immediately — as a natural-born soldier endowed with precisely the gifts needed for combat. "He was kind of a warrior-type person," said Pete Conners, a Company E veteran, recalling Eversole many years later. "He didn't have an air about him of being fearless . . . but he was. He *was* fearless. . . . He was just such a solid guy, and the people under him — they would follow him any place."[20]

It was Eversole's contradictions that so appealed to Ernie — his fierceness combined with a tender, even self-torturing side. Though the two men spent only a few days together, Ernie placed Eversole in the very small category of G.I.'s who were more to him than passing friendly acquaintances. Several days after his visit with Company E, Ernie sought out Eversole at a rest camp at Caserta. Telling the Army he needed Buck's help with research on front-line combat, Ernie finagled a special pass for him to visit Naples, which was then off-limits to enlisted men and non-commissioned officers, and proceeded to spend five days showing Eversole a grand time. When Ernie needed to spend a day at his typewriter, he packed Eversole off for a sight-seeing trip to Pompeii with an officer friend and a pair of nurses. Eversole was pleasantly bewildered. "I couldn't see why he picked me to write about," he told Lee Miller after the war. "I suppose when we met, that we felt pretty much the same towards each other. . . . He was the best friend I ever had, and I am very thankful for the Reputation he gave me."[21]

That reputation was of a hero in the mold of the American western, with the contradictions and ambiguities inherent in the role. "He is to me," Ernie wrote, "and to all those with whom he serves, one of the great men of the war."

Ernie introduced Buck by enumerating traits recognizable to any home-front reader as quintessentially American. Not only was he a westerner — always a mark of distinction for Ernie — but he had followed the pioneer trail, venturing west to seek his fortune. He was literally a cowboy who "made the rodeos in season," though an egalitarian one, as "he was never a star or anything." He hearkened to the American dream of moving up a notch after the war; "he wants to go get a little place and feed a few head of cattle, and be independent."

He had "outdoor hands, strong and rough." In the routine of daily affairs at the front he was practical and reliable, "the kind of man you instinctively feel safer with than with other people.

He is not helpless like most of us. . . . He can improvise, patch things, fix things." But he was also and foremost a warrior, "cold and deliberate in battle. His commanders depend more on him than any other man. He has been wounded once, and had countless narrow escapes. He has killed many Germans. . . . War is old to him and he has become almost the master of it, a senior partner in the institution of death."

In Sicily, Ernie had pondered the question of what thoughts, if any, propelled soldiers into battle. Now he engaged a related but deeper question. In view of what such men were doing and having done to them by other men — in view of the towering facts of industrialized combat's effects on the bodies and minds of fragile mortals — what were we? Undeniably, these American men were now killing. Had the war changed them fundamentally? Had they become killers at heart? Or had they — and by implication all of us — been savages to begin with, freed by war's special circumstances to satisfy lusts and hatred? In short, why did they fight, and what did that say about human nature?

Neither Ernie's assignment nor his journalistic breeding encouraged philosophical speculation. Nonetheless, his private preoccupations were reflected in the things he chose to report. In his portrait of Eversole, they reached their fullest form. In Sicily, Ernie's earlier notion that soldiers fought out of love of country had given way to a belief that they fought "at least for each

241

other." Now he recognized the mute pragmatism and fatalism with which most soldiers weathered the war, their utter lack of idealism or ideology. On one level Buck Eversole operated by the simplest principle: "He kills because he's trying to keep alive himself." But there was more to it than that. The front, as Ernie tried repeatedly to tell readers, was "another world," with separate norms and rules. At the front, killing was a job; you were judged not by the job's morality but by how effectively you did it. "The years roll over him and the war becomes his only world, and battle his only profession. . . . 'I'm mighty sick of it all,' he says very quietly, 'but there ain't no use to complain. I just figure it this way, that I've been given a job to do and I've got to do it. . . .' " It was a cold duty but better than killing out of hatred, and "Buck Eversole had no hatred for Germans."

In fact, a sympathetic kindness and fellow feeling lay under this hard shell. Twice Buck had been responsible for the death of a mountain mule: once to relieve an animal's pain from a shell wound; once by accident, and "Buck still feels guilty about it." For the forty or so soldiers who fought under him he felt a far deeper angst.

His platoon has turned over many times as battle whittles down the old ones and the replacement system brings up the new ones. Only a handful now are veterans.

"It gets so it kinda gets you, seein' these

242

new kids come up," Buck told me one night in his slow, barely audible Western voice, so full of honesty and sincerity.

"Some of them have just got fuzz on their faces, and don't know what it's all about, and they're scared to death. No matter what, some of them are bound to get killed."

We talked about some of the other old-time non-coms who could take battle themselves, but had gradually grown morose under the responsibility of leading green boys to their slaughter. . . .

"I know it ain't my fault that they get killed," Buck finally said. "And I do the best I can for them, but I've got so I feel like it's me killin' 'em instead of a German. I've got so I feel like a murderer. I hate to look at them when the new ones come in."[22]

Like the men gathered by the body of Captain Waskow, Eversole and his comrades were joined by a species of love that could be kindled only in war's ashes. Ernie's underlying theme was this: despite the ferocity all around these men — indeed, because of it — goodness grew among them. "The ties that grow between men who live savagely together, relentlessly communing with Death, are ties of great strength. There is a sense of fidelity to each other in a little corps of men who have endured so long, and whose hope in the end can be so small."[23] Ernie made this evident in his rendering of Eversole's departure from the company for a rest.

The company was due to attack that night. Buck went to Sheehy and said, "Lieutenant, I don't think I better go. I'll stay if you need me."

The lieutenant said, "Of course I need you, Buck, I always need you. But it's your turn and I want you to go. In fact, you're ordered to go."

The truck taking the few boys away to rest camp left just at dusk. It was drizzling and the valleys were swathed in a dismal mist. Artillery of both sides flashed and rumbled around the horizon. The encroaching darkness was heavy and foreboding.

Buck came to the little group of old-timers in the company with whom I was standing, to say goodbye. You'd have thought he was leaving forever. He shook hands all around, and his smile seemed sick and vulnerable. He was a man stalling off his departure.

He said, "Well, good luck to you all." And then he said, "I'll be back in just five days." He said goodbye all around and slowly started away. But he stopped and said goodbye all around again, and he said, "Well, good luck to you all."

I walked with him toward the truck in the dusk. He kept his eyes on the ground, and I think he would have cried if he knew how, and he said to me very quietly, "This is the first battle I've ever missed that this battalion has been in . . . I sure do hope they have good luck."

And then he said: "I feel like a deserter."

He climbed in, and the truck dissolved into the blackness. I went back and lay down on the ground among my other friends, waiting for the night orders to march. I lay there in the darkness thinking — terribly touched by the great simple devotion of this soldier who was a cowboy — and thinking of the millions far away at home who must remain forever unaware of the powerful fraternalism in the ghastly brotherhood of war.[24]

The "cold and deliberate" predator in Eversole's nature was balanced by essential human goodness. Eversole, the prototypical Pyle hero, was hard and soft, killer and saint. This above all was the image of the American soldier that Pyle conveyed to his vast readership. This image of the G.I. as suffering servant — coldly effective yet warm-hearted — served in place of the idealism of World War I. If Americans could no longer believe wholeheartedly in a war to save the world for democracy, they at least could believe in men such as this.

After the Eversole columns, Ernie wrote a three-part narrative of his last night with Company E. On the day of Buck's departure the company was ordered to move to the front and attack. (Though censors' rules made it impossible for Ernie to specify the action at the time, it was in fact the Americans' first strike across the Rapido River, a bloody fight in which Company E's regiment was the first to cross the river.) This was another of Ernie's "night march" stories, a little genre he seemed to invent, perhaps because they offered the best chance short of actual battle to convey something of the drama, difficulty and mystery of life at the front. It was an effective series. But Pyle left out a part of the story. He had wanted to go with the company into the battle itself.

Even Lieutenant Sheehy apparently was not aware of Ernie's hopes in this regard. He believed Ernie desired to go only as far as the "jumping-off" point, where the company would change formation to go on the attack. But while still in behind the lines, Ernie told his little band of eight veterans that he would like to go farther than that. "He wanted to go with us," recalled Pete Conners. "We told him what it would be like if we had that choice to make. . . . Everybody was saying, 'Hey, Ernie, get back where you belong. It's all right for you to be here with us now, but when we go into the next one, several are not coming back, and if you went with us, you might be one of those.' " Nonetheless, he said, he wanted to see what it was like to have no one between him and the German line. The company had seen war correspondents before, and read their accounts of battle based on after-the-fact interviews. "It was all right," Conners remembered, "but most of it was kind of doctored up a little bit, we thought, for reading purposes. But being with this guy, and knowing that he was sincere about it, I guess every guy right there said, 'Hey, this guy's not fooling. I think he would really go.' "

Someone up the line said no, the Army couldn't be responsible for it. So Ernie asked to follow the company as far as possible. He waited with them through a "night full of distant warfare," then walked just behind Conners through deep darkness, negotiating the sharp ups and downs of the terrain by watching the bobbing whiteness of the map in Conners' rear pocket.

When the soldiers reached a point perhaps two hundred yards from the Germans, they scooped shallow foxholes in the wet ground. "They attacked just after dawn . . . ," Ernie wrote. "I stayed behind when the company went forward. In the continuously circulating nature of my job, I may never again see the men in this outfit. But to me they will always be 'my' company."[25]

Of Ernie's little band of veterans in Company E, one was killed near the fiercely contested abbey on Monte Cassino the day after Ernie's departure; two were wounded on the slopes of the mountain; one was captured by Germans at the abbey. Sheehy and Allumbaugh were soon hospitalized with trench foot. Buck Eversole,

too, contracted trench foot but refused hospitalization; eventually his feet were so swollen he
had to be carried off the slopes around the
abbey.[26]

High school graduation, 1918. "I was a farm boy, and town kids can make you feel awfully backward when you're young . . ." (*Lilly Library, Indiana University*)

Ernie and Jerry early in their marriage. Later he wrote her: "When you were what to me was 'normal' . . . it seemed to me that our companionship was the most ideal thing that ever happened." (*Ernie Pyle State Historic Site*)

Pyle learned the reporting trade and developed his writing style during four years as the *Washington Daily News'* aviation correspondent, flying 100,000 miles and writing more than 1.5 million words. (*Ernie Pyle State Historic Site*)

Jerry Pyle at her beloved piano. (*Ernie Pyle State Historic Site*)

Feats of geographical mastery delighted Ernie, whose wanderlust drove him to five of the seven continents. He crossed from Colorado into Utah — his 48th state — in September 1936, less than a year after becoming a roving columnist for Scripps-Howard. "I did considerable gloating over that girl who rides with me, because she is just a home-body and has only been in 45 states." (*Ernie Pyle State Historic Site*)

"Dear Folks and Auntie" — Ernie's widowed aunt, Mary Bales, "tall and straight despite a lifetime of killing work," his mother Marie, who "would rather drive a team of horses in the field than cook a dinner," and his father, Will, who "has never lived anywhere but on a farm, and yet I don't think he ever liked the farm very well." (*Ernie Pyle State Historic Site*)

After two years of writing his roving column six days a week, Ernie concluded the assignment was "too much for a human being. It becomes an ogre and you fight it day and night." Yet he persisted for four more years. (*Ernie Pyle State Historic Site*)

The Rolling Stones

wish you lots

of Holiday moss -

The Pyles' 1939 Christmas card. (*Ernie Pyle State Historic Site*)

In Albuquerque: "A regular little boxed-up mass production shack." (*Ernie Pyle State Historic Site*)

"They understood each other extremely well," a friend said of Pyle and Paige Cavanaugh. "Ernie never had any relationship with . . . another person that was as profound and close as the one that he had with Paige." (*Ernie Pyle State Historic Site*)

In the wake of victory in Tunisia, Ernie joy-rode through the U.S. camps in a commandeered German Army Volkswagen. "I've written . . . that war is not romantic when you're in the midst of it . . . But I will have to admit there is an exhilaration in it; an inner excitement that builds up into a buoyant tenseness which is seldom achieved in peacetime." (*Ernie Pyle State Historic Site*)

With GIs. "He just came up and said, 'Hi, I'm Ernie Pyle,' " a veteran recalled. No great pronouncement about his being a member of the press . . . He was very easy to talk to, and one felt at ease immediately with him. It was his modesty, his natural modesty, and a feeling that you wanted to help this guy along somehow." (*Ernie Pyle State Historic Site; Lilly Library, Indiana University*)

The assault correspondent in helmet and Mae West life-jacket, approaching the invasion beaches of Sicily aboard the U.S.S. *Biscayne.* "Everything in this world has stopped except war and we are all men of new professions out in some strange night caring for each other." (*Ernie Pyle State Historic Site*)

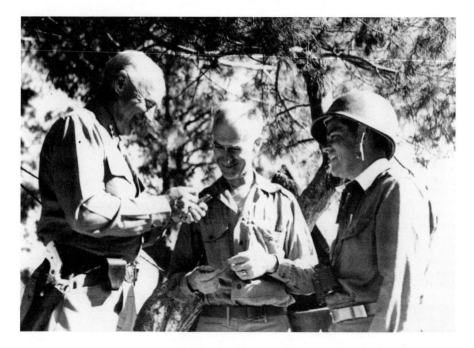

With General George Patton and United Press correspondent Chris Cunningham. "Ernie . . . hated Patton's guts," a friend wrote. "Patton's bluster, show and complete disregard for the dignity of the individual was the direct antithesis of Ernie's gentle character." The general's name never appeared in a Pyle column. (*Ernie Pyle State Historic Site*)

Ernie relaxing with an Air Corps acquaintance in Italy, early 1944. "I've been drinking far more than I should . . ." he told his editor. "In our correspondents crowd, we're all so damn homesick and weary of the war that it seems like a disease, and you take to the bottle now and then without planning on it." (*Courtesy of Jack Gross*)

Exhausted and depressed after a stay at the front north of Naples, Pyle went sightseeing in the ruins of Pompeii with a friend, flier Ed Bland. (*Ernie Pyle State Historic Site*)

261

On the narrow Anzio beachhead, "nobody is wholly safe, and nobody who says he has been around Anzio two days without having a shell hit within a hundred yards of him is just bragging." (*Lilly Library, Indiana University*)

A collapsing wall nearly killed Pyle during a bombing at Anzio. "Much to my surprise, I wasn't weak or shaky after it was all over. In fact I felt fine — partly buoyed up by elation over still being alive, I suppose. But . . . by mid- afternoon I felt very old and 'beat up' . . ." (*Ernie Pyle State Historic Site*)

Pyle with colleagues (from left) Hal Boyle of AP, Gordon Gammack of the *Des Moines Register*, Don Whitehead of AP. "The war correspondent has his stake — his life — in his own hands . . ." the photographer Robert Capa wrote. "Having the freedom to choose his spot and being allowed to be a coward and not be executed for it is his torture." (*Ernie Pyle State Historic Site*)

In Normandy: "Just the same old field routine again, miserable but not too dangerous." (*Ernie Pyle State Historic Site*)

(Below) In Paris, with Hal Boyle of the Associated Press: "I had thought that for me there could never again be any elation in war. But I had reckoned without the liberation of Paris . . ." (*Ernie Pyle State Historic Site*)

On the home front, Ernie was inundated with requests for public-service announcements and endorsements. Among the few he agreed to was a War Bond promotion with Treasury Secretary Henry Morgenthau. (*Ernie Pyle State Historic Site*)

With Lester Cowan, producer of *Ernie Pyle's Story of GI Joe*, and Lee Miller. (*Ernie Pyle State Historic Site*)

After a long talent search, Cowan chose the young actor
Burgess Meredith to play the part of Pyle. The two met
on the movie set. In publicity photos, as in the film,
Meredith attempted to mirror Pyle's writings with deter-
minedly soulful expressions. (*Ernie Pyle State Historic
Site*)

Moran Livingstone.
(*Courtesy of John S. Cooper*)

The Navy, eager for the reflected glow of Pyle's fame, shadowed him for "photo opportunities" throughout the Pacific. (*Ernie Pyle State Historic Site*)

Aboard the aircraft carrier U.S.S. *Cabot.* (*Ernie Pyle State Historic Site*)

(Photo by Alfred Eisenstaedt/Ernie Pyle State Historic Site)

8

★★★★

"An Awful Knowledge . . ."

ITALY AND BRITAIN: FEBRUARY–MAY 1944

The compelling fact about Pyle's suffering soldiers was that they were still alive. They endured. His endless night marches were made by men defeating death. That was the essence of the myth.

But myth and reality were different, of course. As the Italian campaign dragged on, death hovered closer and closer to Ernie's consciousness, and fear became his constant companion.

". . . sometimes I feel it sinful if I should survive . . ."

On the morning of February 4, 1944, a familiar name in a *Stars and Stripes* headline caught Ernie's eye. The next instant his eyes were riveted to the page. Raymond Clapper had been killed in an airplane crash while covering the war in the South Pacific. Ernie had ceased to be shocked by the death of friends, he wrote later, but with this news he took the day off to recover. He tried to write but could produce nothing. "I'm just floored by it . . ." he wrote Lee

Miller that evening.

> What a waste of intelligence and character —
> as the whole war is. It gives me the creeps.
>   The whole thing is getting pretty badly
> under my skin, Lee. I've got so I brood about
> it, about the whole thing, I mean, and I have
> a personal reluctance to die that is always in
> my mind, like a weight. Instead of growing
> stronger and hard as good veterans do, I've
> become weaker and more frightened. I'm
> allright when I'm actually at the front, but it's
> when I pull back and start thinking and visu-
> alizing that it almost overwhelms me. I've
> even got so I don't sleep well, and have
> half-awake hideous dreams about the war.[1]

Pyle's friend Tom Treanor, a gifted freelancer who was soon hired by the *Los Angeles Times*, said he glimpsed war's essence when men in whom he had great confidence were killed. "Then, it seemed, I would sense, as at no other time, the blind, unthinking, and overwhelming power of war . . . ," Treanor wrote. "There would break upon me this desolating and terri-fying feeling that war was something so much greater and more all-powerful than the men who make it. It certainly cracked and weakened any belief in my own indestructibility."[2]

In North Africa, where Pyle had been a green-horn and American casualties relatively low, the presence of death in the distance had charged

271

the air around him. The threat of it had offered a setting for exciting, boy's-magazine stories of "near things" and "close calls." As the months passed and more bodies lay along the roads and in the fields, he felt a numbness in their presence. At other times he appraised destructive scenes like an art critic, as when he watched American artillerymen fire shells over a mountain just before dawn. As light spread from the eastern horizon and the firing ceased, a rainbow formed over the mountain,

> standing out radiantly against the moist green hillsides and drifting white-gray clouds. . . .
> As we watched, that other end of the rainbow became gradually framed by a rising plume of white smoke — caused by the shells we had just sent over. The smoke didn't obscure the rainbow. Rather it seemed to rise enfoldingly around it, like honeysuckle climbing a porch column. Men newly dead lay at the foot of that smoke. We couldn't help thinking what a strange pot of gold that beautiful rainbow was pointing to.[3]

It wasn't heartless to report the scene this way; Pyle was like many who could not help but notice war's occasional beauty. But starting with Ray Clapper's demise, Ernie increasingly regarded death less as a curious spectacle than as a sinister personal adversary. His career and Clapper's had intersected at many points, and for several days he could not shake off thoughts of times and places they had known together in Washington. Clapper, solid and dependable, symbolized home. In an introduction to a posthumous collection of Clapper's writings, Ernie wrote: "There was something in him so normal, so like other people who live in houses and have families and dogs and fireplaces, that when he came to the wars somehow it always seemed impossible that anything could ever happen to him."[4] This, of course, was the sort of thing people always said about Ernie himself, and his own description of Clapper — "a sound man . . . [with] vast experience and good common sense . . . who worked like a dog" — may have reflected his private estimate of his own best qualities.[5]

In other words, if Clapper could die, so could he. Perhaps he had never fully realized it until then.

The day after Ernie learned of Clapper's death, a "sweet little . . . letter" arrived from Moran Livingstone. "I had been very low," he replied, "and your hieroglyphics tickled me and helped my waning spirits . . ." Moran's letter does not survive, but it is apparent from Ernie's reply that she had expressed a sense of shame for being unable to "realize the war" — to comprehend it as Ernie did. He reassured her. "Nobody blames you for not *realizing* the war darling; anybody in America who pretends he does is lying."

It was not a comprehension to envy; "there are times when the perpetual misery and death of war, and what seems the inevitable doom of all things, has me on the ropes. I get to losing my perspective and sometimes feel it sinful if I should survive the war myself."

He wished he could abandon it, he said, "and yet some perverseness in my nature keeps me hypnotized and glued to it . . ."[6]

Ernie scolded his friend Don Whitehead for going along on the amphibious landings at Anzio, the Italian coastal town where General Mark Clark hoped to bypass the stalemate at Cassino. "You're a damned fool," he told Whitehead. "Why should you keep on sticking your neck out like that? It's not worth it." But on February 25, when Anzio had bogged down in a stalemate worse than Cassino, Ernie followed Whitehead to the beachhead. "He would tell you, and convince you, that he was absolutely washed up — he simply couldn't stand the sound of another shell or bullet, or the sight of another bleeding guy," Whitehead remembered later. "And the next thing he would turn up with some assault force, or with some landing troops, or at Anzio, or on the front somewhere, all the time protesting that he just couldn't take any more."[7]

The difference this time was that his fears were nearly realized.

Anzio and Nettuno were contiguous resort towns linked by a long business street that ran along a bluff overlooking the water. There was no "rear" at Anzio: the entire beachhead lay within easy reach of German shells, and casualties were enormous. The American and British troops could do little but sit helpless under an industrial rain of shells and bombs, incapable of retreat or advance. There were no armored thrusts for reporters to see, not even a heroic defense — just stolid, miserable stamina, the trait Ernie admired above all others and chronicled at Anzio for four weeks.

To house the correspondents, Fifth Army's public relations staff found an odd, rambling villa with four stories rising from the water's edge connected by a maze of stairways to three stories built on the bluff above. About thirty men bunked there — officers, enlisted men, and a dozen reporters. Most lived on the lowest floor at the level of the beach, which was thought to have an advantage in safety, but Ernie chose a room on the top floor because its windows allowed in more light for writing. "We called it 'Shell Alley' up there because the Anzio-bound shells seemed to come in a groove right past our eaves day and night."[8]

The reporters living on the first floor were still in their beds on the morning of March 17 when the ceilings above them broke open. Blast followed blast, choking the rooms and hallways with plaster and bricks. Still in their underwear or stark naked, the men jumped up and ran from room to room, checking for casualties. On the first floor they found everyone alive, but they assumed the upper floors had been destroyed.

"Well," said one, "they got Ernie."

A moment later Pyle came down the stairs with blood trickling from a single tiny cut on his face. His narrow escape made headlines the next day throughout the United States, followed by his own account two days later.[9]

He had been lying awake in bed when he heard antiaircraft fire nearby. Normally he stayed in bed during an air raid, but today he rose, donned his helmet and slippers, and crossed the room to look out at the harbor and the sky. "I had just reached the window when a terrible blast swirled me around and threw me into the middle of the room. I don't remember whether I heard any noise or not." The window frame blew inward, spraying the room with thousands of glass shards. Wood and plaster and pieces of furniture flew back and forth under the force of "one gigantic explosion" after another. Ernie found a corner and huddled there. "The concussion was terrific. It was like a great blast of air in which your body felt as light and as helpless as a leaf tossed in a whirlwind." Suddenly a wall collapsed on the bed where he had been lying only seconds before, breaking and twisting the steel frame. Doors crashed down. Half of another wall fell in broken hunks of stone and brick. Sheets of unfinished columns shot off his table and were punctured with holes, and Ernie remembered thinking, " 'Well, it won't make any difference now anyhow.' . . . I definitely thought it was the end."

An entire stick of 500-pound bombs had landed within thirty feet of the villa. Ernie felt "very old and 'beat up' " by midafternoon, and for the next two days the passage of shells over-head "really gave me the woolies." Several re-porters who had been in the villa during the bombing left Anzio as soon as they could, but Ernie stayed on for a week, "just purposely to get my nerve back," as he confided to Cavanaugh. "Finally left full of self respect and feeling on top of the world. . . . I seemed to be able to take it even better than before. Had several mighty close calls from shells, as well as the bombs. Piss on it."[10]

Back in Naples, the war seemed once more to widen out to encompass continental schemes and grand strategy. Ernie spoke with his old friend Ira Eaker, now commander of Allied air forces in the Mediterranean, about the course of the campaign in Italy. General Clark summoned Ernie to dinner and talked of "some things I can't print." For weeks correspondents had been leaving Italy for London to be on hand for the invasion of northwest Europe. Now the most illustrious of them was leaving, too.

"I didn't realize it meant so much to me . . ."

In the middle days of April 1944, Ernie emerged from the plush Dorchester Hotel into the mild spring sunshine of London to be stared at wherever he went. This owed less to his fame than his attire — Army pants, British battle jacket and the disintegrating infantry boots he had worn from Sicily to Monte Cassino. In London, where the sidewalks teemed with British and American officers hurrying to their office bivouacs in dress blouses and "pinks," Ernie's garb violated Army regulations so flagrantly that he had to buy an official blouse and dark trousers to avoid the clutches of zealous MPs. "They apparently never saw a guy before who looked like he might have come from the front," he grumbled with ill-concealed pride. Finally he dug through storage at the Mount Royal for the brown civilian suit he had packed away on the eve of TORCH — the suit he had longed for the afternoon of his visit to the White House — and from then on was noticed only for who he was, not what he wore. Most people "just think I'm a bedraggled bank clerk, and it's much better."[11]

Americans swarmed in the streets. Ernie heard that three hundred war correspondents had arrived in London already, most of them neophytes whom he regarded with a veteran's smug amusement. ("If 'Dog News' doesn't get a man over here pretty quickly to cover the dog angle of the invasion I personally will never buy another copy.")[12] Hotel vacancies were extremely scarce, but W. P. Simms, Scripps-Howard's longtime man in London, secured Ernie a room directly across the hall from his own suite at the Dorchester. The room was tiny, but after five months in Italy it seemed baronial with its soft bed, hot water, and "three buttons to press to bring running either a waiter, a valet, or a maid." Life in the war-weary city that Ernie cherished as "my overseas home" had eased during his eighteen-month absence. Shoppers strolled the sidewalks, and the English seemed "as kind and polite to each other as they always were." The coming of spring affected his good impression, for "the buds are out and flowers are blooming, and everything always seems kind of wonderful to me in springtime."[13]

That was his public report. Privately, his plunge back into urban life was "[giving] me the jerks." His eyes were " 'crossed' and blurry," his stomach churned, "and after the winter's months of beastliness, I have a terribly guilty feeling about being here."[14] Compared to Italy, London was safety itself, of course, but when British antiaircraft batteries took aim at the occasional German planes over the city, he could not relax muscles and reflexes that had stayed tightly coiled for months. "I find that after the [Anzio] beachhead I'm very allergic to raids," he confided to Miller, "and can hardly get my breath when the guns start."[15]

Wisely, he had built up a fat column cushion during his last weeks in Italy. He needed it now. When he had been in England nearly three weeks he had written only three columns, so distracted was he by officials, friends, acquaintances, total strangers and endless minor but essential errands. Letters jammed his mailbox at the rate of two hundred a week, including many from servicemen in Italy which he could not bear to leave unanswered. The burden of mail got so heavy by the middle of May that he accepted the loan of a young officer from Army Public Relations to act as his secretary. As always, he could make progress on his columns only during long, quiet stretches of concentration. Yet, day after day, try as he might, he could not put together ninety uninterrupted minutes, "largely due to my constitutional inability to say no to anybody or anything." He gave Moran a list of intrusions from just two consecutive days at the end of April:

> . . . a soldier whose sister I met once in my life, eight years ago, comes and sits two hours to chat; the embassy calls up and wants me to talk with a Belgian something or other who was pleased with my columns about the Belgian Congo a year ago; the Italian division of the Foreign Office wants me to come and tell them all about Italy, as if I knew anything about it; two different Special Service Branches want me to go make talks at fighter bases; the Army radio wants me to talk; Special Service men come and actually talk me into writing a long special piece for Stars & Stripes (put to me in a

way that I couldn't refuse without seeming like a slacker); an ass who is now a captain and used to be a newspaperman drops in with a Canadian major and stays half an hour (the major is very nice, but what of it?), the British Vogue or Harpers Bazaar or something wants to come take pictures for a layout; a gal from The [London] Standard comes for a half hour; Air Force Public Relations men come for an hour and a half about my next trip, which could have been done in ten minutes . . . oh hell I'm tired of recounting them, but you get the idea. It sounds big-shotish I know, but it isn't. . . . [I]t's about to drive me crazy.[16]

Six years earlier, Lee Miller had submitted a selection of Ernie's travel columns to the advisory board of the Columbia University Graduate School of Journalism, which met each spring to award the Pulitzer Prize in nine categories of journalism. It had been a long shot, as the Pulitzers were unofficially reserved for "serious" and "important" work. For his trouble, Miller received nothing more than a postcard from Carl W. Ackerman, secretary to the board, to "acknowledge receipt of your nomination."[17]

But early in 1944, the same Carl W. Ackerman now wrote a warm little note to George Carlin of United Feature, informing him that "it has been suggested that the dispatches of Ernie Pyle from the war fronts would make a worthy entry for a

Pulitzer Prize."[18] Carlin and Miller, who had never heard of the Pulitzer board soliciting a particular entry, were delighted. But Ernie, remembering twenty years of serious types winning the prize, professed doubt: "My stuff just doesn't fit their rules."[19]

"Wanna bet?" Miller fired back across the Atlantic. "I hereby bet you $100 that you win a Pulitzer prize this year."[20]

Ernie took it.

He was in his room at the Dorchester on a morning early in May when his noisy phone rang yet again. He picked it up and heard Don Whitehead say, "Congratulations, you bastard, you won the Pulitzer Prize."

A pause followed.

"You wouldn't shit me, would you, Don?"

Whitehead read aloud from the Associated Press cable in his hand. "Well, I'll be goddamned!" Ernie said. "Now I lose a hundred dollars."[21]

"I didn't realize it meant so much to me," he wrote Miller. "I never enjoyed losing a bet more. . . ."[22]

In the fraternity of war correspondents, everyone knew Pyle was preeminent at home, and Ernie watched his colleagues for signs of resentment or envy. To his relief, he found none. All the evidence suggests he was liked and admired by every other member of this tough, tight little guild, with the possible exception of A. J. Liebling, the erudite *New Yorker* man who suspected Pyle's country-boy image was an inspired piece of acting. "He was a hard guy to be jealous of," recalled Chalmers Roberts, who knew Ernie in Europe. "He wasn't a blowhard or a show-off or a name dropper. . . . He was such a sweet guy. Everybody liked Ernie."[23] His colleagues' goodwill undoubtedly stemmed in part from Pyle's feature assignment, which meant he never competed with them for breaking news, but also from the way he wore his fame in a mock cloak of conceit. Once when Clark Lee of the Hearst chain pleaded with Ernie for a slug of whiskey, Pyle insisted that in exchange Lee must read the Captain Waskow story aloud three times.[24] Another time a reporter grabbed an Indiana University alumni monthly from Ernie's mail and began to read aloud from an article praising him to the skies. When Pyle's prose was compared to "the rugged simplicity of the Bible," Ernie affected an elaborate pout. Didn't he feel honored, another reporter asked. "Hell, no," he snapped. "I never did think the Bible was very well written."[25]

From December through March, Ernie received only one letter from Jerry. Finally he received a sketchy second-hand report of her condition from a friend in Albuquerque. It was not reassuring. Since the first of the year she had been struggling through another crisis — more drinking followed by "a complete nervous collapse"; toxic effects from a sedative; another hospitalization; another trip to Denver to be nursed by her mother and sister. Her hands shook so badly that her handwriting looked like forgery. This, evidently, was her reason for not writing to Ernie: she knew her painful scrawl would give away her condition. By the time Ernie reached London, she was back in Albuquerque, alone in the little house. Her doctor, having insisted that Jerry quit her job at the air base, now had apparently washed his hands of her.[26]

Whenever Jerry went into a crisis, Ernie's usual reflex was to conjure up at least some small reason for optimism. But this time the reflex was sluggish. "I can't see anything for it but one swing of the pendulum after another until it's all over," he told Cavanaugh. Clearly she was not safe alone, yet Jerry hated having a nurse live with her. And Ernie, remembering the disastrous experience of trying to care for her himself in 1941, believed his presence would likely only make matters worse. (Jerry's closest friends agreed.) "I feel so goddam sorry for her I could weep, and it haunts me to think of her there in the house alone, tortured in her mind as she is, and sick," he said. "But I don't know what the hell to do about it. . . . It's been proved that me being there doesn't help any, so there's no use for me to quit and come home and go nuts too."[27]

For several years, as the number of people she could tolerate shrank to a bare handful, Jerry had kept up her friendship with the Albuquerque editor E. H. Shaffer, his wife, Liz, and their three children. During Ernie's absences the Shaffers had shared holidays with Jerry, helped her through crises, and kept a watchful eye out during her spells of relative tranquility. But Shaffer had been plagued by worsening alcoholism and illness, and in the spring of 1944 he entered a crisis and died.

Jerry's reaction revealed her fears for Ernie. On the night of Shaffer's death, she decided suddenly that she must see her friend's body; she was driven to the mortuary and did so, seeming to find comfort in the act. The next morning, though Liz did not expect her at the funeral, Jerry's wan figure appeared, "so tense that you could literally see her holding herself together." All that day she maintained a rigid self-control. The next morning she put herself back in the hospital.

These events occurred just as Shaffer's *Albuquerque Tribune*, like the rest of the nation's newspapers, carried frequent stories of the immense buildup of American troops in England for a great strike across the English Channel. Everyone knew the invasion was coming, and every report made it obvious it would dwarf all previous operations of the war. Jerry knew Ernie was to be in the midst of it, and she must have known that, bearing the mantle of "America's greatest war correspondent," he could not possibly hang back in the rear echelons. Less than a week after Shaffer's death, Liz Shaffer sent off an anxious letter to Lee Miller in Washington. Knowing Lee held Ernie's power-of-attorney, with discretion over his bank account, she pleaded with Miller to release enough money to pay for electroshock treatments for Jerry, but without telling Ernie enough of the details to induce him to come home. Liz had become convinced that there was "a lot more involved" in Jerry's tailspin of the last few months than her alcoholism alone. "The more I thought about it," she told Miller, "the more it seemed probable to me that she had tried to face that fact that Ernie might not come back — in fact she probably went so far as to be certain that he wouldn't. And she just can't" face it. Her condition had improved; then Shaffer had died. "As you know," Liz told Miller, "she was deeply fond of Shafe and his death would have been a blow to her at any time, even if Ernie were safe in this country. Now, in addition to her own sorrow and concern for the children and me — well, I don't know whether I can quite explain it or not. But I think that for her the week [of Shaffer's death and funeral] has been almost like a rehearsal of something that she fears may happen to her at any minute."[28]

"An operation is pending . . ."

Ernie left London for the country on May 2, the day after the Pulitzers were announced. With his cushion now flat after two weeks of unproductive days, he badly needed column fodder. He spent a couple of days with a tank-destroyer unit, then several more days with a B-26 bomber squadron at an American airfield. The contrast to the drab, improvised airfields he had known in North Africa was sharp, for this was "a lovely place . . . wonderfully green, as is all England now. . . . You walk from one barracks to another under elms and chestnuts, big-trunked and wide-branched, and it gives you a feeling of beautiful peace and contentment." Nearby were quiet villages, "the lovely kind you read about in books," where fifteen Americans from one squadron alone had already found English girls to marry.[29] The serenity of the place, when contrasted with the airfield's destructive purpose, played on the mind. Ernie had been invited to the base by a couple of airmen, in London on evening passes, who had recognized him in the bar at the Dorchester. "It's a funny war," one of them had said. "Here I am this afternoon in London, having a drink in a supercivilized place like this and going to the theatre tonight. And this morning I was out on a short mission across the Channel, dropping bombs to beat hell and killing everyone in sight. I can't figure it out."[30]

A sense of going through the motions while awaiting a catastrophic change pervades Ernie's dispatches from England. There was no theme to cover that he hadn't covered before, no topic to match what he had gone through in Italy or what he knew was to come across the Channel. Yet his readers were hardly disappointed, for he instinctively reverted to the entertaining fluff and personal narrative that had always charmed them, even when he lacked a big topic. Ernie turned up all sorts of entertaining scraps. One was about Lieutenant General Carl "Tooey" Spaatz, the commander of Army Air Forces in Europe, who got so mad watching some German pilots botch a raid over London one night that he finally yelled, "The damn fools! They're setting bombing back twenty years!" He told stories about the mixing of Yanks and Brits, like the one G.I. who said to another, "These English are beginning to act as if this country belonged to them."[31] "Small world" and "funny coincidence" stories — always Pyle staples — proliferated on this small island where Americans were congregating by the hundreds of thousands. Ernie told of running into the G.I. son of a coffeeshop owner he knew in San Francisco; the G.I. husband of a girl from the farm next door to his parents' place in Dana; his friend Arthur McCollum, the contractor who had built his house in Albuquerque.[32] Familiar faces seemed to appear at every pub and on every street corner — soldiers he had last seen in Cairo, the Belgian Congo, Ireland, Tunisia, Washington or Albuquerque. They'd softened in the months away from combat, he remarked, but "when our trails cross again their paunches will be down, and their faces thin and brown and dirty, and they will look hard and alive and like the friends I used to know. They'll look better. It's a silly world."[33]

During these weeks of agonizing suspense in the United States, the column came as light and diverting tonic. The pleasant tone bore no relation to the author's state of mind. So many of the thousands of people gathered in Britain — officers, enlisted men, support staff, inexperienced reporters — knew what was about to happen only in an academic sense; he listened to them talk about the war with a grim and private foreboding. One newcomer was Lee Miller's ex-wife, Katie Hillyer, who was in London with the Office of War Information. After dining with her one night, Ernie told Miller: "Your Katie is full of war ideologies or something, but I don't believe she really knows people get killed."[34]

Ernie dropped in regularly at the massive office building where the Army's public relations branch had set up shop. The operation filled four floors and burst into adjacent buildings. A huge room had been designated as headquarters for the correspondents covering the invasion, who now numbered some four hundred and fifty. Most of their faces were unfamiliar to Ernie; in fact, "half of them [are] not even newspapermen. I don't know who the hell they are."[35] The reporters were managed by a battalion of press relations officers. They had laid plans for coverage of the invasion as detailed as the planning of paratroop drops and artificial harbors. Their briefing papers bulged with secret memoranda on how correspondents would be called up and transported to witness the invasion, and diagrams of "press copy flow" — from the beachhead to a dispatch point to a command ship to the London copy room at Supreme Headquarters, Allied Expeditionary Force (SHAEF), where each dispatch would pass through a "news controller," a censor and a cable operator for transmission to New York.[36] Their talks with reporters reflected the Army's fears that many people at home were naive about the Herculean battles that lay ahead. Correspondents were asked to emphasize that "the first hammer blow cannot be expected to cause more than an indentation. . . . In other words, the fact that we have landed on the continent can be recorded as a great feat, taken all by itself. . . ."[37]

Day by day portents mounted. The effects on Ernie were predictable: "queer vague pains" in his stomach; eyes "crossed and blurry."[38] At a meeting with fifty-five top British and American reporters, including the twenty-eight designated as "assault correspondents" who would go ashore in the very first days, Army public relations officers issued chilling reminders: "Have your blood type marked on your identification tags"; "Have your gas mask where you can get at it"; "The Judge Advocate General will assist you in making out wills or any other legal papers you have put off until the last minute." The reporters were not yet told of the exact timing of the invasion, but they were warned to be ready to leave London at a moment's notice. Once or twice the Army bundled them into cars for brief tours of southeastern England — an attempt to deceive any German spies who might be watching them. General Bradley, in command of the American forces, met with the correspondents briefly. He said he would not see them again as a group on the English side of the Channel.

On May 22, all correspondents accredited to SHAEF were herded into the theater of an officers' club, where General Eisenhower, the supreme commander, stepped to the podium. Ike tried a joke — "I've been informed by the newspapers that an operation is pending" — then reiterated his view that correspondents were quasi-staff officers integral to the process of making war. "Our countries fight best when our people are best informed. You will be allowed to report everything possible, consistent, of course, with military security. I will never tell you anything false. . . .

"I have no doubt as to the outcome of the future," Eisenhower warned, "but I have no illusions as to the magnitude of the task. . . . It will be no basket of roses."[39]

Each correspondent was allowed 125 pounds of baggage plus whatever he could carry. Ernie assembled his gear. The carriage of his Remington typewriter had broken in Italy, forcing him to turn it by hand at the end of every line. But he had gotten so accustomed to this that he did not bother to have it fixed, even when Remington, learning of the mishap through one of Ernie's columns, had offered to send a replacement.[40] For fortification he packed no fewer than eleven bottles of good liquor secured through friends in London, plus a handful of good-luck trinkets sent to him by readers. "I believe in nothing," he told Moran, "but make sure to have my pockets filled with my quota of rabbits feet, St. Christopher medals, rams-horns and what not."[41]

"Obviously I can't go into any of our very well-laid plans for covering the invasion," he wrote Miller, "but I can say that all preparations are finished and we are ready. Censorship will be very tight at first, so some of my first columns may arrive pretty badly butchered up. I won't be able to get stuff out right away, so don't expect to hear from me for several days after the landings."[42] In the last week of May he surrendered his bedroll to an Army PRO, who whisked it off to a secret destination for packing in an unseen hold. By May 26 he was "tied up in knots in the back of my neck," as he told Cavanaugh. "All I do is drink and work and wait." Later that day, without regard for his cushion, he simply stopped writing: "To hell with it."[43]

"For Christ's sake take it easy, and don't get too damned heroic," Miller had warned Ernie early in the spring. "About the tenth echelon of the invasion will be soon enough."[44]

Ernie meant to take the advice. He had missed the worst landings in North Africa, Sicily and Italy, and he had no wish to press his luck now, in what promised to be a landing far more violent and dangerous than any other in the European theater. Four correspondents had just been killed in a single week in Italy. "I have not yet made plans on what I'll do in the invasion," he told Moran in April. "I think a smart thing would be to get on the underground in London and keep riding for four or five days, back and forth."[45] In fact, he was fearful enough to consider waiting for two or three weeks after D-Day before crossing the Channel. But sometime in May, Bradley's aide, Chester Hansen, invited Ernie to accompany the general on the command ship *Augusta*. Under this plan, Ernie would go ashore on the second or third day. He had no taste for the honor, for it meant sailing in the lead convoy, then lying offshore all the first day to be targeted by German defenders. But as he told Jerry, it was "something like an invitation from the White House — something you don't refuse."[46]

He was downplaying a decision of immense consequence. Of all the men who would participate in the invasion — some 175,000 the first day alone — only the tiniest fraction held the power to decide not to go. The great Time-Life photographer Robert Capa, whose photographs of the landings on Omaha Beach would become perhaps the most famous of the entire war, reflected later on the choice he was offered just before D-Day: to go in with a regimental staff, "a pretty safe bet," or to accompany one of the first waves. "I would say that the war correspondent gets more drinks, more girls, better pay, and greater freedom than the soldier, but that at this stage of the game, having the freedom to choose his spot and being allowed to be a coward and not be executed for it is his torture. The war correspondent has his stake — his life — in his own hands, and he can put it on this horse or that horse, or he can put it back in his pocket at the very last minute."[47]

As May drew to a close, a handful of correspondents exercised Capa's option and pulled out of the invasion. Ernie sympathized, but it was not in him to turn away. His fame had raised the stakes so high that he could not pull out without risking humiliation for himself and Scripps-Howard. Perhaps, too, he was determined to pass another test of courage. Certainly he felt bound to the soldiers going in. About the reporters who had pulled out, he wrote Miller: "I guess all of us feel that way, but there's nothing to do for it but to go on and go."[48]

In the last days of waiting, a kind of fog settled over him. Gravitating toward the little group of reporters who had been through as much as he had — Don Whitehead, Clark Lee, Jack Thompson, Bill Stoneman of the *Chicago Daily News* — he would catch himself in a trance, unaware of what his friends were saying. He spent at least one night drinking himself into a stupor. He suffered "terrible periods of depression" and had "hideous dreams" of the invasion. The others reported similar feelings; even Whitehead and Lee, swashbucklers who had seemed fearless in Africa and Italy, "began to get nerves."

"All the time fear lay blackly deep upon our consciousness," Ernie wrote later. "It bore down on your heart like an all-consuming weight. . . . And frankly I was the worst of the lot."[49]

The Army had promised the assault correspondents twenty-four hours' notice. But when the phone call finally came at nine o'clock on the morning of May 28, Ernie was told to appear in ninety minutes outside the office of a lieutenant colonel in the Public Relations Division. The caller said this was just another exercise, "but we knew inside ourselves that this was it."[50] His colleagues were already there when "a cab drew up and a bedding roll, duffle bag, typewriter, and assorted odds and ends of gear with legs stumbled out. It was Ernie — with a terrific hangover."

He gave them a look and said, "Well, well! Imagine meeting all you interesting people here. All of you look horrible."[51]

Stoneman, who had been shot in North Africa, whipped out his notebook and pencil and approached Ernie briskly.

"Tell me, Mr. Pyle," he said, "how does it feel to be an assault correspondent?"

"Awful," Ernie admitted.[52]

They were driven by jeep to an assembly area — a "sausage," in Army parlance, because of the areas' curvilinear shapes on the map. Here they spent the night and picked up their official battle kit: "clothing impregnated against gas attack,[53] a shovel to dig foxholes, seasickness capsules, a carton of cigarets, a medical kit, rations and one funny little item which I can't mention but which was good for many purposes" — condoms, no doubt, which many G.I.'s used that week to keep rain and saltwater spray out of their rifle barrels. Deprived of their bedrolls, the reporters were issued three blankets, but Ernie could hardly sleep for the cold. Until now he had felt physically quite well in Britain, despite his nerves; he had even gained eight or ten pounds. But now, he realized, "We had got a little soft, and here we were again starting back to the old horrible life we had known for so long — sleeping on the ground, only cold water, rations . . . and dirt."[54] There was little inspiration among the thousands of soldiers moving to their embarkation ports. "They have no great faith in the new world, they have no belief in any great liberating mission," a British captain wrote to his wife that night. "They know it's going to be a charnel house. All they want is to put an end to it all. . . ."[55]

Another day of driving brought Ernie, half-frozen, to General Bradley's headquarters at the western port of Bristol, where he looked up Colonel Samuel Myers, whom he had known in Africa. Myers's task was to get Bradley's first cross-Channel command post established in the field. Ernie now changed his plans. He told Myers about Bradley's invitation to sail aboard the *Augusta,* but he said he preferred not to return to war with "too much brass." He said he wanted "to ride with the boys that were going in the hard way," according to Myers. So it was decided Ernie would sail on the LST (landing ship, tank) designated for Myers and other First Army headquarters staff, along with several hundred G.I.'s.[56]

Early the next morning he took the last land leg of the journey through a "dismal, cold, cruel rain." Myers's convoy was bound for the little port of Falmouth near the tip of the Cornwall peninsula at Britain's southwestern corner. Civilian traffic had been cleared from the roads; they saw only Army green trucks, jeeps and motorcycles. When the convoy stopped for a stretch, Ernie watched a little wire-haired terrier jump from a truck and romp in a field "with never any worry. It seemed wonderful to be a dog."

That evening, May 31, Ernie waded a few yards through English Channel surf to his LST, which was already burdened with the armored cars and soldiers of an armored reconnaissance unit. Minutes later, the ship edged into Falmouth Harbor and let down its anchor to wait for the final signal. Later that night the colonel commanding the Army troops aboard told Ernie the entire plan for Operation OVERLORD, the Allied invasion of four broad beaches on the northern coast of France. Now he knew "the secret the whole world had waited years to hear," Ernie wrote later,

and once you have heard it you become permanently a part of it. Now you were committed. It was too late to back out now, even if your heart failed you.

I asked a good many questions, and I realized my voice was shaking when I spoke but I couldn't help it. . . . From a vague anticipatory dread the invasion now turned into a horrible reality for me.

In a matter of hours this holocaust of our own planning would swirl over us. No man could guarantee his own fate. It was almost too much for me. A feeling of utter desperation obsessed me throughout the night. It was nearly 4 A.M. before I got to sleep, and then it was a sleep harassed and torn by an awful knowledge.[57]

9
⭐⭐⭐⭐

"You Alone Are Left Alive . . ."
FRANCE: JUNE–SEPTEMBER 1944

The din of a newspaper city room in the 1940s was the same from coast to coast: telephones ringing, typewriters clattering, questions and answers hollered through a haze of cigarette smoke across rooms crowded with scarred desks and crumpled paper. The noise rose or fell according to the rhythm of the daily news cycle, but always it was underlaid by the soft chugging of the wire machines, the "press tickers" that patiently printed infinite streams of dispatches from all over the world.

Often, the chugging was punctuated by a sharp little bell. This was meant to draw the attention of busy telegraph editors to a wire story considered slightly out of the ordinary by the issuing office. Once in a great while, the bell would ring five times in quick staccato. That was the code for a terse bulletin known as a "flash." A flash was history in the making. One bell barely raised editors' eyebrows. Five bells set off a stampede to every wire machine in America.

In the first days of June 1944, editors came to

work knowing the next flash could ring at any moment.

A flash came on Monday, June 5: Rome had fallen. President Roosevelt spoke to the nation by radio at eight-thirty that evening eastern time, saluting the Fifth Army.

Just after midnight, five bells rang again. The flash came from the Associated Press in New York: "German Trans-Ocean agency claims invasion has begun." The *New York Times* squeezed a headline but no story into its next edition, which reached the sidewalks at 1:30 A.M. At 2:00 A.M., radio announcers began to interrupt programs to read the AP bulletin, and at 3:32, the few listeners awake heard the voice of Colonel Ernest Dupuy, Eisenhower's press aide, confirm the early reports: "Under the command of General Eisenhower, Allied naval forces, supported by strong air forces, began landing Allied armies this morning on the northern coast of France." That was all.

Gradually Americans awakened to the news. For their grandchildren and great-grandchildren living in the era of twenty-four-hour live television coverage of great events, a leap of the imagination is required to understand the extent of Americans' ignorance that morning. They were told only that the invasion of Western Europe had begun, nothing more. No images of invasion beaches flashed on television screens. Radio carried no reports from the scene. People didn't even know precisely where that scene was; the Allies censored the exact location of the landings to comply with elaborate efforts to protect the troops as long as possible. Nor did Americans learn which divisions were involved, or how many men. There was to be no report of casualties for several weeks. Place names that would later toll like foghorns in the American memory — Utah Beach, Pointe du Hoc, Omaha Beach — went unspoken. Were the landings in cities, as in North Africa? On sandy beaches? Cliffs? No one knew. For those trying to visualize what was happening on the morning of D-Day, the mind's eye found only a misty void. Many felt the simple passion to *see* expressed by a woman in Marietta, Georgia. She, like everyone else, knew that an event without parallel or precedent was occurring. "Even if it meant I had to die," she said, "I should like to be a part of that invasion. It is the biggest and greatest and most spectacular thing in all history."[1]

D-Day was a day of noise in America: car horns honking, church bells pealing, factory and train whistles shrieking, headlines screaming "invasion!" But there was very little more news. A few radio correspondents who had been aboard invading planes in the morning rushed to file reports, but they had seen only "a lot of smoke, ships, and planes, little else. There was nothing from the beaches."[2]

Nothing.

With nothing new to tell, radio announcers were reduced to endless repetitions of old bulletins, plus inspirational messages from Eisenhower and other leaders. Reporters with Reuters, the British press association, sent a few words via carrier pigeons, one from a ship, another from land. Just before midnight, listeners finally heard a recording of an almost-on-the-scene report made early in the morning by George Hicks, a correspondent for the fledgling ABC, who had been aboard a cruiser off the invasion beaches. Hicks's nerves spilled into the broadcast, giving the report a thrilling note of tension: "At this very moment . . . the platform on which I am standing is vibrating to concussion of the guns and the exploding shells . . . . If you'll excuse me, I'll just take a deep breath for the moment and stop speaking."[3] It was the nation's first authentic glimpse of what had happened. People yearned for more.

But newspapers didn't deliver much more the next day or that whole week. The leading stories were based on press releases, dignified as "communiqués," issued at Eisenhower's Supreme Headquarters, Allied Expeditionary Force, or SHAEF. Until SHAEF crossed the Channel to France, its offices were in London, many miles from the fighting, and the communiqués were written by Army and Navy press officers picking and choosing from official reports. To write his daily dispatch about the day's battles, a correspondent assigned to

SHAEF first would read the day's communiqués. Then, if he had time, he might scrounge a few quotes from officers who had been no closer to the fighting than he. Finally he spent a frantic hour or two assembling a dispatch summarizing the day's highlights in time for transmission.

To erect his column of type, he had perhaps eight or ten essential facts plus an unvarying small stock of punchy adjectives and verbs. Allied advances were always "relentless" and "merciless." "Fighting" was always "fierce." Present participles were popular — American columns "were hammering," "were striking," "were filtering," "were cutting," "were thrusting," and the beachhead was always "steadily expanding." The double-barreled hyperbole was the reporters' trustiest weapon, especially on D-Day itself. In its June 7 edition alone, the *New York Times*, without really seeing any of it, reported "the greatest airborne force ever launched," "the greatest air and sea bombardment of history," "the greatest mine-sweeping operation in history," and "the greatest military venture of all time." In short, reading newspaper accounts of Normandy (indeed, of most military operations in World War II) was like reading an account of a football game written by a sportswriter sitting outside the stadium who derives his only knowledge of the game from the hurried accounts from one team's assistant coach who runs out after each quarter to give brief and self-serving updates. It was barely better than nothing.

There were correspondents on the narrow beachhead, of course, but they were terribly rushed, hamstrung by censorship, and in paralyzing danger. The scarcity of front-line coverage was compounded by a colossal blunder by the Army's Public Relations Division, which somehow left nine of the designated assault correspondents in England, "about ready to commit mass hari-kiri," as one of them said.[4] For many days the sole representative of the Associated Press in Normandy was Pyle's friend Don Whitehead. His colleague Hal Boyle, stuck in England, had predicted just such a fiasco, "simply because the fatheads whose job in the army is to annoy correspondents had here their biggest, most golden opportunity in history to screw up," and "the prediction has come true."[5] Boyle may have drawn solace from the fact that his competitors across the Channel were tearing out their own hair over delays in transmission that ran to four and five days.

Yet even if hundreds of reporters had come ashore on June 6 under conditions ideal for writing and transmitting, the result might not have been much different. "The correspondents sent some 700,000 words on the first day," the historian Phillip Knightley notes, "and yet, reading their reports . . . one cannot escape the impression that the sheer size of the operation overwhelmed most of them."[6] Really they had little to be ashamed of, for it is a simple fact that the invasion of Normandy defied description.

Between the lines of the myriad accounts of D-Day — which later became one of the most written about days in history — one glimpses a certain frustration. It is the frustration of witnesses to a scene so overpowering to the senses that, try as one might, it simply could not be conveyed to a person who was not there.

Pyle's friend Tom Treanor, the freelancer who had just joined the *Los Angeles Times,* was perhaps the only reporter to acknowledge the irony of the assault correspondent's assignment on D-Day. To file one of the first beachhead dispatches, Treanor scrambled up the bluff at Omaha Beach, glanced out to sea, scrambled back down, then wrote: "It was too much to describe."[7] A few weeks later, shortly before he was killed near Paris, Treanor elaborated. When people at home asked him what war was like, he confessed, "I couldn't help them. Like life in the big city, war is composed of all things, and can't be disposed of in a club luncheon. There's no formula for reducing the whole mystery to understandable terms. There are only flashes which light up a little corner of the fog and make you think, momentarily at least, that you are beginning to see."[8]

"I took a walk . . ."

Ernie Pyle came ashore at Omaha Beach on a landing craft early on the morning of June 7. Thousands of infantrymen moved past him

305

across the gravelly terrain of the beach and up the bluffs beyond. The front lay a couple of miles inland. Exploding mines in and near the water sent up "geysers of brown earth."

Pyle faced an irony: on this beach where the century's biggest story had just broken, his options as a reporter were dismayingly limited. He was not supposed to write the news of what was happening that day; that was for the boys at SHAEF in London. Besides, he had only the barest notion of the broader military situation, as he readily admitted to readers: "Indeed it will be some time before we have a really clear picture of what has happened or what is happening at the moment. You must experience the terrible confusion of warfare and the frantic nightmarish thunder and smoke and bedlam of battle to realize this."[9] Other reporters were required to scour the beachhead for hometown heros. The result could be pretty threadbare, as when Jack Thompson of the *Chicago Tribune* trumpeted his discovery of a Chicagoan in the Signal Corps who had been "virtually the only officer successful in getting . . . hand-carried signal equipment ashore."[10]

Ernie might have scuttled up to the front lines, but it was no mean feat to write something worth reading directly from the front. One of the earliest such reports came from Leonard Mosley, a fine British writer who on June 6 could manage little more than this: "There is a helluva battle going on here as I write and bullets and mortar bombs, not to mention a couple of snipers, are producing conditions in my vicinity not conducive to consecutive thinking."[11] In any case, Ernie knew the fighting front inland would be much like other fronts, and he wanted to convey what was unique about this place and time.

Thus, with few alternatives, he began simply to walk. He did not explore the bluffs but stayed along the water's edge. When men rushed across his path, he would pause to let them pass like a stroller on a city sidewalk crowded with hurrying office workers. Sometimes he looked out to sea, taking in the view of ships filling the ocean from the beach to the horizon, waiting to unload their cargoes. But mostly he trained his eyes downward, looking at things on the sand. He walked for several hours. Officers and enlisted men recognized him; he talked with some of them. Late in the day he boarded an outbound boat to return to the LST for the night, looking "very tired [and] very sad" to one officer who saw him.[12] Over the next day — perhaps two days — he wrote three columns derived from his few hours on the beach. They comprised the first substantive account to reach American readers from any correspondent on the beachhead. They were significant not only because they provided powerful mental images to millions of readers hungry for such images, but also because they offered lessons about what the images meant.[13]

Pyle began by giving readers their first explanation of how great had been the feat of getting ashore against the German defenses, for "now that it is over it seems to me a pure miracle that we ever took the beach at all." He listed the Germans' advantages: "evil devices" hiding underwater "to catch our boats"; the one hundred-foot bluff studded with "great concrete gun emplacements" that enfiladed the beach; the well-protected machine-gun nests and concrete walls; the gaping ditch dug to stymie Allied tanks; checkerboards of mines; and "four men on shore for every three men we had approaching the shore.

"And yet we got on."

Soldiers had told Ernie about the near disaster at Omaha — how their men "simply could not get past the beach" in the face of "an inhuman wall of fire from the bluff." But the defenses had been cracked. There had been "terrific and wonderful naval gunfire" and "epic stories of destroyers that ran right up into shallow water and had it out point-blank with the big guns in those concrete emplacements ashore." Then came the move that latter-day historians would confirm as the turning point at Omaha: ". . . our men were organized by their officers and pushed on inland, circling machine-gun nests and taking them from the rear. As one officer said, the only way to take a beach is to face it and keep going. . . . Our men were pinned down for a while, but finally they stood up and went through. . . . In the light of a couple of days of retrospection, we sit and talk and call it a miracle that our men ever got on at all or were able to stay on."

Pyle addressed readers' fears directly. Yes, he had seen "the bodies of soldiers lying in rows . . . and other bodies, uncollected, still sprawling grotesquely in the sand or half hidden by the high grass. . . ." But there was reassurance, too. Casualties had been lower than expected, he reported, and "these units that were so battered and went through such hell are still, right at this moment, pushing on inland without rest, their spirits high, their egotism in victory almost reaching the smart-alecky stage," driven by "the spirit that wins battles and eventually wars."

This was Pyle the patriot. Doing his part as he saw it for the invasion, he steered public opinion along the path between complacency and defeatism. It had been tough but not too tough, he was telling the home front. Be grateful, not despairing. Be confident but not overconfident. Everyone at home got the point. The "miracle" column, distributed to all U.S. papers as part of the Normandy "pool" arrangement, was played on scores of front pages, including those of such Scripps-Howard competitors as the *Washington Post*, under giant headlines like the *New York World-Telegram*'s: "PYLE GIVES VIVID CLOSEUP OF SCENE ON BEACHHEAD HARD-WON BY ALLIES." On the same day that Republican Senator Carl Hatch inserted the column in the *Congressional Record*, it was accorded respectful play by the Communist editors of the *Daily Worker*. Pyle's account was quoted as an authority on battle *sine qua non* in editorials in both the *New York Herald Tribune* and the *New York Times.* "It's getting so you can't pick up any damned publication at all without seeing you mentioned," Miller told him.[14]

With this introduction out of his way, Pyle shifted to the challenge of somehow conveying the immense scale of the assault, both its size and its costs. For this he conceived a stroke of brilliant simplicity. He chose to write, as usual, about "what I see."

I took a walk along the historic coast of Normandy in the country of France.

It was a lovely day for strolling along the seashore. Men were sleeping on the sand, some of them sleeping forever. Men were floating in the water, but they didn't know they were in the water, for they were dead.

The water was full of squishy little jellyfish about the size of your hand. Millions of them. In the center each of them had a green design exactly like a four-leaf clover. The good-luck emblem. Sure. Hell yes.

I walked for a mile and a half along the water's edge of our many-miled invasion beach. You wanted to walk slowly, for the detail on that beach was infinite.

The wreckage was vast and startling. The awful waste and destruction of war, even aside from the loss of human life, has always been one of its outstanding features to those who are in it. Anything and everything is expendable. And we did expend on our beachhead in Normandy during those first few hours.

He described the material wreckage that lay in the surf — ruined trucks and barges, swamped boats and landing craft, burnt jeeps and tanks, "half-tracks carrying office equipment that had been made into a shambles by a single shell hit, their interiors still holding their useless equipage of smashed typewriters, telephones, office files . . . smashed bulldozers and big stacks of thrown-away lifebelts," abandoned rolls of barbed wire and steel matting, and "stacks of broken, rusting rifles." This wastage was

enough for a small war. . . . And yet we could afford it. We could afford it because we were on, we had our toehold, and behind us there were such enormous replacements for this wreckage on the beach that you could hardly conceive of their sum total. Men and equipment were flowing from England in such a gigantic stream that it made the waste on the beachhead seem like nothing at all, really nothing at all.

But there is another and more human litter. It extends in a thin little line, just like a high-water mark, for miles along the beach. This is the strewn personal gear, gear that will never be needed again, of those who

311

fought and died to give us our entrance into Europe.

Here in a jumbled row for mile on mile are soldiers' packs. Here are socks and shoe polish, sewing kits, diaries, Bibles and hand grenades. Here are the latest letters from home, with the address on each one neatly razored out — one of the security precautions enforced before the boys embarked.

Here are toothbrushes and razors, and snapshots of families back home staring up at you from the sand. Here are pocketbooks, metal mirrors, extra trousers, and bloody, abandoned shoes. Here are broken-handled shovels, and portable radios smashed almost beyond recognition. . . .

I picked up a pocket Bible with a soldier's name in it, and put it in my jacket. I carried it half a mile or so and then put it back down on the beach. I don't know why I picked it up, or why I put it back down. . . .

I stepped over the form of one youngster whom I thought dead. But when I looked down I saw he was only sleeping. He was very young, and very tired. He lay on one elbow, his hand suspended in the air about six inches from the ground. And in the palm of his hand he held a large, smooth rock.

I stood and looked at him a long time. He seemed in his sleep to hold that rock lovingly, as though it were his last link with a vanishing world. . . .

The strong, swirling tides of the Normandy coastline shift the contours of the sandy beach as they move in and out. They carry soldiers' bodies out to sea, and later they return them. They cover the corpses of heroes with sand, and then in their whims they uncover them.

As I plowed out over the wet sand of the beach . . . I walked around what seemed to be a couple of pieces of driftwood sticking out of the sand. But they weren't driftwood.

They were a soldier's two feet. . . . The toes of his G.I. shoes pointed toward the land he had come so far to see, and which he saw so briefly.

The story of the walk on the beach drew still more feverish praise at home, but the author shrugged it off. "I think America must be very emotional about the invasion, to compare that beachhead litter piece with the Waskow piece," he told Miller. "It was very inadequate in expressing what you really saw."[15]

Yet by lingering over minutiae, Pyle had gotten across a sense of D-Day's enormity where most writers had failed. He was like an anthropologist evoking some great past metropolis by analyzing scraps of its fossilized garbage. At the same time he compressed the gigantic canvas into a comprehensible human scale, evoking not just awe but love as well. The sleeping soldier with the rock in one hand is described as a parent would describe an exhausted little boy found sprawled asleep in a corner after a day of play; he is vulnerable, pathetic, lovable. There is comfort here, too. The shifting sands and the "swirling tides" are the healing movements of time, and the dead have already joined its current.

Of course Pyle saw selectively. There was much wreckage on Omaha Beach that he did not write about — blasted-off human limbs, pulpy chunks of flesh, shell-shocked weeping men. He kept the dead and mutilated under a discreet shroud. Hundreds of bodies lay on Omaha Beach on D-Day, but the particular corpse in his account is literally buried in sand, out of sight, while others are merely "sleeping forever." Probably understatement made the point better than raw realism. That wasn't Ernie's style, nor, in all probability, would it have passed the censors, nor was it what people wanted at home. Instead, the tone of the beach walk columns is sad, shocked poignancy, a mood that suited him. Whether one calls the motive propaganda or patriotism, Ernie's D-Day columns were intended in part to aid the war effort; he never entertained doubts about that role. But his main aim went beyond that; it was more subtle and complicated.

He never articulated it quite this way, yet the inescapable force of Pyle's war writings is to establish an unwritten covenant between the soldier at the front and the civilian at home. War, he was saying, demands recompense. The experience of the combat soldier is so terrible that you, the civilian, can never redeem it, but you must at least try to see it and know it, and return your humble gratitude and love. He sounded this theme plainly in the first of his D-Day columns — "I want to tell you what the opening of the second front in this one sector entailed, so that you can know and appreciate and forever be humbly grateful to those both dead and alive who did it for you" — and all the pictures of suffering and waste that follow are meant to give it weight. More weight would have accrued had he gone farther in describing the beaches' horrors, but this would have violated the unspoken norms of taste that pervaded the war correspondents' ranks, and it risked evoking the dreaded "defeatist" reaction. It was the same theme he had groped for when composing last words for *Here Is Your War.* "When we leave here for the next shore," he had written, "there is nothing we can do for the ones beneath the wooden crosses, except perhaps to pause and murmur, 'Thanks, pal.' "[16]

"An awful lot of dead people . . ."

The mountain campaign around Cassino had been worse for sheer physical misery, but the ferocity of the fighting in Normandy outstripped anything Ernie had ever seen, and he began to slide into emotional and physical exhaustion.

315

Death, hovering nearby in Italy, now closed in and overwhelmed him.

From the beginning of the campaign in France, he had had great difficulty sleeping. In North Africa and Italy he had been able to sleep through the worst imaginable noise, but now the mere drone of an occasional Luftwaffe plane at night kept him agonizingly awake. "Instead of getting used to it," he told another reporter, "I become less used to it as the years go by . . . I am much more afraid of a plane overhead now than I was during the London blitz, or even during our early dive-bombing days in Africa."[17] Many nights in June were "so noisy that it's almost impossible to get any sleep unless you go to bed drunk, so that's what I try to do as often as we can conscript some cognac."[18] Ten days after D-Day, he had knots in his stomach from "constant tenseness and lack of sleep."[19] What had been an exhilarating adventure in North Africa was now awful, slogging drudgery. He felt old. "I find I cant take as much as I could a year or two ago," he told Lee Miller. "Out in the field I wear out awfully easily, and when I come back I have to rest a day before writing."[20]

In the weeks just after D-Day the First Army's drive for Cherbourg was the big news, and for once Ernie decided he should stay abreast of breaking events. He hooked up with the Ninth Division, one of two divisions assigned to take the port. He had covered the division in North

316

Africa, but censors had prevented him from naming it, a deprivation of publicity that divisional PR officers had stewed about ever since. Now, with a highly efficient PR setup and restrictions removed, they seized upon Ernie and paraded him from one camp to another. He was proud of his role in giving publicity to a deserving outfit — "not publicity in the manufactured sense, but a public report to the folks back home on what an outfit endures and what it accomplishes." But he resented the usurpation of his own person for the purpose, fuming to Miller, "I completely lost 24 hours through being trundled against my will . . . around to battalion after battalion just allegedly because they thought it was good for morale."[21]

Such interruptions and distractions dogged his every movement. Each day brought new invitations from soldiers ranging from privates to generals yearning to have Pyle's recognition bestowed upon their units. "He could have had a limousine to take him wherever he wanted to go," Don Whitehead recalled.[22] Ernie politely sidestepped fawning brass on principle, but the G.I.'s, whom he had no wish to avoid, were nonetheless becoming a nuisance. He was literally attracting crowds. A Pathé newsreel cameraman riding behind Pyle in a convoy on the Cotentin Peninsula was dumbfounded to see soldiers stopping traffic to search out Ernie's jeep, calling, "Hey, Ernie!" and brandishing franc notes and rifle stocks to be autographed.[23]

Every bag of mail from the U.S. to Army post offices in France was made heavier by Pyle columns clipped and sent to soldiers from relatives. These were constantly being proffered to the author for autographs. "Ernie had to fake a little when a newly-met soldier would say, 'Why, this is the damnedest coincidence! Just today I get a letter from home with this clipping of your column, and now here you turn up in the flesh!' " Miller wrote later. "This happened hundreds of times, but Ernie didn't have the heart to say so."[24] Nor did he always have the heart to say no when G.I.'s in trouble with wives or sweethearts beseeched him to get a quick message across the Atlantic. In the midst of the Normandy beachhead in early July, Ernie found time to ask Miller to "Please wire Mrs. Murray Hughes Junior Eleven South Main Green South Carolina QUOTE ALL MY LOVE DARLING LETTERS FOLLOW SOON SIGNED MURRAY UNQUOTE."[25] Near the front in the Cotentin, Pyle's jeep entered a forest where soldiers were actually firing on the enemy, yet when the word spread that Pyle was there, they ran from their positions to see him.[26]

On one level, his popularity with the G.I.'s was no mystery. They enjoyed the attention. As Ernie said himself, "Soldiers like to read about themselves. . . ." And in one of his columns: "Your average doughfoot will go through his normal hell a lot more willingly if he knows that he is getting some credit for it and that the home folks know about it."[27] But the intensity of their loyalty, like the intensity of Pyle's fans at home, demands a closer look. After all, he was not the only reporter of the "worm's-eye view" of the war. But he was the only correspondent to gain universal G.I. approval. In fact, G.I.'s saw him as a stellar exception. As a rule, they distrusted correspondents as flashy cowards without the guts to stay near the front any longer than was necessary to grab a quick quote. The average reporter's "jubilant interpretations and hopped-up style," declared a G.I. reporter in *Stars and Stripes*, "tended to widen the breach between civilians and soldiers and to destroy the latter's confidence in the press."[28] The average G.I. was outraged by headline hype about dashing columns and effortless gains. These underestimated his agonies. Pyle never committed journalistic felonies of that type. He was universally regarded as "a guy who knows how it is" because he lived at the front; in fact, many soldiers believed he spent more time in combat than he actually did. "Most of these news men over here give me a healthy pain," a soldier in the First Armored Division wrote his father, "but Ernie Pyle is different. . . . He lived and traveled right along with all of us, did the things we did, slept and sweated out all the things we did."[29]

Any argument that Pyle sugarcoated the realities of war must be tempered by his status with veterans — a point that Ernie angrily raised himself after a deskbound officer in the United

States criticized *Here Is Your War* as a "brilliantly naive" soft-soaping of the war. "I wish the cocksucker could take a trip or two to the front with me," Ernie steamed to Miller, "and see the receptions I get from the frontline soldiers who read the column all the time, and see what they think of it."[30] G.I.'s knew the war was worse than it appeared in Ernie's columns, but they knew he knew it, too, because he had been there, and because he hinted at it. G.I.'s were not notorious for complete candor in their own letters home; they observed the same canons of taste that Ernie did. "I can not say much about the war," one sergeant confided to a friend at home, "but Ernie Pyle is giving a real good picture of it."[31]

Perhaps, too, Ernie served the same function for soldiers in Europe that the picture-magazine story about North Africa had served for him — the story that, "for some perverse reason," made the war seem "thrilling," though the actual experience ran from mundane to horrible. Soldiers could see an image of themselves that they liked in his heroic depiction of the war. If it was not one hundred percent of the truth, it was real enough, and it offered them a chance to see themselves as part of something large and noble, in sharp contrast to the boredom and drudgery of their actual lives. The G.I. myth worked for them, too.

In the Cherbourg campaign Ernie spent nine

days with the Ninth Division in a state of perpetual tension, deliberately exposing himself to enemy fire as never before. Unlike more cautious outfits, he said, the Ninth "kept tenaciously on the enemy's neck," which meant camps were uprooted nearly every day in a furious pursuit. Ernie stuck mostly with the headquarters staff, which normally would be far enough from the fighting for safety. But with the Ninth, headquarters stayed nearly on top of the front, and some of its staff were killed by shells and snipers. There was never a peaceful night. American artillery kept up an intermittent roar, and "usually German planes were over too, droning around in the darkness and making us tense and nervous."[32]

Though a veteran of far longer standing than nearly all the men he was with, Ernie had lost none of his talent for self-deprecation. Sitting up in a tent one night, he and an officer friend heard an explosion nearby and

a shrill whine through the treetops over our heads. But we didn't jump, or hit the dirt. Instead I said: "I know what that is. That's the rotating band off one of our shells. As an old artilleryman I've heard lots of rotating bands. Sometimes they sound like a dog howling. There's nothing to be afraid of."

"Sure," said Captain Nelson, "that's what it was, a rotating band."

But our harmless rotating band, we found

a few minutes later, was a jagged, red-hot, foot-square fragment of steel from a 240-mm. German shell which had landed a hundred yards away from us. It's wonderful to be a wise guy.[33]

As the Ninth's leading elements moved into the suburbs of Cherbourg — which looked "so much like the Hollywood sets of old European cities that you get your perspective reversed and feel that Cherbourg has just been copied from a movie set" — Ernie, Robert Capa and Charles Wertenbaker of Time-Life were with a company of infantrymen.[34] "The city around us was still full of sound and fury. You couldn't tell where anything was coming from or going to." To the east and west, other units had already moved forward, but no Americans had yet been up this street, which was under rifle fire from a fortified stand of German pillboxes and machine-gun nests half a mile away. A lieutenant approached Ernie and explained how the strongpoint must be approached and assaulted.

"We don't know what we'll run into, and I don't want to stick you right out in front" [the officer told Pyle]. "So why don't you come along with me? We'll go in the middle of the company."
I said, "Okay." By this time I wasn't scared. You seldom are once you're into something. Anticipation is the worst. Fortunately this

little foray came up so suddenly there wasn't time for much anticipation.

As they paused behind a high wall, a hard rain soaked the men's clothes and "vicious little shells" spurted over their heads. Then an order was given, and Ernie found himself where he had asked to be with Company E of the 34th Division at the Rapido River — out where there was nothing between him and the enemy. He narrated the company's movements for his readers: a crouching dash one by one across "a little culvert right out in the open," then up the road, resisting the dangerous but "almost irresistible pull to get close to somebody when you are in danger."

The men didn't talk any. They just went.

They weren't heroic figures as they moved forward one at a time, a few seconds apart. You think of attackers as being savage and bold. These men were hesitant and cautious. They were really the hunters, but they looked like the hunted. There was a confused excitement and a grim anxiety in their faces.

They seemed terribly pathetic to me. They weren't warriors. They were American boys who by mere chance of fate had wound up with guns in their hands sneaking up a death-laden street in a strange and shattered city in a faraway country in a driving rain. They were afraid, but it was beyond their power to quit. They had no choice.

They were good boys. I talked with them all afternoon as we sneaked slowly forward along the mysterious and rubbled street, and I know they were good boys.

And even though they aren't warriors born to the kill, they win their battles. That's the point.

He went on to record the company's halting progress up the street, ducking in doorways as they went (with G.I.'s calling, "Hey, Ernie!" every few yards); his own close call when a German shell pierced an American tank just a few yards from his hiding place; the reduction of a German pillbox. His account was fractured and confusing, just as he intended; Pyle counted it a success whenever he contradicted the common image of battle as an orderly conjunction of tidy, tin-soldier lines. "I hope this has given you a faint idea of what street fighting is like," he concluded. "If you got out of it much more than a headful of confusion then you've got out of it exactly the same thing as the soldiers who do it."[35]

The hedgerow country of Normandy was a killing field such as Ernie had never seen, and as the weeks passed, the constant presence of "too much death" whittled down his will to persist.[36] He was feeling the effects after just a week, though he tried to be offhand about it. "The country is lovely to look at, but . . . spoiled by the climate," he remarked in his first letter to Jerry. "And there are an awful lot of dead people, which of course warps one's viewpoint."[37] By the time he reached Cherbourg, he had to damp down his revulsion. In a letter to Lee Miller, he sounded as if he might be courting an order to come home. "Although I don't often stick my neck out," he confided to Miller, "just the normal presence in the zone is precarious. . . . I still get moody about it. Also sometimes I get so obsessed with the tragedy and horror of seeing dead men that I can hardly stand it. But I guess there's nothing to do but keep going."[38] A day later, on June 30, he spilled out his feelings in a long letter, one of his frankest of the war, to Moran Livingstone, who apparently had speculated on the virtues of "catching the white boat" — a homeward-bound hospital ship — with a "million-dollar wound."

This hedge to hedge stuff is a type of warfare we've never run into before, and I've seen more dead Germans than ever in my life. Americans too, but not nearly so many as the Germans. One day I'll think I'm getting hardened to dead people, dead young people in vast numbers, and then next day I'll realize I'm not and never could be. I have continually to fight an inner depression over the ghastliness of it all that almost whips me a good part of the time. I frankly have fears for myself too, but I think that's probably a weakness which is the result of an accumulation of close calls and fear, rather than any plausibility of my chances being any less than they ever were.

Ernie could repeatedly reassure American readers that their "good boys" in the rifle companies were not being changed by the war, but he was not so confident about the state of his own psyche.

I think the danger of me being utterly warped and distorted inside by all this horror is as great as actually getting killed. You weren't alone in vaguely admitting to yourself the good points of catching a slight one — I've often thought of it myself — the trouble is you never could know ahead of time, and that one that brushes your cheek is the same one that would have killed you if you hadn't turned your head unexplainably half a second earlier.[39]

It was not just the anonymous bodies he saw that preyed on his mind. The D-Day ordeal suffered by his friends Don Whitehead and Jack Thompson, who had lain at the water's edge on Omaha Beach for hours, convinced him they had "no right to be alive at all," yet he knew Whitehead, especially, felt "such a sense of duty and loyalty to his office" that he would continue to risk his life indefinitely. On July 1 he learned that Kay Garland, a friend from the British Ministry of Information since the Blitz of 1940–41, had died in a "buzz bomb" attack while attending church in London. "We feel pretty badly about it," Ernie told Jerry. "I suppose I've seen 500 dead men just since landing in France, but when someone you know who isn't really connected with war gets killed by war, you seem to feel it more."[40] One day Arthur McCollum, the friend who had built the Pyles' home in Albuquerque, appeared at Ernie's camp, and they spent the better part of a day drinking and commiserating about the death of McCollum's son, a flier lost over Germany.

Unable to write a single page of copy after he finished his Cherbourg columns, Ernie told his contacts among the Army PROs that he wanted to cover units in the rear echelon for a while. Privately, he admitted that the front had become so exhausting to body and mind that he had no choice but to back off for a while.[41] A kind of blankness was coming upon him even when he tried to write letters. "The early part of the invasion was so fast and so consuming that I didnt write a single letter to anybody . . . ," he told Jerry. "And then when I did try to write, I found I couldnt say anything. Nothing would come out."[42]

He decided to cover ordnance, the unglamorous branch that fixed trucks and tanks and supplied the ammunition, for though "the layman doesn't hear much about [it] . . . the war couldn't keep going without it." After all, there were "more vehicles in the American sector of our beachhead than in the average-sized American city."[43] Ernie's brief stay with the mechanics may have given him a break, but it also rendered a fine journalistic service that many reporters would have sneered at. It was a grievous distortion to imply, as all newspapers did, that the only parts of the war that mattered were the high commands and the line of battle. This was an industrial war. All the tankers and riflemen and bombardiers put together made up only the sharp point of a long, long spear constructed of signalmen, cooks, quartermasters, engineers, drivers and clerks. Americans who now know the war only through Hollywood lenses are always startled to learn that some 90 percent of American troops in World War II never came close to a front line.

After all his time crafting glowing articles from the dramatic materials provided by battle itself, his little series on ordnance, written with only "a faint rumble of big guns . . . in the far distance," proved he had not lost his ability to work wonders with the ordinary. As always, Ernie knew the literary value of simple, solid fact — for instance, that the ordnance branch's parts catalogue included 275,000 items; that artillerymen in Normandy could easily fire $10 million worth of shells in a day; that the average IQ in ordnance far exceeded that of the Army as a whole; that ordnance companies fixed things for four days at a time, then followed the front, leapfrogging each other at times of swift advances. He included the odd touches of human sympathy and identification that no other reporter, no matter how loudly his editor demanded "Pyle-type stuff," could duplicate: "You'll find great soberness and sincerity [in ordnance units], plus the normal satisfaction that comes from making things whole again instead of destroying them." Few writers could fuse information, inspiration and emotion as Pyle did after spending a few hours on the long grass at the edge of a Norman pasture, watching a dozen men in greasy coveralls fix a pile of rusted, broken rifles.

The first few hours of the morning are given to taking broken rifles apart. They don't try to keep the parts of each gun together. All parts are alike and transferable, hence they throw each type into a big steel pan full of similar parts. At the end of the job they have a dozen or so pans, each filled with the same kind of part.

Then the whole gang shifts over and scrubs the parts. They scrub in gasoline, using sandpaper for guns in bad condition after lying out in the rain and mud.

When everything is clean they take the good parts and start putting them back together and making guns out of them again.

When all the pans are empty they have a stack of rifles — good rifles, all ready to be taken back to the front. . . . And believe me, during the first few days of our invasion men at the front needed these rifles with desperation. Repairmen tell you how our paratroopers and infantrymen would straggle back, dirty and hazy-eyed with fatigue, and plead like a child for a new rifle immediately so they could get back to the front and "get at them sonsabitches." . . .

As gun after gun comes off the stack you look to see what is the matter with it —

Rifle butt split by fragments; barrel dented by bullet; trigger knocked off; whole barrel splattered with shrapnel marks; guns gray from the slime of weeks in swamp mud; faint dark splotches of blood still showing.

You wonder what became of each owner; you pretty well know . . .

The boys said the most heart-breaking rifle they'd found was one of a soldier who had carved a hole about silver dollar size and put his wife's or girl's picture in it, and sealed it over with a crystal of flexiglass.

They don't, of course, know who he was or what happened to him. They only know the rifle was repaired and somebody else is carrying it now, picture and all.

Then as now, the cover of *Time* magazine, launched twenty years earlier by the legendary

Henry Luce, ranked among American society's most hallowed status symbols. Ideas for *Time* covers seldom originated with the magazine's correspondents in the field. The lot of these overtalented and underappreciated souls was merely to obey orders from mahogany-desk-bound editors in New York, who cabled directives to the field with few if any gestures in the direction of creative collaboration.

Time's man in Normandy was Charles Wertenbaker. Near the end of June 1944, about ten days after the publication of Pyle's Omaha Beach columns, a cable demanding material for an Ernie Pyle cover found Wertenbaker in the Cotentin, where he happened to be traveling with Pyle. The *Time* man showed the cable to his sleepy-eyed friend, who could only mutter: "Jesus. The country . . . must have gone nuts."[44] Of course, the cover of *Time* would flatter the most modest soul, especially when one could crow about it to the likes of Paige Cavanaugh, whom Ernie needled delightedly: "They say I'm to be on the front cover of Time in about three weeks. I suppose that will make you throw up."[45]

"Ain't that colossal?" he wrote Jerry.[46]

Actually, the thought of Jerry's part in the story troubled him. As *Time*'s reporters sniffed for "background" among Pyle cronies and acquaintances from Washington to Dana to Albuquerque to Hollywood, Ernie imagined a trashy tell-all about Jerry's problems and their marital ordeal. It worried him enough that he hurried off a cable to Miller, requesting that his boss pass a discreet request to friends at *Time* to "soft-pedal the divorce if they would — for both our sakes."[47]

Time's sausagemakers in New York managed to stuff the story into the edition dated July 17. Thanks to a reporter just arriving in France from London and the States, Ernie got his hands on the magazine July 18. He surveyed the cover — a broad-smiling facial portrait set against a collage of war illustrations and the headline "He loves people and hates war." Then he studied the text. There was the obligatory praise — "a great reporter . . . well on his way toward becoming a living legend" — and Ernie was relieved to find nothing embarrassing about his marriage. But the story of his rise to fame dripped with condescension.

> Four years ago he was an obscure roving reporter whose syndicated column of trivial travelogues appeared in an unimpressive total of 40 newspapers. At that time almost any class of war correspondents would have voted him least likely to succeed. . . . He stood in awe of professional war correspondents and firmly believed himself incompetent to become one.

No more than an "average man" himself, Pyle was said to identify with soldiers' hopes and fears "because he shares them as no exceptionally fearless or exceptionally brilliant man ever could." His "artless" writing was commended to aspiring journalists as "a profitable study both of skills acquired and handicaps overcome."

By now Ernie was hardened against ill-informed slights directed at the old travel column, which he knew included much work that rivaled any of his war coverage. But he was bewildered and appalled by *Time*'s tales of his career since Pearl Harbor. In a North Africa foxhole, after an unsuccessful spell of trying "to be a more or less conventional war correspondent," he was said to have experienced an epiphany. It seemed that Scripps-Howard had ordered Pyle to interview the French admiral, Jean Darlan.

[Pyle] was hurrying across an airfield to the interview when a swarm of Stukas swooped down . . . splattering bullets around him. He dived into a ditch just behind a G.I. When the strafing was over he tapped his companion on the shoulder and said, "Whew, that was close, eh?" There was no answer. The soldier was dead.

Pyle sat through the interview in a daze, went back to his tent and brooded for hours. Finally he cabled his New York office that he could not write the Darlan story. Instead he wrote about the stranger who had died in the ditch beside him. For days he talked of giving up and going home. But when the shock wore off, he knew for sure that his job was not with the generals and their stratagems but with the little onetime drugstore cowboys, clerks and mechanics who had no one else to tell their stories.

This anecdote — an utter fantasy, though retold ever after as solemn truth — was not half as embarrassing as the passage that followed, which cast Pyle as the pitiful target of practical-joking soldiers who "plagued the funny-looking little man unmercifully, 'scrounging' (i.e., swiping) his blankets and water, knocking off his helmet to reveal the wad of toilet paper always kept there, ridiculing his passion for orderliness and his perpetual puttering, pouncing on him in howling droves when he modestly retired behind a bush to relieve himself." Their affection for him had arisen only after "they saw Pyle force himself to share their dangers [which] sometimes made him scream in his sleep. . . ."[48]

Lee Miller, perhaps guessing his charge might need soothing, pronounced the article "on the whole a really marvelous job, except for the crap . . . about how we ordered you to cover a Darlan press conference and so on. . . . This spread would be worth plenty in [syndication] sales — if there were any papers left, to speak of, that aren't running you already."[49] This failed to appease Ernie. He kept quiet among his friends in France, but he was insulted and incensed. He suspected — correctly — that someone from

Time had been reading the latest work of Lester Cowan's scriptwriters and seized on their fictions as fact. (This, of course, made him all the more anxious about Hollywood's looming portrayal of him on screen.) He shot off a searing telegram to Miller, who was about to visit Cowan's set, pleading with his boss to "ELIMINATE ALL MONKEY BUSINESS RE PORTRAYING ME . . . ." and quash "OUTRAGEOUS CHARACTERIZATIONS DEPICTING ME ALMOST AS BUFFOON. . . . EYE [*sic*] NEVER BEEN GREENHORN OR JOKE AMONG SOLDIERS OR CORRESPONDENTS. MY FEAR ALWAYS BEEN INWARD AND NOT DEMONSTRABLE AND HAVE ALWAYS GONE THICK THINGS REGARDLESS AND STILL GO MUCHS ANYBODY ELSE. . . ."[50] The article was just the sort of heavy-handed journalism he despised — a slick concoction of fake wisdom based on shabby reporting. "They had to try to be so damned analytical and their analysis, it seems to me, results in an absolute distortion," he fumed to Jerry. "Somehow it seemed to leave me without any dignity, and I believe I do have a little."[51]

Jerry, in the midst of another rally, took the piece in stride. But she was chagrined to learn of Ernie's deep embarrassment. "I was *so hurt* because he was," she told Miller. "He was just starting out for the front . . . and he had just read the piece. . . ."[52] Perhaps that explained why, despite his growing fatigue, Pyle gave up the rear echelons and took a great risk just a few days later. "It wouldnt be fair to the troops who are doing the real fighting" to stay in the safe zone, he told Jerry. "If you stay away from them very long you get ashamed of yourself, and back up you go again."[53]

Delay and defeat stalled the Allied advance in Normandy for six weeks after D-Day. Repeated attempts to break out of the beachhead were thrown back by the Germans. In mid-July, Bradley prepared Operation COBRA, an all-out concentration of air and land forces aimed at piercing the German lines and breaking through to the hedge-free terrain leading to Paris and beyond. One evening Bradley himself appeared at the correspondents' camp to outline his plan: to attack a segment of the German line about two-and-a-third miles across just west of the town of Saint-Lô. First there would be an air bombardment of unprecedented magnitude to crack the German shell, he said, followed by three entire infantry divisions massed side by side, then two armored divisions and a fourth infantry division, whose aim would be to ram through the expected gap and run free, shattering the Germans' cohesion in a reverse version of the *Blitzkrieg* of 1940. The cautious Bradley did not use the word "breakthrough," but he didn't have to. "This is no limited-objective drive," another officer confirmed to the reporters after the general had gone. "This is it."[54]

Bradley was waiting for a forecast of three cloud-free morning hours for the bombers. After several cloudy days, some sixteen hundred bombers left their airfields in Britain on July 24, but when the clouds returned they had to be recalled. Disastrous errors in bombing that morning killed twenty-five Americans in the 30th Division, some elements of which shot at their own planes in disbelief and fury — "a not uncommon practice among all the armies in Normandy when suffering at the hands of their own pilots," according to one historian of the campaign.[55]

The next morning dawned clear. Ernie stood with a group of officers by a stone farmhouse in a shell-battered orchard. Given his choice of service arms to accompany, he had, to no one's surprise, picked the infantry, "because it is my love and because I suspected the tanks, being spectacular, might smother the credit due the infantry." He went with the Fourth Division, which would be the assault's spearhead.

An hour remained before the bombers were due, three hours before the infantry would move. The men dug in a bit deeper. "A cessation of motion seemed to come over the countryside and all its brown-clad inhabitants — a sense of last minute sitting in silence before the holocaust." The road out of Saint-Lô ran across the regiment's front; this was to be the line of demarcation for the bombardiers, who would aim their payloads just beyond the road. (In fact,

Bradley had pushed his commanders to reach the road with just such a line of demarcation for the bombers in mind.) G.I.'s laid colored strips of cloth and prepared yellow smoke canisters all along the road to make sure it was visible from bomber altitude.

Because the country was flat and lined with tall hedgerows, there was no place for Pyle to get a grandstand view unless he watched from the bomb line itself. Having no wish to risk being so close, he walked back through the fields, through crowds of waiting soldiers, until he found another stone farmhouse about eight hundred yards behind the front. There he stood with a small group of men, watching the sky.

"And before the next two hours had passed," he wrote later, "I would have given every penny, every desire, every hope I've ever had to have been just another 800 yards further back."[56]

Years after the war, an obscure professor of philosophy at a small western college wrote a book entitled *The Warriors*. Part memoir, part meditation on men in battle, the work comprised J. Glenn Gray's deeply considered reflections on the months he spent as an infantry and counterintelligence officer in the European theater in 1944–45. It is now regarded as among the most perceptive explorations of war ever written. Among "the enduring appeals of battle," Gray wrote, "war as a spectacle, as something to see," was perhaps the most powerful. "There is a popular conviction that war and battle are the sphere of ugliness, and, since aesthetic delight is associated with the beautiful, it may be concluded that war is the natural enemy of the aesthetic. I fear that this is in large part an illusion." Along with beauty, Gray said, war attracted "the fascination that manifestations of power and magnitude hold for the human spirit." In battle the soldier sometimes achieves "an awareness of power that far surpasses his limited imagination," and he reaches "a state of mind unknown in his everyday experiences."[57]

Ernie Pyle's account of the great bombardment at Saint-Lô captured these elements of wonder in a single narrative of the sensual experience of full-blown modern warfare. The account remains persuasive evidence of why humans are attracted to war — of the emotions that compelled Robert E. Lee to remark as he watched the Confederate advance at Fredericksburg, "It is well that war is so terrible — we would grow too fond of it."

In Pyle's re-creation, the experience began with an extraordinary concert of sound. American dive bombers "everywhere you looked" filled the air with "sharp and distinct sounds of cracking bombs and the heavy rip of the planes' machine guns and the splitting screams of diving wings . . . all fast and furious, but yet distinct, as in a musical show in which you could distinguish throaty tunes and words. And then a new sound gradually droned into our ears. . . ." Ernie called it "a sound deep and all encompassing with no notes in it — just a gigantic faraway surge of doom-like sound." The distant "heavies" came into view as "the merest dots in the sky," becoming "clots . . . against the far heavens, too tiny to count individually," then

gigantic waves in a constant procession and I thought it would never end.

Their march across the sky was slow and studied. I've never known a storm, or a machine, or any resolve of man that had about it the aura of such a ghastly relentlessness. You had the feeling that even had God appeared beseechingly before them in the sky with palms outward to persuade them back they would not have had within them the power to turn from their irresistible course.

In flights of twelve planes, three flights to a group, with the "groups stretched out across the sky," the bombers passed over the men, who leaned far back to look straight up, cupping their hands at the sides of their eyes. A moment later they heard the first bombs exploding past the road, a "crackle of popcorn" that "swelled into a monstrous fury of noise" and continued for an hour and a half, "an indescribable cauldron of sounds. Individual noises did not exist. The thundering of the motors in the sky and the roar of bombs ahead filled all the space for noise on earth." The bombardment all but crushed one of the great German armored divisions, the Panzer Lehr, whose commander wrote later of the assault: "It was hell. . . . My front lines looked like a landscape on the moon, and at least seventy percent of my personnel were out of action — dead, wounded, crazed or numbed."[58]

As German antiaircraft batteries speckled the high blue dome above with puffs of smoke, the spectacle's enchantments shifted from the ear to the eye. One bomber trailed smoke,

> and as we watched there was a gigantic sweep of flame over the plane. . . . It slanted slowly down and banked around the sky in great wide curves, this way and that way, as rhythmically and gracefully as in a slow motion waltz.
>
> Then suddenly it seemed to change its mind and it swept upward, steeper and steeper and ever slower until finally it seemed poised motionless on its own black pillar of smoke. And then just as slowly it turned over and dived for the earth — a golden spearhead on the straight black shaft of its own creation — and it disappeared behind the treetops.

Here and there human specks dropped from crippled bombers, some sprouting parachutes, some plummeting fast without chutes. One flier could be seen struggling to free a parachute snagged on the tail of his plane, but then flames clothed him, and

> a tiny black dot fell through space, all alone.
>   And all that time the great flat ceiling of the sky was roofed by all the others that didn't go down, plowing their way forward as if there were no turmoil in the world. . . . They stalked on, slowly and with a dreadful pall of sound, as though they were seeing only something at a great distance and nothing existed in between. God, how you admired those men up there and sickened for the ones who fell.

In war, J. Glenn Gray believed, "seeing sometimes absorbs us utterly; it is as though the human being became one great eye." The result is a rare emotional experience that Gray called "ecstasy," not in the sense of intense joy, but "in the original meaning of the term, namely, a state of being outside the self." For a moment one rises out of the realm of selfish concern and mingles with forces beyond common reckoning. Ernie put the same idea this way: "It is possible to become so enthralled by some of the spectacles of war that you are momentarily captivated away from your own danger."

Typing his account a few days later, Ernie left readers hanging off the end of one column in "that benign state" of transcendence, staring vicariously at an overhead wonderland. He began the next column by yanking them back into selfish, seamy reality, reminding them this scene was no artist's dreamscape. Pyle and his fellows in the farmyard were not as one with the machines above. They were tiny, vulnerable atoms encased in soft shells of mortal flesh.

> As we watched, there crept into our consciousness a realization that windrows of exploding bombs were easing back toward us, flight by flight, instead of gradually forward, as the plan called for.
>
> Then we were horrified by the suspicion that those machines, high in the sky and completely detached from us, were aiming their bombs at the smokeline on the ground — and a gentle breeze was drifting the smokeline back over us!
>
> An indescribable kind of panic comes over you at such times. We stood tensed in muscle and frozen in intellect, watching each flight approach and pass over us. . . . And then all of an instant the universe became filled with a gigantic rattling as of huge, dry seeds in a mammoth dry gourd. . . . It was bombs by the hundred, hurtling down through the air above us.

The men dived. Ernie found himself spread-eagled under a heavy cart in a shed, staring into the eyes of an officer beside him, both of them silent, "our heads slightly up — like two snakes . . . gaping at each other in a futile appeal . . . ."

343

He remembered "chaos, and a waiting for darkness."

> The feeling of the blast was sensational. The air struck you in hundreds of continuing flutters. Your ears drummed and rang. You could feel quick little waves of concussions on your chest and in your eyes. . . .
>
> I can't record what any of us actually felt or thought during those horrible climaxes. I believe a person's feelings at such times are kaleidoscopic and uncatalogable. You just wait, that's all. You do remember an inhuman tenseness of muscle and nerves.

After the cascades of bombs finally edged forward again and it was over, Ernie learned that no one in his little group had been hurt. But in the fields around him one hundred and eleven men died, including Bede Irvin, an AP photographer, and Lieutenant General Lesley McNair, commander of all Army ground forces, who had come far forward against the urgings of staff to watch COBRA begin. Nearly five hundred were wounded. "Maddened men were forcibly carried to the rear," one historian writes. "Others merely ran blindly from the battlefield. Maimed men lay screaming for aid." [59] Yet despite the bombing shortfall, the ground attack proceeded. The breakthrough was accomplished, and a great open-field run toward Paris began.

Men in the 9th and 30th divisions seethed with anger at the Air Corps. Before the bombardment, ground commanders had beseeched the fliers to follow a course parallel to the front rather than across it, precisely in order to minimize the risk of bombing "creepback." General Courtney Hodges found General Leland Hobbs, commander of the 30th Division, at his command post, "terribly upset" and unwilling to follow the dictates of courtesy between the ferociously competitive ground forces and Air Corps. "We're good soldiers, Courtney, I know," Hobbs raged, "but there's absolutely no excuse, no excuse at all. I wish I could show some of those air boys, decorated with everything a man can be decorated with, some of our casualty clearing stations." [60]

One can easily imagine how reporters covering the Persian Gulf War or the latter stages of the Vietnam War might have interpreted such a horrific American blunder. It is a measure of how differently the World War II correspondent conceived of his role that Pyle, though he acknowledged "bitterness" among the infantry that day, stepped unhesitatingly into the role of conciliator, even if he had to gloss over the infantry's genuine feelings. "After the bitterness," he wrote, "came the sober remembrance that the Air Corps is the strong right arm in front of us. . . . Anybody makes mistakes. . . . The smoke and confusion of battle bewilder us all on the ground as well as in the air. And in this case the percentage of error was really very small compared with the colossal storm of bombs that fell upon the enemy. The Air Corps has been wonderful throughout this invasion, and the men on the ground appreciate it."

On this note, Ernie finished his columns on the breakout. He sent them off to Miller, then took to his cot with stomach pains, fever, diarrhea and "a hell of a period of depression." [61] It was four days before he could get out of bed and another four before he could muster strength enough to write anything. His malady, he told Miller, was "a 'collapse' reaction from being so long under such strain and tension, during the big attack. . . . That bombing . . . was the most sustained horrible thing I've ever gone through. I really dont believe I could go through the whole thing again and keep my sanity." [62] He soothed his nerves by conjuring homecoming images of Albuquerque — "coming over the rim of the mesa from the west," or "flying in over the Sandias and looking down on the valley and *home*." Like many others that August, he watched the breakout from Saint-Lô and Patton's swift advance across Brittany with rising hopes of an end to the European war by Christmas, perhaps even earlier. By August 9 he was back at his typewriter, feeling "a second wind that will carry me on through to the finish, which cant be too far away now."

"I hope to be home within a month after the

last shot is fired," he told Jerry. "And then a nice long rest." [63]

But the finish was indeed far away, and Ernie's second wind did not last.

One afternoon Ernie was making his careful way up a dirt road lined with squatting G.I.'s when a shell struck just twenty feet behind him, so close that it seemed to hit the ground "not with a crash, but with a ring as though you'd struck a high-toned bell." Moments later, he joined an officer who was looking for a command post in a stone farmhouse nearby. Not sure where the house was, they wandered in an orchard for five minutes, looking for it. Spotting it, they approached, only to see it take a direct hit from a shell just fifty yards away. Shells began to fall so fast that Ernie had to dive into a ditch over and over, "just a bewildered guy in brown, part of a thin line of other bewildered guys as far up and down the ditch as you could see." Later in the afternoon he left a command post, then learned ten minutes later that it, too, had been hit. A third command post took a hit and burned to the ground just before he arrived there. [64]

This afternoon "full of might-have-beens" seemed emblematic of Pyle's entire experience in the last weeks in Normandy, where the intensity of combat reached its peak. Punch-drunk from close calls and scenes of carnage, he could find no heroes of endurance to offer readers in reassurance. To convey this new reality, he made another stab at reporting on battle fatigue, and this time penetrated the censors with an account of

> two shock cases . . . staggering down the road. . . .
> They were not wounded but were completely broken — the kind that stab into your heart. They were shaking all over, and had to hold onto each other like little girls when they walked. The doctor stopped them. They could barely talk, barely understand. He told them to wait down at the next corner until we came back, and then they could ride.
> When they turned away from the jeep, they turned slowly and unsteadily, a step at a time, like men who were awfully drunk. Their mouths hung open and their eyes stared, and they still held onto each other. They were just like idiots. They had found more war than the human spirit can endure.[65]

Buck Eversole had been the infantry's mythical man in Italy. But the myth was breaking down in France, where Ernie found a different sort of prototype to profile: Private Tommy Clayton, who had landed on Omaha Beach and spent thirty-seven straight days in the front lines without rest. Ernie met him in the press camp, where Clayton had been assigned after spending several days in an "exhaustion camp" after he shot a German three times at close range before realizing the man was already dead. But "the worst experience of all" for such men, Ernie said, "is just the accumulated blur, and hurting vagueness of [being] too long in the lines, the everlasting alertness, the noise and fear, the cell-by-cell exhaustion, the thinning of the ranks around you as day follows nameless day. And the constant march into eternity of your own small quota of chances for survival." [66]

In August 1944, the front became fluid. The Germans still fought with great effectiveness, but they had given up Normandy and were falling back swiftly toward Paris. They would stand and fight, then run. The Allied fighting columns would follow, leaving a silent vacuum between the front and the giant rear-echelon units. Ernie drove into such an area one day in August. It was "a sweet old stone village," where not one of the fifty or so buildings remained whole. He could tell the battle had just moved on because the destruction was so fresh — pools of blood that had "only begun to congeal and turn black"; "gray, burned-powder rims of the shell craters in the gravel roads, their edges not yet smoothed by the pounding of military traffic"; "cows in the fields, lying grotesquely with their feet to the sky"; and men whose bodies had not yet begun to show the look of death.

"There is nothing left behind but the remains — the lifeless debris, the sunshine and the flowers, and utter silence. An amateur who wanders in this vacuum at the rear of a battle has a terrible sense of loneliness. Everything is dead — the men, the machines, the animals — and you alone are left alive." [67]

On August 25, Ernie and Hank Gorrell of the United Press talked their way past a roadblock and joined soldiers entering a liberated Paris. Scores of correspondents were entering the city at the same time. Each was frantic to dispatch an early report from the City of Light, a dateline second in prestige only to Berlin itself, but few had any expectation of the scenes that greeted them. Danger mingled with overwhelming joy. Over the roar of the crowd the reporters recognized the whine of German shells and the rattle of machine-gun fire up the street. Yet Parisians surged into the streets and swarmed around the jeeps and trucks of Free French soldiers and the U.S. Ninth Division, which Bradley had designated for the honor of entering the city. Six radio correspondents, swept up by some pyrotechnical combination of emotion and competition, put their credentials at risk by making uncensored broadcasts — a deed that landed them all in serious trouble with SHAEF. The colors of the day shine through their sober letters of explanation and apology to the Army. "I realize I did wrong," wrote Paul Manning of the Mutual Broadcasting System. "It is hard to place on paper what really happened in Paris that Friday. . . . The city was like a champagne dream. . . ." [68]

From a third-floor hotel balcony, Ernie and several colleagues gazed down on the street theater below them for a long time, watching French women grasping soldiers' hands and faces, kissing them on both cheeks, leaping up onto tanks and trucks. Finally Ernie pronounced a verdict: "Any G.I. who doesn't get laid tonight is a sissy."[69]

The liberation of Paris was depicted again and again as the greatest moment of the war. But Ernie was privately repelled by the spectacle; among the crowds of cheering Parisians he glimpsed the specter of collaboration. "I am glad you share my rather low opinion of Paris," he wrote a soldier friend several months afterward. "When I was there I felt as though I were living in a whorehouse — not physically but spiritually."[70]

Perhaps he made his decision that day. Perhaps it had been the day before, or a day or two later. He was going home. Amid "the pent-up semi-delirium" of Paris, he could not imagine returning to the front. Perhaps the upsurge of real joy made the prospect of another plunge unbearable. After the trauma at Saint-Lô and the constant drumbeat of death in Normandy, he told a reporter later, "I damn near had a war neurosis. About two weeks more and I'd have been in a hospital. I'd become so revolted, so nauseated by the sight of swell kids having their heads blown off, I'd lost track of the whole point of the war. I'd reached a point where I felt that

351

no ideal was worth the death of one more man."[71]

His explanation to readers was nearly as frank: "I've been immersed in it too long. My spirit is wobbly and my mind is confused. The hurt has finally become too great. . . . It may be that a few months of peace will restore some vim to my spirit, and I can go warhorsing off to the Pacific. We'll see what a little New Mexico sunshine does along that line."[72]

10

★★★★

"The Pyle Phenomenon"

SEPTEMBER 1944–JANUARY 1945

The letters arrived at hometown newspapers, at Scripps-Howard's offices in New York and Washington, at Army post offices. They came from all over.

From New York:

". . . would you Be So Kind to Look up my Boy and Let us know in your paper How He is getting along. It would be a grate favor . . . I havent Herd from Him Since Feb 22/43 . . ."[1]

From a town in Ohio:

"I know it is a 1000 to 1 shot but if you should stumble into the 504th M.P. Bn. will you please look up Sgt. Charles R. Sparnon . . . and tell him all the family and friends said HELLO DICK and wish him . . . the Best of Luck also that POP said he had nothing to worry about at this end of the line."[2]

From Pittsburgh:

"Mr. Pyle my sweetheart is now in North Africa. I don't know if he is dead or alive. . . . I've tried so hard to get word of him. I work in a defense plant here. Sometimes I work two shifts without any sleep. . . . I have two children & have gone with this boy three years. . . . Mr. Pyle if it would be possible for you too find out if he is close too you . . . tell him the girls Joan and Shirley are waiting for him and still love him. It would help him I know. . . . If you see him tell him I love him & am waiting. . . . Sir a few words from you would give him courage. . . . [H]e is a good boy one of the best. . . . Please Mr. Pyle keep writing about the boys as you have been doing. Your words bring happiness to thousands just like me."[3]

"One of Us"

Soon after D-Day, shaking his head, Lee Miller confided to an associate that "silly as it may seem, I think it is literally true that millions in this country were more concerned about what happened to Ernie Pyle than about what happened to our invading armies."[4]

After all, people *knew* the public figure named Ernie Pyle, knew him intimately. "I don't ever expect to know you," a Massachusetts housewife wrote him, "but I feel that I already know you, and it's all quite comfortable."[5] Observing his fellow devotees of Pyle's column, Randall Jarrell

354

concluded that "the illusion that he was a personal friend of theirs" was nearly universal; and "actually he was — we meet only a few people in our lives whom we ever know as well or love as much."[6] Of course what they knew was an image — an image that by 1944 was "as much a part of [Americans'] daily lives as ration-points and the butter shortage."[7] The image had been born in the daily lines of the column; but now as the war went on, the popular image grew and flourished beyond the writer's control, nourished by the imaginations of a readership that by this time numbered, by one reliable estimate, some 40 million.

People close to Ernie recognized that the person and the public image were diverging. Scripps-Howard spoke of "the Pyle phenomenon." Miller began calling him simply "the Pyle," an image composed of several parts.

There was Ernie Pyle the seer. "Somehow when I read it I feel as if I can almost see the war," wrote a fan. It was a sentiment echoed again and again. A veteran of World War I said to read Pyle was to "be back again in the lines — trudging along in single file." Diana Trilling identified the same quality, noting that "the photographic eye and ear of the reporter turn out to be more creative than the ostensibly creative mind. . . . The soldiers who appear in Ernie Pyle's [articles] live and flower in our imagination long after most of the characters in recent fiction vanish back into air."[8] To see through

Pyle's eyes was to feel through him as well. Pyle offered "no mere intellectual comprehension" of the war, a magazine editor said, "but an emotional grasp that I sometimes find almost unbearably potent."[9] This interior vision was a dense packet of feelings for the soldiers — pity, compassion, empathy, pride, tragedy, all suffused with a will to keep a stiff upper lip.

Then there was Saint Ernie, a "noble soul," "90 percent heart and the rest intestinal fortitude," who seemed to suffer and sorrow on behalf of everyone, yet who affirmed the survival of the good amid the horror of war.[10] "Ernie has come to be envisaged as a frail old poet," observed the author of a perceptive profile, "a kind of St. Francis of Assisi wandering sadly among the foxholes."[11] On a face that one reporter called "sweet and kind, and haunted by memories," he seemed to bear all the nation's war sorrows. This was precisely the expression captured by Alfred Eisenstadt in a much-circulated photograph taken upon Ernie's return from France.[12] No other reporter would deign to notice the "little homey facts" of war, readers believed, yet these facts held a meaning far beyond mere human interest. "They matter even more than the war matters," an admirer told Ernie, "because they are eternal and beyond the reach of war."[13] Only an essentially benevolent spirit would view the war this way. Indeed, one woman testified that "God is in Ernie's column."[14] One letter came unsigned from a

average, in antecedents, education, position
. . . no records hung up, just plugging along
trying to do the best I can, see my family
through, be as useful as I can and somehow
hope the final score will not be too bad.

Through the years, like most everyone, I've
often wondered what it was all about,
sometimes inclined to the cynical, always
with a big question mark, in fact, many of
them. . . . I've read the ancient and modern
writers, listened to the orators and was not
satisfied. I knew life was good, though well
mixed up, and looked for something tan-
gible that would would prove my point. . . .

Without any label, I have found the outline
of what I have been looking for in [your]
clear pictures of human lives. . . . It has
helped me a lot. . . .

This is a bit cryptic but I am sure it will
convey my thoughts to you without being
spelled out. Please accept my appreciation
of a series of lessons in life.[15]

Finally, there was Ernie Pyle the common
man.

Ernie was anything but handsome, yet from
1943 on he attracted photographers like a Hollywood star, at home and overseas. Here was the
Common Man incarnate. A man so celebrated
yet so emphatically ordinary in appearance

could hardly help but become an object of Americans' traditional veneration of the little guy, the underdog, the man on the street. He was "the sort of a fellow you'd never notice in a crowd," "not a big man physically," "a scrawny little chap with an enchantingly homely mug," "a short scarecrow with too much feet in G.I. boots."[16] The point was not his actual size but the obvious contrast — little man, giant stature. The public delighted in it, as they did in Ernie's championship of the humblest among the G.I.'s. It was lost on no one that Ernie preferred the company of dogface privates to well-educated Army bigwigs. "The nice thing about you," one woman wrote, "is you talk of the plain soldiers and that makes you one of us."[17] At a time when movie stars' props and costumes were sold to raise funds at War Bond auctions, Ernie's notorious out-at-the-elbows sport jacket brought a large sum early in 1944. This was thanks to Lee Miller, who understood that the holes in an old jacket worn to tea at the White House were the epaulets of an American folk hero.[18]

Contemplating Pyle and what he stood for — his sad eyes, his virtue, his democratic commonness — Americans of the 1940s embraced their particular understanding of what the war was all about. It was not a true war of self-defense, as in England or the Soviet Union, nor a war for race mastery, as in Germany. Pyle's war might not be "a war to save the world for democracy," as Woodrow Wilson had said of World War I, but it was a war that reinforced and celebrated what people felt it meant to be American. What a commentator once said of the great cow-boy-vaudevillian Will Rogers applied equally well to Ernie: "He is what Americans think other Americans are like."[19]

Just how firmly Pyle's man-of-the-people image had taken hold of Americans high and low was strikingly apparent in New York, where he spent several days upon his arrival in the United States in mid-September 1944. On orders from Scripps-Howard, which had commissioned the eminent sculptor Jo Davidson to do a bust, Ernie posed for several hours in Davidson's Manhattan studio. He stayed long enough to glimpse the emerging likeness — a Lincolnesque head, strong and wise, with a slight, knowing smile over an open-collar Army shirt. Afterward, on the street outside, a reporter watched Ernie struggling to hail a cab amid the gathering crowd.

For the mounting excitement he created you'd think he was Errol Flynn. Girls and children rush up to Flynn, but men, women and children rush up to Pyle. "Are you — you are — may I just shake your hand — thank you, thank you, I read you every day — my wife throws me out of the house if I leave the paper on the subway — Mr. Pyle, I'm from Cleveland and I read you in the Cleveland — My God, that's Ernie Pyle. It is too. Jeez, Ernie

Pyle! Mr. Pyle, if I may, I would like to ask you —" is the way it goes . . . accompanied by looks of such affectionate admiration and deep respect as are awarded only your very best friend.[20]

"A baffled little fellow being pushed around by events . . ."

This sort of goodwill and prestige alighted upon few people indeed, as anyone with something to sell realized long before Ernie himself fully appreciated the fact. No sooner had he erected his wartime image than bidders began to circle around it, hoping to harness it to their own causes. They offered him chances he could not have dreamed of two years earlier. Yet the price they asked was his most valued creation — his public image.

Among the first to come courting were other newspaper interests. The giant Hearst chain, the North American Newspaper Alliance and the Chicago Sun syndicate all made quiet attempts to buy Pyle away from Scripps-Howard. But Ernie placed a high value on bosses he liked and trusted; he rebuffed each corporate suitor with firm assurances that he was already happily married. (Late one summer night in 1944, Lee Miller found himself sharing a Chicago cab with the head of the Hearst syndicate, Joe Connally, who tipsily informed Miller that "for my money, Pyle is the No. 1 guy in this war." Miller smiled obligingly and replied, "Not for *your* money, Connally, although I understand you made some overtures.")[21]

Even within Scripps-Howard, exasperating pressures sometimes arose to make more hay from Ernie's reputation. In England he got a cable from Louis Seltzer, editor of the chain's big *Cleveland Press*, battling for circulation as always against the rival *Plain Dealer*. Seltzer beseeched Ernie to seek out soldiers from Cleveland to feature in the column — a penny-ante request of the kind that had harried Pyle for years. Once he would have gone along, but no more. "I know his reason — [John] McDermott is over here for the Plain-Dealer," he fumed to Miller. "But Christ I can't drop the column — or convert the column — just for Cleveland. . . . Hell, I'm trying to describe the war and the war is made up of people from everywhere. I've always just written about whomever I run onto, and they turn out eventually to cover the whole U.S. If I started doing anything like that the column would sink in two months."[22]

That was that. But entreaties from friends like Seltzer were nothing compared to those that flowed in from strangers, who approached Miller with sonorous overtures under the most prestigious corporate letterheads. Ernie felt no pangs when spurning a commercial pitch, as he usually did, but it was harder when the supplicant was a charitable organization such as the Red Cross, which he had often praised. "These things are so damned hard to turn down," he told Miller on one such occasion, "and yet if I do them it eventually adds up to something awful."[23]

Radio raised a new challenge. It was one thing for Pyle simply to lend his face or name to a page in a magazine; it was quite another to authorize what radio sponsors wanted — to put his column (or "excerpts" or "dramatizations") on the air. The column, as always, was Ernie's sacred cow, and anyone proposing to "monkey" with it was automatically suspect.

He had had brushes with radio before. During his months in Great Britain before the North African campaign, no less than Edward R. Murrow had peppered him with invitations to do a weekly broadcast over the CBS network. Though tempted, as it would mean "a little money" and "a nice feather in my cap," he had said no, fearing the commitment would impede his freedom of movement and consume too much of his time.[24] He had the same worry when radio offers multiplied in the winter of 1943–44, only now the risks and rewards were greater. When DuPont purchased the rights to dramatize *Here Is Your War* on the NBC program *Cavalcade of America*, Miller raised a host of concerns, from quibbles over single words in the script to forbidding an anti-strike passage on grounds that Pyle must not be "put in any position of being 'used' for anti-labor purposes." Miller's main fear was corniness. When the Pyle character was given the line "When there's trouble, you can't lose me," Miller nixed it as "bombast, and quite out of character." And what if "some cluck of a stomach-turning variety" was hired to play Ernie?[25] When the ad agency reneged on its promise to cut the anti-strike passage, Miller was incensed — "You can't trust these fucking advertising and radio people out of your sight" — and in no mood to look kindly on any new radio proposals.[26]

But in the spring of 1944, with public attention to the war reaching a peak in anticipation of D-Day, radio raised the ante. First, the advertising firm of Young & Rubicam approached Miller with a deal for a weekly Pyle dramatization on NBC that would give Ernie "a damned nice piece of income." (The amount is uncertain.)[27] The sponsor was a major dairy firm. As Pyle dithered over the proposal in Europe — "I'm still scared of radio" — Miller tossed it upstairs for corporate consideration.[28] "The concern" made it clear that all such decisions ultimately lay with Ernie himself, but Scripps-Howard's chieftains, particularly John Sorrells and Deac Parker, were strongly opposed. These men had stuck by Ernie's travel column in the face of widespread indifference among the chain's editors, had paid him during his frequent sabbaticals to care for Jerry, and their support had continued through the fizzling of Carlin's syndication efforts before 1942. They were not without self-interest in scowling at radio's courtship of their star; they feared a poor job by radio could diminish Ernie's value to the chain.[29] But they also understood his magic as well as anyone.

Sorrells felt certain "no program could possibly catch the spirit and the flavor of Ernie's columns." But the danger was greater than that:

> It might result in something so foreign to the peculiar quality of Ernie's writings it might very well destroy the image which the reading public has created of Ernie. . . .
>
> Ernie's appeal almost defies analysis. His pieces are letters back home; he symbolizes to those back here their own GI Joe over there. There is drama aplenty in Ernie's stuff, but it's the drama that takes place within a man's mind and heart. These boys are thrown together physically and live together on the closest and most intimate terms, and yet each stands apart and alone with his own thoughts locked within him. . . . [O]utwardly he's a soldier, battle-wise, cunning, tough, dangerous, but inwardly they're still civilians in uniform — just boys a long way from home.
>
> It seems to me that Ernie manages to portray — or perhaps mirror — these boys, inside and out at the same time. It seems to me that is the unique quality of his appeal. No radio show, with planes whining and guns going off and "voices" interpolating here and

there can possibly catch that elusive, intangible, subtle thing in Ernie's pieces.[30]

Thanks partly to Sorrells's analysis, Young & Rubicam were politely sent packing. Miller concurred for the moment, fearing radio would "tend to make Ernie into a Boy Scout or . . . just a plain ass."[31] But less than a week later, at the end of May 1944, a far more tempting proposal convinced Miller to argue in the opposite direction.

It came from Westinghouse Electric, which enjoyed a dignified reputation for sponsoring programs of only the highest quality and good taste. There would be no dramatization; instead, Ernie himself would simply record material from his columns for broadcast three times a week *after* the material had been published in newspapers. He would be asked to do no extra writing. There would be no fancy embellishments — just an announcer, Ernie's voice, and a purely "institutional" ad for Westinghouse. The fee would be no less than $3,000 per week, far higher than the undisclosed Young & Rubicam offer. Just as Ernie was moodily walking the deck of his LST in the English Channel, a sharp little debate about his future was played out through the mails between Washington and New York.

Miller passed the Westinghouse pitch along to the top brass and to Ernie, adding his own strong endorsement. It was "too much money for a small boy from the country to turn his back on," he told Ernie. "I am sure it is the best proposition ever made to any commentator or reporter." The "promotion value to Scripps-Howard is potentially enormous," and the format eliminated the "problem of corny dramatization."[32]

Roy Howard rumbled in opposition. He didn't like the idea of radio "skimming the cream" off Scripps-Howard's number-one property. He also firmly believed radio broadcasts would "dilute" Ernie's talents or even seduce him away from newspapers entirely.[33] Miller fired right back, hinting Pyle might bolt the chain if he felt ill-used in this matter. Since Ernie had already rejected scores of outside offers, Miller said, it was "illogical" to fear that he

would go the way of all newspapermen who dabble in radio. . . .

It is perfectly true that Scripps-Howard made Ernie's success possible. But it is also perfectly true that Scripps-Howard is now envied by every syndicate in the country for the possession of this "property." Ernie is not naive; he knows he is at the top of the heap. While I believe he would acquiesce in any decision of the management against his picking up this big money, I cannot help feeling that if I were in a similar position I would be sore as hell to see a potential $156,000 a year vetoed on the ground that I couldn't be trusted to stick to the newspaper business.[34]

Roy Howard's fears may have been "illogical," but the concerns of other executives were not. The money at stake looked impressive, they admitted, but wartime taxation would shrink the sum considerably. They wondered how a big Pyle radio show would be received by readers who appreciated "the fact that his head has not been turned by success."[35] And they wondered about Ernie's speaking voice, which was less than impressive. Approaching this point carefully, Deac Parker wrote Ernie:

I have never heard you over the radio. Therefore I am not sure whether you are good or lousy. I do know about you as a writer. At the risk of flattery, I'll say you are not lousy. . . . A writer is one personality. That personality may or may not duplicate itself over the air. If it doesn't, then there is a letdown to those who have become acquainted with the personality in type. . . . So there is chance-taking involved, having to do directly with your prestige, the character you have developed in the mind of millions of American readers; and the old, old question of a personality, great in one line, getting – perhaps – out of focus and out of cast.

With that, Parker told Ernie, "the decision is now up to you — without prejudice."[36]

By the time Ernie read all this in his mail, his distractions included the Luftwaffe and the liberation of Normandy. He was leery of bucking Roy Howard's wishes, though he felt that "Roy is a little free with his objections to my making some money. These offers will never come again, and I still don't have enough piled up to live on happily ever after."[37] He thought it over for an hour. Then he cabled Miller to turn the offer down. "Maybe I'm making a mistake, I don't know . . . ," he wrote Jerry. "But I'm a little afraid of anything extra-curricular. And I've been out in this other world so long I guess I've sort of lost my perspective about what money means. Somehow it just seemed to me like a good joke to turn down $150,000 a year for doing nothing. People are getting killed for 50 bucks a month, so what the hell. I suppose I'll regret it in my old age."[38]

A few days later, Ernie suddenly cabled Miller again and asked him to reopen talks with Westinghouse: "HAVE DOWNTURNED SO MUCH AM BEGINNING FEEL IT HARDLY FAIR FOR OFFICE ASK ME FORGO SOMETHING THIS SIZE." But it was too late; Westinghouse already had cut a deal with someone else — news that left Ernie "relieved" in the end.[39] In the aftermath, even the imperious Howard hastened to smooth any ruffled feelings his star might be harboring. "I hope you elect to remain with Scripps-Howard as long as you work for a living," he wrote Ernie, "but . . . we [will] allow no selfish interest of ours to run counter to any purpose of yours. . . . Scripps-Howard did not make you or give you fame. The most we can take credit for is having had the brains to realize what you had on the ball . . ."[40]

As "visions of an extra three grand a week for Ernie" went "floating away," Miller felt momentarily as if he might "go down the street and quietly hang myself."[41] But the disappointment was mightily softened by growing evidence that Ernie would not need radio to become wealthy. Ernie's publishers at Henry Holt and Co. were well on their way toward bringing out a second collection of Ernie's columns in time for Christmas 1944 — this one to cover the campaigns in Sicily, Italy and France — and they were predicting another enormous sale. But these rewards paled in comparison to what Lester Cowan was promising.

Accompanied by a blast of publicity, camera work for the Pyle movie began in March 1944 at an Arizona location hastily touched up to more closely resemble the battlefields of Tunisia. " 'Here Is Your War,' " the press release trumpeted, "will be Hollywood's first gesture to glorify the infantryman, the foot-slogging soldier for whom General Eisenhower asked a 'bit of glory' and who was overlooked in Filmland's concentration on the more spectacular arms of the services . . ."[42]

But long before he could fulfill that boast, Cowan had to master a task of great complexity with numerous so-called experts peering over his shoulder — Ernie and his surrogates (Lee Miller, Paige Cavanaugh, and correspondent friends whom Ernie dispatched to the set as consultants); the Army; and fiendishly loyal Pyle fans. As Cowan and his writers got to work, "we could see millions of fingers pointing at us, charging us with mutilation. . . . It is almost impossible to conceive a picture of Pyle that will please everyone, as he has apparently become all things to all men."[43] The war itself was among Cowan's headaches. For weeks during the spring of 1944, the developing script was bogged down, like the Fifth Army, in the mud of Italy. He needed Europe to be invaded soon, and successfully, to give the script its necessary "up" conclusion — and he needed Pyle not to miss out on "the Big Show." When the invasion of Normandy showed early signs of success, with Pyle along, he pronounced himself "eternally grateful to General Eisenhower. . . ."[44]

Even Eisenhower was less troubled by delays than Cowan. Choosing a lead actor became a comically long ordeal. For months, the Hollywood press traded leaks and rumors about who was to get the part of Pyle. All manner of names circulated: Fred Astaire, Gary Cooper, Bing Crosby, Fred MacMurray, Gene Kelly, Walter Huston, Jimmy Durante, Gene Kelly, even a Pittsburgh Pirates announcer whom Cowan heard was a dead ringer for Pyle, not to mention a fine after-dinner speaker.[45] When the name of the tough-guy star James Cagney arose briefly,

Ernie was horrified. "Get him the hell out of the running pronto," he instructed Cavanaugh. "Anybody else."[46]

Cowan hoped to find a talented unknown for the part, a choice in which Ernie concurred. But after an early talent search failed, Cowan narrowed the choice to three professionals: a character actor named Jimmy Gleason, whose chief advantage was a close resemblance to Pyle; Walter Brennan, a veteran of "mellow, hoosier type roles"; and Burgess Meredith, who was serving as an Army captain but had been brought in as a technical adviser to Cowan. Believing Gleason and Brennan to be too well known, Cowan settled on Meredith, but the Army refused to release him from duty.[47] This sent Cowan back on the trail of an unknown, a search which his publicist believed could "create even more national interest than the search for Scarlett O'Hara." Cowan's people were inundated with letters from hundreds of people offering their services as Pyle, including a Philadelphia janitor, a professor of French at the University of Missouri, a taxi driver from Bangor, Maine, an amateur boxer from Cleveland and one skinny, smooth-skulled man whose wife attached a photograph and a note saying, "Like Ernie, to know him is to love him."[48] "People find it easy to imagine themselves in [Pyle's] shoes," Cowan's publicity man observed. "He represents any one of the countless middle-aged, bald, under-sized men. In a sense his eminence in the journalistic field represents the victory of the commonplace over the glamourous."[49] From a list of some two hundred Cowan chose ten for screen tests, but he still was unsatisfied. A final plea to the Army managed to spring Meredith, though the choice was not made official until October 1944. As Meredith remembered it long afterward, his escape was engineered by none other than Harry Hopkins, President Roosevelt's special assistant, who called Meredith from the White House, said Pyle had specifically asked for him, and that General George Marshall, chief of staff of the Army, "was anxious to do anything Ernie Pyle wanted — so if I cared to play the role they would give me an honorable discharge."[50]

More daunting than the search for a Pyle was the search for a story line. Arthur Miller had quit, convinced that Cowan had abandoned his commitment to innovation. The job had been turned over to writer after writer. Cowan looked for inspiration to a string of war correspondents for whom Ernie had finagled jobs as script consultants. When Don Whitehead left England for a pre-invasion trip to Hollywood, Ernie pleaded with him, "For God's sake, don't let 'em make me look like a fool."[51] Unfortunately, it was the hard-drinking Chris Cunningham of United Press, not the level-headed Whitehead, who was the first correspondent to reach the set. Cunningham's hungover rambles on the subject of Pyle included liberal portions of exaggeration, half-truth and utter fantasy. His memories of Ernie in the early weeks of the North Africa campaign were especially hazy. Describing Pyle as "kinda funny looking and out of place," and knowledgeable only about "flowers and nature," Cunningham recalled Ernie as "frankly scared to go to the front" and intimidated into fecklessness by "expert military correspondents." He so bungled the story of Ernie's celebrated scoop on the "soft-gloving" of Nazi sympathizers in Algeria that it sounded like a stroke of dumb luck. Finally, he reported that Ernie had stumbled upon the formula of writing about lowly privates only because he was too "humble" in the face of expert correspondents to assay "the big stuff."[52]

The scriptwriters lapped up Cunningham's stories — partly because they were in desperate need of "realistic" details, partly because the reporter's version of Pyle dovetailed nicely with the plot they already were crafting. Cowan and his director, William Wellman, were delighted. Among their difficulties had been the question of how to portray a character who was half man, half legend. He "writes better than any of us," Cowan confessed, "but in a form and style which is almost impossible to translate into the usual conventional drama."[53] At long last, the moviemakers found their handle. "I see the thing now," Wellman told Cavanaugh. "It's a love story. Ernie falls in love with the lousy infantry, and leaves it, and finds he has to go back to it."[54] Stretched over this dramatic frame would be an uplifting theme: "the progress to *commitment* of civilian Ernie Pyle on the one hand and the military personnel on the other — the progressive shedding of illusions and ignorance concerning the war and its demands — and the final realization of the duties and sacrifices involved."[55] With this conception, Cowan crowed, "we have licked the story. . . ."

In a series of synopses written in June 1944, a screenplay took shape. Its image of Pyle was like a circus mirror — some parts recognizable, some weirdly distorted. Act I was to begin in a hotel room in war-torn London, circa 1942, where the "small pathetic figure of Ernie Pyle . . . a born 4F plagued by his conscience to enter the 1A world of a war correspondent," contemplates his role in the impending invasion of North Africa. "Plagued . . . by doubts about whether he will be able to do the job," he recalls a conversation with "his boss . . . Lee Miller" back in the United States.

BOSS: How much do you weigh, Ernie?

ERNIE: Hundred and ten pounds. (*He sees the boss looking at him askance.*) Well, almost!

The boss's laugh is loud and genuine . . .

BOSS (*seriously*): Ernie, you've always done the little, homey, everyday sort of thing. Do you think you can cover the war?

ERNIE: I admit that bothers me, but I'll never know till I try.

BOSS: I'm warning you. War is big and tough.

ERNIE: That scares me too.

In Africa, Ernie is "overawed by the immensity of war," and among the "expert" correspondents (thanks to Chris Cunningham), he "didn't even know what questions to ask." On the eve of battle, he teams up with an infantry company led by a Captain Walker (a stand-in for Waskow, with add-ons from Buck Eversole), whose naive, inexperienced underlings long to be "home by Christmas." "Ernie's heart sinks" when the soldiers are called to the front, but he swallows his fear and distinguishes himself with his tribute to "the goddamned infantry." Through further battles in Africa, his "deep awe and reverence for our combat troops grows constantly as he witnesses ever more proof of the quality of these former grocery clerks and gas-station attendants . . . just 'ordinary run-of-the-mill' Americans" who soon prove their superiority to the German "supermen."

In Act II, which opens in Italy, Ernie becomes so horrified and exhausted by the slaughter around Cassino that he suspects he has become "just a literary parasite on the GI's who are dying." Unable to write further, he gives up and goes home to the United States. There, unnerved by his fame, he encounters Stephens, a sensitive and intelligent soldier friend who has been sent home for officer training. Stephens, frustrated by the home front's incomprehension of the infantry's plight, unburdens himself to Ernie.

> I thought, when I first went into battle, I was
> going to come out a murderer. I was so
> wrong! . . . Friendship is the greatest thing
> out there — not killing. People here don't get
> it. . . . Listen, Ernie: I would die for any one of
> thirty or forty guys out there, just as easily as
> I flick out this match. They don't understand
> that, but I swear it's true. . . . I was afraid I'd
> come out a murderer, but what I brought
> out of it was love. You've got to understand
> that, Ernie, because if you don't, nobody
> will. . . .
> Do you suppose, Ernie . . . some day . . .
> after we get to Berlin and Tokyo . . . do you
> think this — this love we've found — this love
> for other guys than ourselves — do you think
> we can make it count? I don't know. I hate
> war. There's only one possible excuse for it.
> If something came out of it — a new feeling
> among people — a new sense of what life is.
> Only death can make you feel it. Maybe I'll
> have to write a book. Or maybe . . . you do it,
> Ernie. You've seen it. You know. I can't.

Ernie returns to his typewriter to write
Stephens's story. When "That Girl," the sympathetic and supportive Jerry, pronounces it one of
his best ever, Ernie "knows there is only one
place for him now . . . back among the combat
GI's." In the climactic act he returns to England

376

in time for D-Day and finds his friends "different now . . . mature, battlewise . . . fighting men," who "know there is no going home short of complete victory." In the drive onward, Captain Walker is killed, and the fraternal scene from Pyle's account of Captain Waskow's death is reenacted. The scene's message, "not explicit but implied," is that "the priceless gift of life is bought with death, a variant on the maxim of losing one's life to save it." From the top of the next hill the G.I.'s glimpse a glittering Paris in the distance, symbolizing "a hope and a promise that the battle worn symbols of equality . . . liberty . . . and fraternity will acquire new meanings in a post-war world."[56]

In keeping with his contractual promise, Cowan duly delivered copies of the script-in-progress to Lee Miller and Lowell Mellett a month after D-Day. Miller, pronouncing himself "extremely dissatisfied" with key passages, ticked off a long list of complaints to Cowan, including the fact that Pyle in Africa was hardly "a 'new boy' at the business" but "a well seasoned foreign correspondent. . . . When you propose to portray Ernie as a small boy who is tremulous and bewildered in the presence of other correspondents, you are simply going off the deep end."[57] Lowell Mellett was equally unhappy with the prospect of his protégé being portrayed as "a simple little sap." In their effort to dramatize Pyle appeal's for a movie audience, Ernie's old boss argued, the scriptwriters were portraying Pyle "as much less of a man than he really is." Mellett was particularly put out by the suggestion that Ernie would ever "run . . . away from his job," as "Ernie never ran away from anything, in my opinion." They simply were getting him wrong, Mellett told Miller.

You and I and a lot of others know that Ernie, with all his odd innocence, is also a tough, resilient, world-wise citizen; we know too that he is a complete, all-around newspaper man [and] one of the best reporters anywhere.

He is not, unless he is putting on an act, a simple little boy from the country who stares in open-eyed awe at war correspondents who have had their names in the paper; he's plenty used to having his own name in the paper. Like any good reporter, he's apt to be worried about the story he's working on at the moment or the situation he's undertaking to cover but he also has an abiding confidence in his own intelligence and resourcefulness. All this does not discount his genuine humility and his natural lack of pretense. . . .

There is going to be no comfort to the millions of families that look for Ernie's stories about their boys, in the picture of a dumb and baffled little fellow being pushed around by events which other correspondents take in their stride. . . .

378

If Cowan can give a suggestion of a tough and resolute little man who is not publicly advertising the fact that he is tough and resolute — a fairly difficult prescription to fill — he will have presented the Ernie that I think I know and the Ernie in whom so many Americans have put their faith.[58]

Here was delicious irony — a case of two journalists schooled in the business of fact butting heads with moviemakers trained in the art of mythmaking. In one sense, Mellett and Miller were perfectly right: the scriptwriters had gotten the real Pyle wrong. He was no bumbling rube but a successful and shrewd professional. But that fact blinded Mellett and Miller to the more important truth, to the entire reason Hollywood had seized upon Pyle in the first place. Ernie Pyle had become a mythical figure, and the scriptwriters had gotten that figure down pat. To be sure, they had oversimplified the persona, but they had nailed the essentials — Pyle the seer, Pyle the saint, Pyle the common man.

This conflict between myth and reality was never quite resolved in *The Story of G.I. Joe*. The script went through more rewrites, with the moviemakers and the journalists continuing their give-and-take. Thanks to the indignant Miller and Mellett, outright inaccuracies about Ernie's career were eliminated. Ernie continued to insist that Cowan and Wellman focus more on the soldier characters and less on the semi-fictional Pyle, and the moviemakers went along, excising Pyle's soul-searching on the home front. In the end, the Pyle character was boiled down to just one element of the public persona: Pyle the seer. Burgess Meredith played the odd role with game determination, staring soulfully at his G.I. buddies but not doing much more than that. Robert Mitchum, in his first major role, played the Waskow/Eversole character with the appropriate blend of tough-guy brusqueness and tenderness for his men. When Mitchum's character dies at the end, his men, with Ernie, walk up the hill toward the light, resolved to carry on toward victory. *The Story of G.I. Joe*, little remembered now, would be judged corny and sentimental by the standards set by later war movies. But it was hailed as a milestone in cinematic realism at the time of its release, just as Pyle was hailed as a realist. In fact, it blended myth and reality in about the same proportions as the column that inspired it.

The real Ernie became indifferent somewhere in Normandy.

"I've lost all interest in the fucking movie," he told Miller one day. "Just want to get me a dog and set in the sun somewhere."[59]

Any hope of rest evaporated the moment Ernie emerged from his plane in Albuquerque. The mayor had assembled a welcoming crowd, and the broad-smiling Lester Cowan was in it.

Intense discussions of the movie — joined the next day by William Wellman, the director — lasted three days. Instantly, the mail became so heavy Ernie had to hire a secretary to take dictation, though he forwarded most letters to Rosamond Goodman, his secretary in Washington, for form replies. Requests for speeches poured in, but he said no to virtually all comers. "I turned down Bob Hope, Eddie Cantor and the Treasury Dept all in one day."[60] Interspersed with these demands upon his time were daily trips to the dentist's office, where he underwent a series of fillings, treatments and tests. Mayor Tingley's plans for an enormous banquet to honor the returning hero spawned a backlash among townspeople who knew of the Pyles' penchant for privacy. The Pyles' defenders included friends at the chamber of commerce who quietly sent over a case of Old Granddad, the only honorarium Ernie accepted that fall with anything more than weary resignation.[61]

Lee Miller, who kept tabs on Jerry through correspondence and friends, had told Ernie her emotional condition seemed to have improved considerably. But her appearance startled Ernie upon his arrival. She seemed to have aged fifteen years since he had left for Italy only ten months earlier. Her isolation, too, had deepened. She had unaccountably shut out her two closest friends, Sister Margaret Jane, who was "terribly hurt" at Jerry's rebuff, and Liz Shaffer. Her only regular human contact was Ella Streger, her nurse, who often stayed late and helped with meals. Yet Ernie saw immediately that Miller had been right. She was seeing a psychiatrist, and "she's been as good as gold," he told his friend, and "like her old self mentally," or at least not "that weird doped-up third person she has been in recent years."[62] Ernie's presence now acted upon Jerry like a toxic agent. Her tiny house suddenly alive with ringing phones and loud men, her rigid routine shattered, she retreated to her bed and lay for days crying, with wrenching muscle pains — "apparently," said Ernie, "a delayed reaction to the excitement of my coming home."[63]

Perhaps, too, her relapse was a response to his plans. Ernie had assured Jerry repeatedly that when he returned from his second sojourn in the European theater, he would be finished with covering the war. "I think everybody, including my own conscience, will feel that I've done enough by the time I get back again," he had written her from Italy.[64] But he had not repeated that promise in many months, and now his conscience was telling him something different. In France he had decided "the only thing" to do after a rest at home "is to go to the Pacific." As a reason, he cited the obligation he felt to sailors, soldiers and Marines in the other theater of war. An additional, private reason may have been his hope that the income from a third best-selling book on the Pacific, combined with royalties from *Here Is Your War* and *Brave Men,* his collection of columns on Sicily, Italy and France, would assure him of an independent income. But his publicly stated rationale was doubtless the more important. The folk hero known as Ernie Pyle had become so much a part of the American war effort that it was simply unthinkable for him to retire while the war continued. The power of his own self-created public persona forced the hand of the flesh-and-blood Ernie.

Sister Margaret Jane pleaded with him not to go, saying Jerry could not survive it. "But what can I do?" he asked Miller. "I dont want to go either, but if I stay at home I suppose I'd get so I couldnt live with myself, for not going. And if I go and she should die, it would haunt me the rest of my life."[65]

Ernie decided suddenly to visit Los Angeles. Cavanaugh believed his presence might help the movie and press Cowan to speed up his production. So for a week Ernie sat in Cavanaugh's backyard in Inglewood, receiving one movie functionary at a time — writers, set designers, cameramen — discussing with each his view of the war and his hopes for the film. He was delighted with both the director, William Wellman, "an enthusiastic guy," and Burgess Meredith, who was "keen to play the part . . . and he's got some brains." He felt the visit did "some good," and Cowan agreed, cabling Miller: "ERNIE'S VISIT HERE OF INESTIMABLE VALUE. HE TOOK TIME TO INFUSE EVERY

TECHNICIAN WITH UNDERSTANDING OF [the] SOLDIER. . . ."[66] Meredith later recalled that Pyle was more the iconoclast than the patriot during these talks. The actor was startled to learn "how antiwar he was — the great chronicler of the G.I. was a Pacifist. . . . He was a very spicy-tongued fellow and was always threatening to break his Christ image, which he felt was undeserved. I remember once he said, 'If I hear another fucking G.I. say "fucking" once more, I'll cut my fucking throat.' "[67]

On October 24, Ernie entrained for Albuquerque, arriving early the next morning, a Tuesday, in time to accept an honorary doctorate at the University of New Mexico. For two days he hacked away at his mountain of mail — "letters from soldiers I know overseas, letters from War Department people, letters from old friends everywhere" — while coping with "an alltime peak wave of callers, calls and unfair interruptions. . . . [F]or the first time I began to get bitter and resentful at the whole thing and to feeling I couldnt take it."[68] From Tuesday through most of Thursday, Jerry appeared stable. But on Thursday evening she sat rigidly on the edge of her bed and stared into space. She ate almost nothing and refused to respond to questions. The next day, she was the same. Her psychiatrist visited several times. He predicted worse to come and prepared to administer electric shock treatments. But there was a slim chance she might rally on her own, he said, and on Sunday evening she seemed to do so. She cooked dinner for Ernie, and they spoke. Ernie felt optimistic.

The next morning Mrs. Streger, the nurse, arrived at 8:30, allowing Ernie to drive the few blocks to downtown for a dental appointment. When he returned at eleven, he saw Mrs. Streger standing in the yard, sobbing.

"Oh, Ernie," she cried. "She's stabbed herself all over . . ."

He had to break down the bathroom door. Jerry, dressed in a blood-drenched linen suit, was staring at herself in the mirror. She turned and looked steadily at her husband, saying nothing. She had gouged three deep holes in her neck with a foot-long pair of scissors. She also had cut her wrist and breast with a razor blade. For a moment Ernie thought she was about to die; then, with an experienced eye, he saw that the wounds were clotting, and that her face lacked the pallor he had seen in the faces of dying men.

That afternoon she was admitted to a sanitarium outside the city. She had barely spoken all day, but now, sitting on her hospital bed, she turned to Ernie and said, "May I ask you something?"

He nodded and leaned close.

"Are you Ernie Pyle?" she whispered in his ear.

He certainly was, he said.

"I don't believe it."[69]

Jerry's psychiatrist, whom Ernie believed "a very smart guy," had done "some pretty good thinking" about Jerry. He proposed that when she had recovered her strength — perhaps as early as December — she should be encouraged to take a trip without Ernie. "He says that I've been going away for years and she is the one to stay behind," Ernie explained to Miller. "This time . . . he wants her to be the one to go away on a trip and me stay behind — even though I'd leave the very next day for the Pacific."[70] He saw no harm in trying it. "I've long ago given up hope for Jerry, yet there's nothing to do but hope."[71]

Jerry was forbidden to have visitors, so Ernie took the chance to go east for essential business in Washington and Indiana. The next several weeks were like a kaleidescopic review of his past. He stopped for a day among the lovely limestone towers of Bloomington, where children were let out of school to see the favorite son of Indiana University receive an honorary doctorate of humane letters. (The citation, omitting mention of Pyle's departure from I.U. before his class's graduation in 1923, said only that he was "educated at Indiana University and the broader school of experience.") After the ceremony — which an observer likened to its guest of honor, "short, modest and not too dignified" — he spotted a small, red-haired woman in a gray suit standing to one side. She was smiling at him. It was Harriett Davidson, now married to the doctor in the red roadster. Beaming, Ernie "kissed her resoundingly."[72]

Late that afternoon, in Dana, Nellie Kuhns Hendrix heard the back gate squeak as she had heard it nearly every day as a girl, when Ernie would come over from the Pyle farm to visit the Kuhns children. Now the house belonged to Nellie and her husband. She got up and looked out. It was Ernie again, walking toward her across the grass. He came in and sat in the dining room, pointing out spots on the wall where various pictures had hung thirty years before.

Neither Will Pyle nor Ernie's aunt, Mary Bales, cared to drive any more, so the next day Nellie drove Ernie the ten miles to Clinton to catch the bus for Terre Haute, where the train would pick him up en route to Washington. He pulled his hat down to avoid being recognized. "It was sad," she remembered. "We didn't do much talking at all. It was a time where you didn't talk. He was going back, you know. He said, 'Nellie, I've got to go back with the boys. I've got to stick with them.' "[73]

In Washington, Ernie spent his days among pressed Army and Navy uniforms, his evenings with Moran Livingstone. There was the usual round of parties, including one at the plush brownstone of Walker Stone, head of the Scripps-Howard Newspaper Alliance. The gathering was "large and wet," with many friends around. Late that evening, Ernie approached an acquaintance named Madeline Markman, the wife of an advertising executive whom the Pyles had known in Albuquerque. Ernie said bluntly that he knew she had spoken to a mutual acquaintance of his affair with Moran. As Moran recalled the encounter long afterward, Ernie then said, "Please don't do things like that. Moran and I love each other very much. But nothing, absolutely nothing, will ever come of it. It would literally kill Jerry." At a party at the Hay-Adams a few weeks later, Moran told her son long afterward, "I got my walking papers from Ernie. We stood out in the hall alone. He tore up the picture he'd carried for years of me . . . and he said I wouldn't hear from him again. . . . [T]he only place I was left was in the [Scripps-Howard] list of special people to be notified in case of his death."[74]

Ernie returned to the West shortly before Christmas 1944 and made his final preparations. At the last minute Jerry asked him to change his mind, but he said it was too late.[75]

11

✯✯✯✯

"An End to This Wandering"

THE PACIFIC: JANUARY–APRIL 1945

Ernie last had slept in a war zone in the forests of northern France as the chill of autumn came into the air. Now, four months later, he spent his first night in the Pacific in a pleasant home in Honolulu, where "the loveliness of everything, and the softness" made him feel farther away from war than he had in New Mexico. He exchanged his winter woolens for tropical khaki and snacked on cool papaya. On the lawn outside a Hawaiian woman wearing blue slacks and a red bandana passed a fine spray of water back and forth over the lawn. "White clouds ran an embroidery over the ridges of the far green hills," he wrote. "Palm trees rustled like rain, and the deep whistles of departing ships came from the harbor below us. This, truly, was the Pacific."[1]

"The islands are a paradise . . ."

The Navy did everything possible to make its new guest comfortable, thanks in part to the direct interest of Navy Secretary James Forrestal himself. A personal escort was assigned to show Ernie the ropes — the writer Max Miller, author of several popular books, now a member of the Navy's public relations staff. Navy photographers snapped Ernie's picture in an endless succession of naval settings. He was given plush officers' quarters, plied with fine liquor, wined and dined by admirals. All this left little doubt of the Navy's basic misunderstanding of what Pyle was about. For many weeks he seemed to understand it little better.

The Navy's photographs showed Ernie smiling broadly at seamen, officers and naval gunnery. But his good humor disguised "an awful inner horror of coming back" to war.[2] He welcomed his escape from the "frenzied goldfish life" of his fame. But once he had made his decision to go, he longed desperately not to do so. When his departure was delayed a few days in California, he said he welcomed each day "with a big embrace. I felt like saying to it, 'Ah, my love, you are the day of my dreams. You are my one more day of security — how I cherish you.' "[3]

Lee Miller, who accompanied Ernie from San Francisco to Hawaii, was bound for the Philippines for his own tour as a war correspondent. From now on Ernie would send his business correspondence to the Washington office of Walker Stone, who would fill in as "vice-president for Pyle" in Miller's absence. Carrying a copy of the Navy's *Guide to the Western Pacific*, Pyle boarded a four-motor Douglas transport for the 3,500-mile flight to Guam. Flying west for many hours, the plane touched down at tiny, treeless Johnston Island, where Ernie glimpsed shorts-clad soldiers and sailors tanned a deep bronze, and at Kwajalein atoll, where he sipped iced fruit juice at a linen-covered table. On January 21 the plane landed at Guam, headquarters of the U.S. Fleet in the central Pacific. It was "green and beautiful — and terribly far from home."[4]

Ernie had expected the crush of fans in Honolulu, but he was surprised to find the neck-craning and autograph-seeking "just as bad" in Guam.[5] No sooner had he walked into his comfortable Bachelor's Officer Quarters than he saw a half dozen Navy Seabees peering at him through his window screen, one of them asking, "For God's sake, aren't you Ernie Pyle?" Even here there were men he knew already — a Navy orderly from the ship that took him to Sicily and a censor from Patton's Seventh Army. "Sometimes the world gets almost ridiculously small. I expected my father and Aunt Mary to climb through the window any minute."[6]

Actually, by Pacific standards, a relative from Dana was almost that close — Aunt Mary's twenty-six-year-old grandson by marriage, Jack Bales, a radioman with a B-29 squadron stationed on the island of Saipan, just one hundred and twenty miles north of Guam at the center of the Marianas chain. Jack was a favorite of

Ernie's. "He isn't exactly a nephew, but it's too complicated to explain," he told his readers. "I used to hold him on my knee and all that sort of thing."[7] Three weeks remained before Ernie was due to join a naval task force for the first of his scheduled series of cruises. Here was a chance not only to become reacquainted with Jack and describe the B-29s, which were bombing Japan, but to pry himself "out of the personal world, and the American world" and reenter "the one-tracked mental world of war."[8] More than ever, he needed a sudden reimmersion in work, for in California and Hawaii, "I felt I just never could force myself to write again."[9]

Saipan was one of three U.S.-occupied islands in the fifteen-island Marianas chain; the others were the big island of Guam and the smaller Tinian, from which the *Enola Gay* would depart for Hiroshima with its atomic cargo several months later. The islands were the crossroads of the western Pacific, offering bases for assaults toward the Philippines to the west and the Volcano Islands and Japan to the north — hence their strategic value to the United States. During Ernie's ordeal in Normandy the summer before, a thunderous struggle for the Marianas had cost the lives of many Marines. But now, only half a year later, the islands had sprouted acres of coarse new warehouses, hospitals, airfields, harbors, training grounds, highways and camps to house scores of thousands of men. Diversions abounded: there were more than two hundred outdoor movie theaters; sixty-five theater stages on one island alone; hundreds of softball diamonds, basketball courts and boxing arenas. The Army had passed out 3,500 radios, then set up a radio station to supply them with music, news and variety shows. In odd hours soldiers waded slowly through the crystalline surf, staring through glass-bottomed boxes at the multiformed marine life.[10] Ernie was agog. Publicly, he professed himself "thrilled by what the Americans are doing." Privately, he could hardly believe a war was being fought here. Recording a first impression he would later have cause to regret, he wrote: "The islands are a paradise and life here is fine. . . ."[11]

Landing on the air strip at Saipan, Ernie looked out upon a lovely place of semi-tropical palms and deciduous trees climbing the slope of the island's small Mount Tapotchan. His cheek felt the perpetual mild breeze — no brutal South Pacific heat in this temperate latitude — and his eyes took in the clean new buildings and barracks. At Jack Bales's steel Quonset hut, Ernie met Jack's hutmates, all fellow fliers who were kind enough to treat him as a comrade rather than a celebrity. Feeling at ease and unharassed for the first time in many months, Ernie allowed himself to drink and loaf with Jack's group for several days. Then he wandered off to a little house on the beach that had been built for the squadron commander — "about the best place I've ever had to write" — and quickly piled up a thick ream of copy. "It's quantity and not quality I'm after now. . . . Maybe they can improve as I get back into the swing."[12]

Jack Bales later recalled his amazement at Ernie's casual reporting methods. For several days Ernie "didn't do a damn thing," just got "half-stoned like the rest of us" and sat around the Quonsets apparently with no purpose greater than to "bullshit with us." He did nothing more journalistic than watch a few planes take off. But when he returned from his writing spell and showed Jack a sheaf of columns about the squadron, "you'd read those things and you'd remember." Ernie had not taken a single note, Bales recalled, yet the quotations were verbatim, "just like he had a recorder with him. His mind was kind of a recorder."[13] One day a young United Press correspondent named Red Valens sought Ernie out, and they talked. Awed by the older man, Valens asked, "How do you write?" Pyle gave a shrug that Valens interpreted to mean, "I really wish I could tell you."

"I sit and talk and listen," Ernie said. "Later . . . I go and sit at the typewriter. Maybe for a long time."

"No notes?" Valens asked.

"If I forget something then it wasn't really worth remembering."[14]

In print, Ernie crowed proudly about Jack Bales, who "had been on more missions than anybody else in his squadron."[15] But he felt "pretty fearful" for his nephew. "I really dont see that he has much chance of coming through alive," he told Jerry.[16] Jack was at least as concerned about Ernie, whom he pulled aside one day and blurted, "You stick your nose in this stuff, you're gonna get killed. For Christ's sake, you've written enough and done enough for the war effort. Turn around and go home."

"I owe it to these guys," Ernie replied.[17]

Yet the life "these guys" were leading, dangerous as it was in brief spurts, seemed incomparably softer to Ernie than the lives of "my friends fighting on the German border."[18] He goaded Jack and his buddies about their comforts — a solid roof, a real bed, someone to cook for them, not to mention the luxury of a hospitable climate. Bales remembered Ernie saying, "Jesus Christ, you guys don't know what war is about." "He was serious about it," Bales recalled, and "we fly boys . . . didn't argue with him."[19]

When Ernie boarded the light aircraft carrier USS *Cabot* for the first of his scheduled cruises, the sailors' lot struck him as scarcely any tougher. The ship was a floating American town, with five barbers, three doctors, two libraries, a general store and a daily newspaper. Indeed, the voyage seemed to Ernie to have all "the calm and repose of a pleasure cruise in peacetime." Pilots lounged bare-chested in the sun. From the flight deck came the soft *thok-thok* of tennis: the executive officer was playing the chaplain. Sailors worked regular hours, shot baskets, laughed at nightly movies, soaked in hot showers, dumped their soiled clothes at the ship's laundry and dined on steak and ice cream. Seeing all this, Ernie could think only of Italy: "It was hard to keep in mind that we were a ship of war, headed for war."[20]

Everything — "the methods of war, the attitude toward it, the homesickness, the distances, the climate" — seemed strange and impossibly remote from the world he had known for three years: "I can't seem to get my mind around it, or my fingers on it."[21] He meditated upon being "twelve thousand miles from Sidi-bou-Zid and Venafro and Troina and Ste.-Mère-Eglise — names as unheard of on the Pacific side of the world as are Kwajalein and Chichi Jima and Ulithi on the other side." Here, the crawling vegetation grew so fast that buildings ruined in battle only a few months earlier already were "festooned with vines and green leaves." The Pacific enemy, too, seemed an alien species. In Europe the Germans, "horrible and deadly as they were, were still people," but the Japanese "are looked upon as something subhuman and repulsive; the way some people feel about cockroaches or mice." And the racism, he confessed, was contagious. Upon seeing some Japanese prisoners, Ernie reported they "gave me the creeps, and I wanted a mental bath after looking at them." [22]

Nothing unnerved him more than the sheer

distances of the Pacific war. Fighting it was "like watching a slow-motion picture," with months of planning followed by days or weeks of sheer travel just to reach the designated field of battle. The huge task force of which the *Cabot* was a tiny part was nothing "like the swarming, pulsing mass that literally blanketed the water when we started to Sicily and to Normandy." It was a dispersed affair spread over a hundred miles of deep blue water, "peaceful and routine," with most ships invisible over the horizon, "so spread out that they didn't seem as overpowering as they actually were."[23] One day Ernie sat with a Navy map entitled "Our Enemy: Geography," and compared Pacific distances to European.

[A]t Anzio, the Third Division set up a rest camp for its exhausted infantrymen; it was less than five miles from the front line, within constant enemy artillery range. But in the Pacific, they bring men clear back from the western islands to Pearl Harbor to rest camps — the equivalent of sending an Anzio beachhead fighter all the way back to Kansas City for his two weeks. It's 3,500 miles from Pearl Harbor to the Marianas, all over water, yet hundreds of people travel it daily by air as casually as you'd go to work every morning. [24]

He tried to sympathize. He knew the Pacific held its own miseries, especially the "endless sameness" that drove men "pineapple crazy." Strange as it seemed to one who had seen many cases of battle fatigue in Europe, he heard repeatedly that "a man doesn't have to be under fire in the front lines to have finally more than he can take without breaking. He can, when isolated and homesick, have more than he can take of warmth and sunshine and good food and safety — when there's nothing else to go with it, and no prospect of anything else."[25] Whenever he pointed out the Pacific's relative comforts, he took care to mention the corresponding monotony of most servicemen's lives there. Yet when he was asked to compare the two theaters of war, as often he was, he did not hesitate to speak his mind, either in person or in print.

> The boys ask you a thousand times how this compares with the other side. I can only answer that this is much better. They seem to expect you to say that, but they are a little disappointed too.
>
> They say, "But it's tough to be away from home for more than a year, and never see anything but water and an occasional atoll." I say yes, I know it is, but there are boys who have been in Europe more than three years, and have slept on the ground a good part of that time. And they say, yes, they guess in contrast their lives are pretty good.
>
> Seaman Paul Begley looks at his wartime

life philosophically . . . "I can stand this monotony all right," he says. "The point with us is that we've got a pretty good chance of living through this. Think of the Marines who have to take the beaches, and the infantry in Germany. . . ." But others yell their heads off about their lot, and feel they're being persecuted by being kept out of America a year. I've heard some boys say, "I'd trade this for a foxhole any day." You just have to keep your mouth shut to a remark like that. [26]

"It was such a contrast to what I'd known for so long in Europe that I felt almost ashamed . . . ," Ernie told Jerry. "They're . . . safe and living like kings and don't know it."[27]

The group portrait that emerged day by day from Ernie's typewriter was not especially attractive. When he had described a dugout in North Africa that some homesick soldier had fixed up into a snug little den, the effect was to evoke sympathy for a resourceful lad prepared to make the best of bad circumstances. But when Ernie described the hot water and clean sheets of the *Cabot*, he only pointed out the glaring contrast between the sailors' lot and the soldiers'. When he said of the sailors that, "taking it all in, they are good boys who do what is asked of them," the impression he left was of slightly spoiled kids — nice enough, he guessed — who simply didn't know how good they had it. [28]

That was a far cry from the sanctified "good boys" who crept up the bloody streets of Cherbourg, doing what no one should ask of anyone. Pyle's unflattering picture of the Navy proves, if proof is necessary, that his tributes to the infantry in Europe sprang from something other than a desire to propagandize on behalf of the Army. If he was a simple propagandist, he certainly lost his skills in the Pacific.

Ernie was repelled by the rigid caste system that lifted Navy officers to an elite sphere above enlisted men, exemplified in signs that said: "Officer Country — Unauthorized Personnel Keep Out."[29] This, too, was a stark contrast to the circle of devoted men around the body of Captain Waskow. "This war, at least in the non-combatant areas, bears no resemblance whatever to the war that you and I know," Ernie confided to Rudolf von Ripper, the Austrian-born war artist he had known well in Italy. "I am afraid it wouldn't appeal to an old war horse like you. . . ."[30]

The *Cabot*, a "baby flat-top," was part of Task Force 58, a naval behemoth comprising hundreds of ships under the command of Admiral Marc Mitscher, with whom Ernie had pitched horseshoes one evening in Hawaii. Ernie asked to be assigned to one of the small carriers, hoping for a more intimate setting than a "big" carrier would provide. The Navy chose the unheralded *Cabot*, perhaps because it had seen lots of action. From the tiny atoll of Ulithi southwest of the Marianas, the task force would trace a giant loop north to the waters off Japan, allowing pilots to make the first air strikes against Tokyo; then steam south to assist in the invasion of the island fortress of Iwo Jima; then return to Japanese waters for more air strikes; and finally steam southwest to reconnoiter the Japanese island of Okinawa in preparation for the great invasion planned there in the spring. The mission sounded, and was, momentous. But Ernie quickly realized that a major action at sea was dispersed across so wide a field of action that no ship's view of it could encompass the whole thing. The *Cabot* came close to both Japan and Iwo Jima, but "never close enough to see anything."[31] Planes took off. Later they landed. It looked little different to Ernie than a training exercise, and by this time he had seen far too much war to be interested in loud airplanes and busy servicemen. When he encountered difficulty filing copy from the *Cabot*, he simply bailed out early, riding by breech's buoy to a destroyer-escort that was headed back to Guam.

The cruise had hardly been an ordeal for him. Indeed, he told Cavanaugh, he "sort of enjoyed being at sea . . . and I at last got back to a kind of normal life, relatively free of grog and people."[32] And the absence of danger was war "the way I like it."[33] But it was hell on the business of producing the "spot war stuff" — up-to-date accounts of breaking events — that editors had come to expect from Ernie in France. In fact, grinding out a series on the placid cruise of the *Cabot* became an exercise in frustration, indeed, one of the most difficult writing experiences Ernie ever had. When a cable from Washington arrived at Guam telling him of Scripps-Howard's keen desire for "spot" news of the Tokyo strikes, he wired back in frustration: "HAVE NO SPOT NEWS ON TOKIO [*sic*] STRIKE. . . . nothing happened to us."[34] He elaborated in a follow-up letter to Walker Stone that expressed all his boredom with the Navy and his worries over boredom's likely effect on his copy. He took pains to remind Stone that

whatever success the column has had over the years, has been considerably due to my being able to resist the old newsman's impulse to shoot into the headlines with spot stuff. . . . I do realize what magic the Tokio strike dateline would be, but I also feel that I would be getting hysterical if I were beguiled out of my own field by that.

Out here things are different. It isn't like the St. Lo breakthrough, where I could drive back 40 miles and get my series started a couple of days after it happened. Here I had to travel by sea for *six* days before I was back where I could write or send anything off with any assurance it would get there.

The whole tempo of war is different out here, and I'm not yet fully adjusted to it. It is slow, and uninspiring. That is, unless you go in on a landing with the Marines. . . . [T]he bulk of the war out here, and the bulk of the men engaged in it, are simply marking time for months on a stretch. Then their war lasts a few hours or a few days, and they mark time again for months. Only a tiny percentage — the Marines and the fliers and the few on ships that get hit — ever engage in war at all. They're just doing a sort of normal, safe, drudgery job away from home. That's what I have to get adjusted to. And it makes damn poor reading while you're adjusting.

As the weeks go by I will, I hope, gradually get a feeling of this war, and be able to do a better job. But I have to feel my way into it, and nothing but the passage of time will solve it. In the future my stuff from out here might conceivably reach the peak tempos that it did in Europe, but by and large and for week after week it is going to be dull as dishwater. It will be human interest stuff about people, but there will be damn little drama of war in it.[35]

To make matters worse, Ernie now stumbled into a contretemps over censorship. Since early in the war, the Navy had enforced a strict policy against allowing the names of its personnel in news reports, with the exception of certain high-ranking officers. This, coupled with severe restrictions against the ability of correspondents to go where they wanted, had led late in 1944 to a virtual revolt against the Navy press relations operation, with reporters and photographers demanding the ouster of the PRO's unpopular head, a contrary old waterfront reporter named Waldo Frank. The abominated Frank had recently been ousted by Captain A. H. "Min" Miller, a capable staff officer sent from London. Miller, able and friendly, quickly made a hit with the correspondents and sympathized with their beefs about unreasonable censorship. But the regulation against names remained, with no explanation, apparently, other than that it had ever been thus.

"The rule had some basis in the early days out here when we were weak, but there is no justification for it now," Ernie complained to Jerry. "The other correspondents and the PRO and the censors themselves have been trying in vain to get it changed for months. There's no personal quarrel about it; everybody is perfectly swell, but the rule is still there."[36] The ban on names threatened to snip the heart out of Ernie's columns; his basic purpose, after all, was "to give the average guy's picture of the war."[37] He had heard of the restrictions in Hawaii, but upon inquiring, he was reassured by the Navy all would be well. So he wrote the first batch of his *Cabot* columns as always, with liberal use of individuals' names, and turned them over to the censors, who politely returned the carbon copies with every name scissored out. At this, the world's best-loved war correspondent strode into the office of CINCPAC public relations and issued a simple ultimatum: Either the Navy would allow him to write about sailors by name, or he would move along to the Philippines, where General MacArthur and the Army would undoubtedly prove more accommodating. For much of one day the Navy scurried and conferred. Then Mr. Pyle was smilingly informed that the ban on names would be relaxed. But the ruling was not official, and Ernie still chafed.[38] "I can hardly keep awake . . . ," he told Jerry. "I'll be glad when I feel I've done enough on the Navy that I can feel justified in stopping going out on different types of ships. . . . You just sweat blood trying to make it interesting."[39] As he sat in his choice room, struggling to write, he slid slowly but inexorably into one of his deep slumps.

"My heart is still in Europe . . ."

The coming of Ernie Pyle had been much anticipated in the Pacific; finally, it was said, this side of the war would get its due. No doubt this accounts for the especially close reading Pyle's first columns received, and the dismay with which they were greeted in some low-echelon quarters. It wasn't as much what he wrote as the company he was obviously keeping — admirals, public relations types, officers, fly-boys. "I honest didn't think *Ernie* would ever end up

405

kissing a brass ass," one G.I. told Red Valens, the young reporter whom Ernie had befriended on Saipan.[40] Among the correspondents' corps at Guam, too, there was quiet sniping about "big shots" from the European theater breezing into the Pacific theater and getting the royal treatment from the Navy. Max Miller recalled that "sly high schoolish criticism" of Pyle from "some of the lesser-trained correspondents" had gotten "under his skin." This "throat-cutting and back-fence gossiping," Ernie told Miller, was what brought him so low at Guam in mid-March.[41]

Doubtless more disturbing than the grousing of Johnny-come-lately reporters were the inklings Ernie picked up that servicemen, too, were entertaining doubts about him. One night at dinner, he ran into some fliers who complained about his portrayal of the central Pacific as a "paradise." He sat with them and "thrashed out . . . the 'misunderstanding.' " But a few days later he got a letter from two other men of the same outfit who made the same complaints. "Some of us are deeply concerned over one of your recent transmissions describing these luxurious paradise islands . . . ," they wrote. "Now hear this, Ernie, we're not bitching, nor are we bitter . . . but come, come, Ernie, how about visiting us sometime, and enjoying our rats' eye view of this Pacific paradise?"[42] Still conciliatory, but with his back up a bit, Ernie replied:

Dear Boys . . .

I have a nephew on the B-29's in Saipan and went up there and lived with him for a week late in January. And, truthfully, they are living well. In fact all the pilots in his hut read the columns before I sent them off and didn't disagree. Naturally they have been set up for some time and are better established than you can be in the early stages. So, I guess I was right and that you were right, too.

Anyhow, I want to see you and have promised your other boys that I met the other night to come down and eat gnats and "C" Rations with you.[43]

A far nastier rebuke was written about the same time for an Air Corps magazine that circulated in the Pacific. "So now it's happened to you, Ernie," the anonymous author began. "We were all glad when we heard that you had decided to come West. . . . We thought here, at last, is a guy who is going to give us a break. Here is somebody who is going to tell the folks at home that there is a war out here too. . . ." Then had come his admission he had "never heard of Kwajalein," an insult that "stopped everybody cold. . . . Out here, Ernie, you speak of Kwajalein the same way you speak of Gettysburg. . . . It was worse than civilian talk." Then had come the comparison of Saipan to "paradise," though "if you had asked around a little

... any PFC could have told you that six or 16 or 26 months on an island like Saipan or smaller than Saipan does something funny to you. . . ." Next he had written of life on an aircraft carrier, "a ship with the best possible living conditions in the Navy," and of "eating with the officers, like all correspondents. . . . It was kind of hard, Ernie . . . knowing that colored GI's were waiting on you and saying, 'Dinner is being served now, Sir.' " The writer knew all about Pyle's firsthand knowledge of "the tough life of the GI." But if he had become "fed up with that life . . . why didn't you just call it quits after you came home? Why come out here and live like no GI ever lived and tell the folks at home this is a 'paradise'? You're making liars out of a lot of soldiers here, Ernie. Or is it the other way around?"[44]

The piece was rife with errors and misreadings. Pyle had not said he had never heard of Kwajalein, only that its name was unfamiliar in Europe. He had not neglected to discuss "island neurosis." He had lived mostly with officers, yes, but he had only arrived in the combat zones a few weeks earlier, and fully intended to portray the "little guy's" view. Yet however unfair the editorial, its burden was essentially true: Pyle had underestimated the difficulties of the Pacific war and given them short shrift in print.

Ernie didn't see the article, but he knew its sentiments were in the air. "So far you haven't been where you belonged out here," Red Valens told him. "It's not good."[45] According to Valens, Ernie agreed. He had gotten off to a "stinking lousy start," Valens recalled him saying one day. "I've been a phony. . . . The boys out here — I've been giving them a lot of crap. . . . If I can just give these bastards . . . a break." Despite his intentions, however, Ernie's loyalties remained half a world away. In February he received a letter of praise from Eisenhower, to whom Ernie had sent a copy of *Brave Men*. The general thanked him for his work in promoting "understanding of what the infantry soldier endures" — an understanding he believed sadly lacking. Ernie responded warmly but wryly, saying,

I think we're fighting a losing cause.

I've found that no matter how much we talk, or write, or show pictures, people who have not actually been in war are incapable of having any real conception of it. I don't really blame the people. Some of them try hard to understand. But the world of the infantryman is a world so far removed from anything normal, that it can be no more than academic to the average person.

As you know, I've spent two and a half years carrying the torch for the foot-soldier, and I think I have helped make America conscious of, and sympathetic toward him, but haven't made them feel what he goes through. I believe it's impossible.[46]

When Jerry asked him to write her not only of what he was doing but what he was "thinking and feeling," he unburdened himself. Often he felt "easy and unconcerned in spirit," he said, "but once in a while I'll get a low spell when the war and its details of death and misery get too real in my mind. . . . It's just that I'd like so much to be home, and not personally ever see any more war ever. I don't expect to see as much out here as I did in Europe, but I'll have to see a little eventually, and I dread that. When I lie and think about it too clearly I feel afraid that if I'm ever in combat again, I'll crack wide open and become a real case of war neurosis."[47]

In the odd, rushed sentences that tumbled from her faint pencil, Jerry responded with warmth:

That you could ever become a victim of war neurosis is one of the things I have believed — and still believe, couldn't happen — I believe it without knowing why — Just as I believe that in spite of everything, you will come through whatever you have to go through — You say when you lie and think about it you feel afraid — It's a different kind of fear — and has an all too real basis — but in a way, it's rather like mine. . . . Ernie, promise me that you will not stay away until you get to the breaking point — and not because of any fear of coming home — There is enough straight in my mind now to make

410

me see that I can keep it that way by trying. . . . In a strange, unclear way, I have always known how greatly I love you. . . ."[48]

She speculated that Ernie might prefer to live separately from her upon his return — an idea he promptly quashed. "You know darling that a separate life . . . is something that I have never wanted and couldnt tolerate. I feel just the same as you do, and always have. All I want you to do is keep on trying just the very best you can until I get home again for keeps, and then we can at last have time to try together."[49]

After the campaign for Iwo Jima in February and March, the next great land challenge was Okinawa, the penultimate step to an invasion of the Japanese Home Islands. Briefings and rumors made it obvious the battle would be one of the bloodiest of the war. With the critical whisperings about him in his ears, Ernie pondered whether to go along. Max Miller and other Navy hands urged him to forgo the campaign, or at least to wait until well after the first landings before going ashore. But at some point in March — exactly when is not clear — Ernie made his decision. He not only would go to Okinawa, but he would accompany a Marine landing, though he chose not to go in with the first waves. According to Max Miller, who saw Ernie often during these weeks, it was the ill-concealed suspicion among some reporters that Pyle had lost his edge, or opted for an easy life among the Navy brass, that tipped his decision. As he put it later to Lee Miller, the "eyebrow-raising" by "the young squirts drove Ernie into making — against all his promises — another landing."[50]

Committed, he felt the familiar, sick depression of fear envelop him, especially when reorganizations of the landing scheme moved his designated place in the operation closer and closer to H-Hour. Again, as before Normandy, he lay awake at night, playing out the coming scenes in his mind. When Cavanaugh wrote about the latest plans for a series of movie sequels to *G.I. Joe*, Ernie reminded him of Lester Cowan's stipulation that any such plans depended on Ernie's surviving the war. "And the way I look at things right now, I wouldnt give you two cents for the likelihood of me being alive a year from now. And I'm not joking."[51]

It became an article of faith in Pyle mythology that he had premonitions of death. Whether this is really so depends on how one regards fears common to the veterans of many campaigns. Men about to go into battle in World War II commonly dwelled on matters of probability and chance. Many had the sense that one was allotted a certain reservoir of good luck, and that the reservoir could not be replenished indefinitely. Ernie said more than once that his fears of coming campaigns were no different from those of many soldiers. Certainly he had said several times in the past that he did not expect to survive the next action. The repetition had a ritualistic quality. Perhaps it was not much more than a superstition; if he announced to the world that he would not make it, perhaps that would purchase another chance. Yet, if his associates were not exaggerating for dramatic effect, his fears about the coming Okinawa campaign seemed to carry a heavier weight of conviction.

Robert Sherwood, the playwright and presidential speechwriter then serving as a kind of global scout for FDR and Harry Hopkins, spent a couple of long, wet evenings with Ernie about this time. On the last of these, the night of March 16–17, there was a party at the officers' club on Guam. Few of the men present knew precisely when the call would come for the Okinawa staging, but all knew it would be soon. Sherwood was leaving the next day for Washington. There was much singing, and Ernie "told a number of cockney and G.I. stories, all featuring that well-known participial form," Sherwood remembered. When Sherwood had to leave, Ernie came out in the corridor with him to exchange drunkenly emotional farewells. They talked briefly of Roosevelt, whom Sherwood would see in a couple of days. "Tell him I love him," Ernie said. When the playwright spoke of a reunion after the war, Ernie shook his head.

"I'm not coming back from this one," he said.

Sherwood tried to laugh off the remark, saying, "You said that about Sicily [and] Normandy and every other operation, and you're still here and doing fine."

Pyle was adamant.

"I always believed it when I said it, and I believe it now, and sometime I have got to be right."[52]

At first, his fears were for nothing. Unbeknownst to the Americans, the one hundred thousand Japanese defenders of Okinawa had withdrawn inland to concentrate their resistance; apart from kamikaze attacks on the ships of the U.S. Fleet, they did little to oppose the landings on the beaches on the morning of April 1 — Easter 1945. The enormous bloodshed of the Okinawa battle lay in the weeks ahead. In Ernie's sector, "the carnage that is almost inevitable on an invasion was wonderfully and beautifully not there. . . . Like a man in the movies who looks away and then suddenly looks back unbelieving, I realized there were no bodies anywhere — and no wounded."[53] He spent several uneventful days ashore with Marines, then returned to the command ship *Panamint* to recover from a cold and write. He wrote twenty quick columns about the Marines and caught up with his mail. "I've got almost a spooky feeling that I've been spared once more and that it would be asking for it to tempt Fate again," he wrote Max Miller. "So I'm going to keep my promise to you and to myself that that was the last one. I'll be on operations in the future, of course, but not on any more landings."[54]

On April 12 he learned via the *Panamint*'s wireless that President Roosevelt had died. The great tide of public grief arose in part from the knowledge that Roosevelt had not lived to see the final victory in Europe, which everyone knew was only a few weeks away. Perhaps this turned Ernie's thoughts to V-E Day and what he ought to write for the occasion. He drafted most of a column and put it away, saving it for revision when the moment actually came. "And so it is over . . . ," he began, writing for once in pencil. "I am as far away from it as it is possible to get. . . . But my heart is still in Europe. . . ."[55]

The *Panamint* served as headquarters at sea for the Army's 77th Division. The division's assignment in the Okinawa campaign was to take the air strip on the ten-square-mile island of Ie Shima, a few miles northwest of the big island. Landings were set for April 16. Ernie heard about a new tank-destroyer being used on Ie; he decided to get a look at it. He went ashore on the 17th, talked with infantrymen during the afternoon and spent the night near the beach in a Japanese ammunition-storage bunker. In the morning he ate cold C-rations, then hitched a ride with Colonel Joseph Coolidge, who was planning to cross the island to find a new site for his regimental command post.

The fighting was inland, so the road from the beach was quiet. At about ten o'clock, a Japanese Nambu machine gun chattered. Pyle, Coo-

415

lidge and the other men in the jeep leaped out and jumped into a ditch along the road. After a moment Ernie raised his head and the machine gunner fired again, hitting him in the left temple just below the line of his helmet.[56]

EPILOGUE
★★★★

"What I See"

Nearly twenty years after Ernie died, his name was invoked in an angry argument on an airport tarmac in Vietnam. It happened in 1963. One of the antagonists was David Halberstam, a brilliant and aggressive war correspondent for the *New York Times.* He was the most powerful and controversial of a small group of reporters who had infuriated official Washington by exposing embarrassing shortcomings and contradictions in U.S. policy in southeast Asia. The other man was Marine Major General Victor "Brute" Krulak, a World War II veteran, adviser to President John F. Kennedy and severe critic of the Vietnam reporters.

Halberstam learned Krulak had spread a fallacious story about Halberstam weeping over photographs of dead Viet Cong. Meeting Krulak's plane as it arrived from the United States, the tall, glowering reporter advanced on the smaller general, identified himself and his business, and shouted: "The story is a bunch of shit! . . . No one ever showed me pictures like that and I did not break into tears and I just want you to fucking know it and don't *ever* put shit out like that again!"

"Well," sputtered Krulak, groping for words, "it's not a G.I. Joe war, is it? It's not a war with an Ernie Pyle, is it?"[1]

Krulak's retort came from the gut of the World War II generation: Ernie and his G.I.'s had made America look good. The Common Man Triumphant, the warrior-with-a-heart-of-gold — this was the self-image Americans carried into the post-war era. And the image endured, passing directly to the correspondents who covered the Korean war; while that conflict lasted, said A.J. Liebling, Ernie was "the most imitated writer in America." As Krulak made obvious, Pyle was the standard of comparison for Halberstam and his Vietnam colleagues, whom the Army warned to "get on the team." The legacy was still powerful even when Americans rushed to the Persian Gulf in 1990–91. There, young reporters for whom even the name "Gomer Pyle" was at most a distant memory scurried from barracks to tents in search of homesick but determined young G.I.'s. Pyle's soldier had become "a stock figure" in "the wax-works gallery of American history as popularly remembered," Liebling believed, an image as durable as "the frontiersman . . . the cowboy, and Babe Ruth."[2]

As a practitioner of the craft of journalism, Pyle was perhaps without peer. After him, no war correspondent could pretend to have gotten the real story without having moved extensively among the front-line soldiers who actually fought. Nor could any credible reporter ever again hint that modern warfare was glorious on the old Victorian pattern, or that soldiers went into battle with patriotic words on their lips, or that war could somehow be waged without producing "an awful lot of dead people."

Yet it would be too much to say Pyle fulfilled his creed — "to make people see what I see." Writing against the grain of "the Pyle phenomenon" late in 1944, Ira Wolfert, a respected correspondent for the North American Newspaper Alliance, said, "Ernie Pyle was telling the truth when he said he tried all the time to tell the folks back home what the war is like, but not he nor me nor the hundreds of others who are in there trying have been able to put down on paper the really ferocious ugliness of war — not only what it does to the bodies of men, but what it does to their minds and spirits . . . [W]ar is not all sweetness and light with only mechanical ugliness, but Ernie Pyle remains . . . all sweetness and light and, in this hour of ordeal for all of us . . . we love him for it. He tells us not only what we want to know, but what we, in our fear and ache, enjoy to know."[3]

Why didn't the war correspondents tell more? As Wolfert implied, Pyle and the others gave Americans about all the realism they wanted. To tell much more was to risk shock, anger, rejection, not to mention censorship. To weave a myth of sacrificial suffering instead was to do one's bit for the war. Pyle's G.I. myth — not an untruth, but a way of bending reality into a sensible and bearable shape — helped Americans through history's most grotesque and deadly ordeal, what Steinbeck called "the crazy hysterical mess." This left truths untold, but perhaps Arthur Miller was right when he said Pyle "told as much of what he saw as people could read without vomiting."

Yet there was perhaps a more important reason for Pyle's reticences. As he admitted to Eisenhower near the end of his life, the ideal of "making people see what I see" simply remained beyond his grasp when what he saw was war. It may lie beyond anyone's grasp. War, the extreme human experience, tests the limits of human communication. Martha Gellhorn, who covered the war for *Collier*'s in Spain, China and France, reflected long afterward that "what you write is never, never good enough. You do your best, but it is always more than you can say. You do your best, but it's incommunicable."[4]

Americans have careened between opposite understandings of war. One views war as glamorous and glorious, the other as unrelieved horror. Pyle challenged the unexamined pieties of both views. In regarding him as a secular saint who only paid homage to the suffering soldiers, Americans misread his basic ambivalence. He felt war's repulsiveness, yet also its attractions.

He was popularly understood only to hate war, which he did, but not to love it, which he did also. "God help me," General Patton is said to have murmured in the killing fields of Europe, "I do love it so." Ernie Pyle might have spoken the same prayer.

Jerry Pyle died in Albuquerque of complications from influenza in November 1945. Several years later, Ernie's body was removed from Ie Shima and reburied among Army and Navy dead in the National Memorial Cemetery of the Pacific, in Punchbowl Crater, Hawaii.

APPENDIX

★★★★

An Ernie Pyle Sampler

Pyle's distinctive voice first emerged in the columns he wrote about aviation from 1928 to 1932. This was Pyle's tribute to a favorite pilot.

What Kind of a Fellow He Was

This is the hardest column I have ever had to write. Every now and then you hear an old flier say: "There's just one trouble with aviation. It's always the best ones that go."

And so it would seem in this case. I mean in the Ludington Line crash last night that killed Pilots Floyd Cox and Vernon Lucas. There weren't any better ones than those two.

They were both pure gold. They had no enemies that I know of, and I don't believe either one of them hated anybody. I don't believe they could.

Floyd Cox was perhaps my closest friend in aviation. We shared confidences and sought each other's advice.

He was sort of a protege of this column, and the column had no greater booster than Floyd. It was a sort of a "you pat my back and I'll pat yours" feeling between us.

George Pomeroy was Floyd's closest friend among the line's pilots. The news hit him terribly. But he steeled himself, and went around talking all evening as tho the dead men were mere acquaintances.

He brought me into town from the field late last night. As I stepped from the car he said: "Well, give him a good send-off, Ernie. He deserves it." I only wish I knew how.

Cox was a perpetual student of flying. He was almost boyish in his enthusiasm to learn more and more about aviation every day.

He studied the weather constantly. He practiced flying by instruments every chance he had. He was studying celestial navigation, and carried his sextant along on his daily trips to New York to practice "shooting" the sun. He flew every new ship he could get his hands on.

He was one of the best pilots on the line, yet he was always saying that he was a mere novice compared to some of the others.

When the line first started, he flew between George Pomeroy and Earl Smith. He liked that combination. They were both old timers, and conservative. He felt that with Pomeroy an hour ahead of him, and Smith an hour behind him, he couldn't get into much trouble.

He had no hobbies, or interests, outside of his wife and his flying.

Going to baseball games was about his only pastime. He said he was raised a farmer, and would always be one. He was uncomfortable in the presence of people who "put on airs." He was genuine.

For several weeks he held the speed record between here and New York. Then one day (it happened to be his day to fly the fast Lockheed) he found that he had a terrific tail wind behind him.

He could have set a new record easily. But he flew throttled back all the way to keep from doing it. He told me later that he was afraid the other pilots would think he was trying to grab the limelight if he broke it again.

About a year and a half ago, when Washington Airport got its first fast Lockheed, Floyd was assigned to carry important news photographs to New York.

Several chartered planes were waiting on the line, and it was a real race. The weather was terrible.

Around Aberdeen, Floyd ran into a hailstorm, and landed. A little later he took off, but couldn't get thru the storm and landed again. The whole side of his face was chewed up by the hailstones.

Every other plane got thru. His boss, instead of being sore, gave him a $20 bonus for his good judgment.

And because I gave him a nice write-up, he came into the office the next day with a new hat, two new shirts and a new tie for me. He wanted me to share his bonus. I mention it merely to show what kind of a fellow he was.

There are many unsolved mysteries in aviation. The exact cause of last night's crash will probably be one of them. And why it had to be Floyd Cox that left us is another . . . .

November 6, 1931[1]

To say Pyle wrote a daily travel column from 1935–42 misses the intensely personal nature of the feature. Through dispatches like the following, readers came to feel they knew Pyle as intimately as a close friend.

That Long, Sad Wind

CEDAR RAPIDS, IOWA — It was soon after crossing into Iowa, coming south from Minnesota, that I gradually became conscious of the wind.

I don't know whether you know that long, sad wind that blows so steadily across the thousands of miles of Midwest flat lands in the summertime. If you don't, it will be hard for you to understand the feeling I have about it. Even if you do know it, you may not understand. Because maybe the wind is only a symbol.

But to me the summer wind in the Midwest is one of the most melancholy things in all life. It comes from so far, and it blows so gently and yet so relentlessly; it rustles the leaves and the branches of the maple trees in a sort of symphony of sadness, and it doesn't pass on and leave them still; no, it just keeps coming, like the infinite flow of Old Man River.

You could, and you do, wear out your life-time on the dusty plains with that wind of fu-tility blowing in your face. And when you are worn out and gone, the wind, still saying nothing, still so gentle and sad and timeless, is still blowing across the prairies, and will blow in the faces of the little men that follow you, for-ever. That is it, the endlessness of it; it is a symbol of eternity.

As soon as I became conscious of the wind in Iowa, I was back in character as an Indiana farm boy again. Like dreams came the memories the wind brought. I lay again on the ground under the shade trees at noon time, with my half-hour for rest before going back to the fields, and the wind and the sun and the hot rural silence made me sleepy, and yet I couldn't sleep for the wind in the trees. For the wind was like the afternoon ahead that would never end, and the days and the summers and even the lifetimes that would flow on forever, tiredly, patiently.

No, I see it's a bad job, me trying to make you see something that only I can ever feel. It is just one of those petty impressions that will form in a child's mind, and grow and stay with him through a lifetime, even playing its part in his character and his manner of thinking, and he can never explain it.

So let's drop the wind, and talk about snakes.

There's another impression that has come up with me out of childhood. I have a horror of snakes that verges on the irrational. I'm not afraid of being killed by a snake. It isn't that kind of fear. It's a horrible, unnatural mania for getting away, and it is induced in equal quantities by a 6-inch garden snake and a 6-foot rattler.

I happened to think about snakes because, in 15,000 miles of driving this year, I had not seen a snake until I drove through southern Minnesota. And there, in less than two hours, I counted 14 snakes on the road.

Ask my mother about snakes. She'll tell you the snake story, probably. In all the years I have been away, she never fails to tell it over again when I am there on a visit.

I was a little fellow, maybe 4 or 5. My father was plowing at the far end of our farm, a half-mile from the house. I was walking along behind the plow, barefooted, in the fresh soft furrow.

He had just started the field, and was plowing near a weedy fence-row. Red, wild roses were growing there. I asked my father for his pocket-knife, so I could cut some of the roses to take back to the house.

He gave it to me, and went on plowing. I sat down in the grass and started cutting off the roses. Then it happened in a flash. A blue racer came looping through the grass at me. I already had my horror of snakes at that tender age. It must have been born in me. I screamed, threw the knife away, and ran as fast as I could.

Then I remembered my father's knife. I crept back over the plowed ground till I found it. He had heard me scream and had stopped. I gave him the knife, and started back to the house.

I approached the house from the west side. There was an old garden there, and it was all grown up in high weeds. I stopped on the far side, and shouted for my mother. She came out and asked what I wanted. I asked her to come and get me. She said for me to come on through by myself. I couldn't have done that if it had killed me not to.

She ordered me to come through, and I began to cry. She told me if I didn't stop crying, and didn't come through, she would whip me. I couldn't stop, and I couldn't come through. So she came and got me. And she whipped me. One of the two times, I believe, that she ever whipped me.

That evening, when my father came in from the fields, she told him about the crazy boy who wouldn't walk through the weeds and had to be whipped. And then my father told her about the roses, and the knife, and the snake. It was the roses, I think, that hurt her so. My mother cried for a long time that night after she went to bed.

It has been more than 30 years since that happened, but to this day when I go home my mother sooner or later will say, "Do you remember the time I whipped you because you wouldn't walk through the weeds?" and then she will tell me the story, just as I have told it here, and along toward the end she always manages to get the hem of her apron up around her eyes, just in case she should need it, which she always does.

September 23, 1935

Pyle wrote this next column in response to an editor friend's request.

A Queer Job

If ever I lose my job as a roving reporter, I'll be in fine practice to be a traveling salesman. For I know the back roads, the jerk-water hotels and the cracker-box vernacular of two-thirds of the states in the Union.

It is my job to travel around over the country for the Scripps-Howard newspapers, covering something specific part of the time — such as TVA, the Dionne Quintuplets, the Florida Canal, or Maj. Bowes' hour; but most of the time just writing about anything interesting I bump into — such as an engineer who plays tunes on his locomotive whistle, or a tobacco auction, or a Broadway newsboy.

In the past year I have covered some 35,000 miles by auto, train, airplane and boat, but mostly by auto. I live in hotels (both good and bad), in private homes, and stop with friends once in a while. When I'm not on a trip, I live in Washington.

There are only a few roving reporters in the world. It is a queer job. My friends think it is an easy job. They think it's just a vacation, they think I'm getting paid just for seeing the world. My poor, simple friends.

They don't know what it is to drive and dig up information all day long, and then work till midnight writing it. One story a day sounds as easy as falling off a log. Try it sometime.

But there are good sides to this job too. You see a lot of fascinating things. And you learn so much. In the past year I have learned more about American history than 16 years of schooling ever taught me. Learned it from hearing people talk, and from reading books about the new places I visited.

As a roving reporter I have learned that the mountaineers of eastern Tennessee are the purest Anglo-Saxon strain in America, and tremendously sharp and capable; that in Nova Scotia they say "good night" as a greeting, just as we say "good evening"; that Texas is the only state with the power to divide itself into smaller states if it wants to; that tourists with Illinois license tags are the wildest drivers on the roads; that in New Orleans masking of the face is allowed by law one day a year, on Mardi Gras; that it costs $750 a day to run the average-sized freight ship; that people in shrimp canneries work from 4 in the morning till 6 and later at night; that Natchitoches in Louisiana is pronounced "Nackitosh."

And as a roving reporter I have seen some wonderful things — the long, soft shadows of the Arizona cactus under a desert moonlight; the awful panic in the eyes of people running before a Canadian forest fire; the slow rising of the Southern Cross into the vast tropical sky as you see it from a freighter at sea; the deep preoccupation on the faces of men and women at the gambling tables in Las Vegas, Nev.; the amazing speed with which a jumble of tin and steel becomes an auto in Detroit; and the amazing speed with which an auto from Detroit becomes a jumble of tin and steel on a slick, snowy road in North Carolina.

In 27,000 miles of driving in one year, I have had only one flat tire. Picked up a nail in Louisiana. Only in one place (on the Gaspe peninsula in eastern Quebec) have I had to go into low gear to get up a hill. I have paid from 12 to 35 cents for gasoline. I have run out of gas twice, and both times it had apparently been syphoned out by thieves, and neither time did I have to walk for gas.

Seldom do I go more than 50 miles an hour any more. I almost never drive at night. Some days I go only 25 miles. Other days 300. I have never been stopped by a cop. I have driven through a blizzard in southern Mississippi, and a dust storm in Nova Scotia.

I have never left anything in a hotel room, except one toothbrush. I have had good hotel rooms for 75 cents, and bad ones for $5. In the back country I have seen pigs hitched to little wagons, hauling wood. And men and women hitched to plows. I have eaten papayas, and cactus candy, and enchiladas, and oranges right off the trees. I have seen (but not eaten) canned rattlesnake meat.

Once in Maine I rounded up half a dozen stories in less than two hours. Another time, in Washington, I worked a whole week on one story. Sometimes I can write a story in half an hour. Other times, when I am out of the mood, I start a story and never do get it finished.

Roving has taught me that people in general are good. Once I stopped at a house in a little village in northwest Florida to ask the direction, and they invited me to stay for lunch. Once, standing high on the precipitous bank of the St. Lawrence River, I talked for ten minutes with a native, and he spoke in French and I in English and neither of us knew a word the other said, but we understood. Once I spent two hours at an abandoned gold mine on a mountain in Arizona, talking with the old watchman who lived alone with his dog. In Ottawa I stood on the sidewalk and chatted with the Premier of Canada for 15 minutes. In Minnesota I picked up the same hitchhiker four times in one day.

How do I find things to write about? Well, some things by design, some by accident. In a strange town, I go to the local newspaper, or the police chief, or a doctor, and they tell me the most interesting people in town. Then I go and talk with the people.

Nobody has ever refused to talk with me. Only one man has ever refused to let me write about him, and even he was friendly and we talked for an hour.

There have been many stories I couldn't write. One was the time I went with a doctor far back into the mountains, to an old log cabin, to see a dying old man. He lay there in his bed like a movie mountaineer, with his shotgun standing at his bedside. When I came in, he raised on his deathbed and held out his feeble hand, and in a whisper welcomed me to his home. It made a lump in my throat, but I couldn't write about it.

There are times when the life of a roving reporter is so thankless and bare that you feel you would rather dig potatoes for a living; but at times such as now, when you sit down and start remembering the things you have done, and seen, and especially the things you have felt — then you know you want to keep going on.

March 18, 1936

In the summer of 1936 Pyle toured the drought-stricken region of the Great Plains known as the Dust Bowl. His feelings about it, recorded in this last column in the series, echoed his sentiments about the farming life he had known as a child and foreshadowed his later feelings about the cumulative emotional effects of war.

BISMARCK, N.D. — This journalistic caravan through the withering land of misery swings to a close, and I am glad.

I am glad, because the world of drought finally becomes an immersion which levels the senses. You arrive at a place where you no longer look and say, "My God, this is awful!" You gradually become accustomed to dried field and burned pasture; it stretches into a dull continuous fact.

Day upon day of driving through this ruined country gradually becomes a sameness which ceases to admit a perspective.

You get to accept it as a vast land that is dry and bare, and was that way yesterday and will be tomorrow, and was that way a hundred miles back and will be a hundred miles ahead. The story is the same everywhere, the farmers say the same thing, the fields look the same — it becomes like the drone of a bee, and after a while you hardly notice it at all.

It is that way all day. It is only at night, when you are alone in the enveloping heat and cannot sleep, and look into the darkness, and the things come back to you like a living dream, that you once more realize the stupendousness of it.

Then you can see something more than field after brown field, or a mere succession of dry water holes, or the matter-of-fact resignation on farm faces.

You can see then the whole backward evolution into oblivion of a great land, and the destruction of a people, and the calamity of long years on end without privilege for those of the soil, and the horror of a life started in emptiness, knowing only struggle, and ending in despair.

I have seen a great deal of this in the last few years. Sometimes at night when I am thinking too hard I feel that there is nothing but leanness everywhere, that nobody has the privilege of a full life, that all existences are things of drudgery that had better be done with. Of course I am wrong about that.

But not only people. I have seen the degradation of great lands, too.

The beautiful valleys and hillsides of Tennessee washing away to the ocean, leaving a slashed and useless landscape.

The raw windy plains of western Kansas, stripped of all flesh, all life driven away, a one-time paradise turned into a whirlpool of suffocation.

And the vast rolling Dakotas where huge herds once grazed with the freedom of the birds, now parched and cramped and manhandled by man and elements into a bed of coals.

July 27, 1936

War's attractions, Pyle's pride in his front-line experience, and the on-the-team status of the Allied war correspondents are all apparent in this column, written near the end of the North Africa campaign.

IN TUNISIA — The war correspondents over here seldom write about themselves, so it may be interesting if I try to tell you how we live.

There are more than 75 American and British correspondents and photographers in North Africa. Since Allied Headquarters is in a big city to the rear [Algiers], that's where most of the correspondents stay. The number actually in Tunisia at any one time fluctuates between half a dozen and two dozen.

Each of the three big press associations has a five-man staff — usually three men back at headquarters and two at the front. They rotate every few weeks.

The correspondents in the city live a life that is pretty close to normal. They live in hotels or apartments, eat at restaurants or officers' messes, work regular hours, get laundry done, dress in regulation uniforms, keep themselves clean, and get their news from communiques and by talking to staff officers at headquarters.

Since their lives are closely akin to the lives of newspapermen at home, we'll deal here only with the correspondents as they live at the front.

Some of us have spent as much as two months in Tunisia without ever returning to the city. When we do it is a great thrill to come back to civilization — for the first day.

But then a reaction sets in, and almost invariably we get the heebie-jeebies and find ourselves nervous and impatient with all the confusion and regimentation of city life, and wish ourselves back at the front again.

The outstanding thing about life at the front is its magnificent simplicity. It is a life consisting only of the essentials — food, sleep, transportation, and what little warmth and safety you can manage to wangle out of it by personal ingenuity.

Ordinarily, when life is stripped to the bare necessities it is an empty life and a boring one. But not at the front. Time for me has never passed so rapidly. You're never aware of the day of the week, and a whole month is gone before you know it.

Up here the usual responsibilities and obligations are gone. You don't have appointments to keep. Nobody cares how you look. Red tape is at a minimum. You have no desk; no designated hours. You don't wash your hands before you eat, nor afterwards either. It would be a heaven for small boys with dirty ears.

Too, it is a healthy life. During those winter months I was constantly miserable from the cold, yet paradoxically I've never felt better in my life. The cold wind burns your face to a deep tan, and your whole system gets toughened. You eat twice as much as usual. I hadn't been hungry for nigh onto 40 years, but in Tunisia I eat like a horse and am so constantly hungry it has got to be a joke.

It is a life that gives you a new sense of accomplishment. In normal life, all the little things are done for us. I make my money by writing, and then use that money to hire people to wash my clothes, shine my shoes, make my beds, clean the bathtub, fill my gas tank, serve my meals, carry my bags, build my fires.

But not up here. You do everything yourself. You are suddenly conscious again that you CAN do things. The fact that another guy can write a better piece than I can is counterbalanced by the fact that I can roll a better bedroll than he can.

And last, and probably most important of all, is that you have a feeling of vitality. You are in the heart of everything, and you are a part of it. You don't feel like an onlooker; you feel that you're a member of the team.

You get into the race, and you resent dropping out even long enough to do what you're up here to do — which is write. You'd rather just keep going all day, every day.

I've written in the past that war is not romantic when you're in the midst of it. Nothing has happened to change my feeling about that. But I will have to admit there is an exhilaration in it; an inner excitement that builds up into a buoyant tenseness which is seldom achieved in peacetime.

Up here the Army accepts us as a part of the family. We correspondents know and are friends with hundreds of individual soldiers. And we know, and are known by, every American general in Tunisia. There is no hedging at the front. I've never known an instance where correspondents were not told with complete frankness what was going on.

In the past no restrictions were put on us; we could go anywhere we pleased at any time. But things are gradually changing, as the established machinery of war catches up with us. There's a new rule that correspondents can't go into the front lines unless accompanied by an officer. Maybe that's a good rule. I don't know. But there are about two dozen of us who will feel ourselves in the odd position of being conducted through our own house.

April 8, 1943

In this dispatch from Tunisia — a mixture of explanation, description, propaganda, and self-revelation — Pyle first declared his allegiance to the infantrymen with whom he became so closely identified.

Now to the Infantry

IN THE FRONTLINES BEFORE MATEUR — We're now with an infantry outfit that has battled ceaselessly for four days and nights.

This northern warfare has been in the mountains. You don't ride much any more. It is walking and climbing and crawling country. The mountains aren't big, but they are constant. They are largely treeless. They are easy to

439

defend and bitter to take. But we are taking them.

The Germans lie on the back slope of every ridge, deeply dug into foxholes. In front of them the fields and pastures are hideous with thousands of hidden mines. The forward slopes are left open, untenanted, and if the Americans tried to scale these slopes they would be murdered wholesale in an inferno of machine-gun crossfire plus mortars and grenades.

Consequently we don't do it that way. We have fallen back to the old warfare of first pulverizing the enemy with artillery, then sweeping around the ends of the hill with infantry and taking them from the sides and behind.

I've written before how the big guns crack and roar almost constantly throughout the day and night. They lay a screen ahead of our troops. By magnificent shooting they drop shells on the back slopes. By means of shells timed to burst in the air a few feet from the ground, they get the Germans even in their foxholes. Our troops have found that the Germans dig foxholes down and then under, trying to get cover from the shell bursts that shower death from above.

Our artillery has been really sensational. For once we have enough of something and at the right time. Officers tell me they actually have more guns than they know what to do with.

All the guns in any one sector can be centered to shoot at one spot. And when we lay the whole business on a German hill the whole slope seems to erupt. It becomes an unbelievable cauldron of fire and smoke and dirt. Veteran German soldiers say they have never been through anything like it.

Now to the infantry — the God-damned infantry, as they like to call themselves.

I love the infantry because they are the underdogs. They are the mud-rain-frost-and-wind boys. They have no comforts, and they even learn to live without the necessities. And in the end they are the guys that wars can't be won without.

I wish you could see just one of the ineradicable pictures I have in my mind today. In this particular picture I am sitting among clumps of sword-grass on a steep and rocky hillside that we have just taken. We are looking out over a vast rolling country to the rear.

A narrow path comes like a ribbon over a hill miles away, down a long slope, across a creek, up a slope and over another hill.

All along the length of this ribbon there is now a thin line of men. For four days and nights they have fought hard, eaten little, washed none, and slept hardly at all. Their nights have been violent with attack, fright, butchery, and their days sleepless and miserable with the crash of artillery.

The men are walking. They are fifty feet apart, for dispersal. Their walk is slow, for they are dead weary, as you can tell even when looking at them from behind. Every line and sag of their bodies speaks their inhuman exhaustion.

On their shoulders and backs they carry heavy steel tripods, machine-gun barrels, leaden boxes of ammunition. Their feet seem to sink into the ground from the overload they are bearing.

They don't slouch. It is the terrible deliberation of each step that spells out their appalling tiredness. Their faces are black and unshaven. They are young men, but the grime and whiskers and exhaustion make them look middle-aged.

In their eyes as they pass is not hatred, not excitement, not despair, not the tonic of their victory — there is just the simple expression of being here as though they had been here doing this forever, and nothing else.

The line moves on, but it never ends. All afternoon men keep coming round the hill and vanishing eventually over the horizon. It is one long tired line of antlike men.

There is an agony in your heart and you almost feel ashamed to look at them. They are just guys from Broadway and Main Street, but you wouldn't remember them. They are too far away now. They are too tired. Their world can never be known to you, but if you could see them just once, just for an instant, you would know that no matter how hard people work back home they are not keeping pace with these infantrymen in Tunisia.

May 1, 1943

Early in July 1943, Pyle sailed from North Africa to Sicily in the greatest armada ever assembled to that time.

Men of New Professions

WITH THE U.S. NAVY IN THE MEDITERRA-NEAN — Our first day at sea on the way to invade Sicily was truly like a peacetime Mediterranean cruise. The weather was something you read about, gently warm and sunny and the sea as smooth as velvet.

We were kept at a sharp alert for at any moment we could be attacked by a submarine, surface ship or airplane and yet any kind of attack — even the fact that anybody would want to attack anybody else — was so utterly out of keeping with the benignity of the sea that it was hard to take seriously the possibility of danger. . . .

Dusk brought a change. Not [a] feeling [of] fear at all but somehow an acute sense of the drama we were playing at that moment on the face of the sea that has known such a major share of the world's great warfare. In the faint light of the dusk, forms became indistinguishable. Nearby ships were only heavier spots against the heavy background of the night. Now you thought you saw something and now there was nothing. The gigantic armada was on all sides of us, there only in knowledge.

Then out of nowhere, a rolling little subchaser took on a dim shape alongside us and with its motors held itself steady about 30 yards away. You could not see the speaker but a megaphoned voice came loudly across the water telling us of the motor breakdown of one of the troop-carrying barges farther back.

We megaphoned advice over to him. His response came back. Out in the darkness the voice was young. You could picture a boyish skipper over there in his blown hair and his life jacket and binoculars, rolling to the sea in the Mediterranean dusk.

Some young man who had so recently been so normally unaware of any sea at all — the book-keeper in your bank, perhaps, and now here he was a strange new man in command of a ship, suddenly transformed into a person with awful responsibilities carrying out with great intentness his special small part of the enormous aggregate that is our war on all the lands and seas of the globe.

In his unnatural presence there in the rolling darkness of the Mediterranean you realized vividly how everybody in America has changed, how every life suddenly stopped and suddenly began again on a different course. Everything in this world has stopped except war and we are all men of new professions out in some strange night caring for each other.

That's the way you felt as you heard this kid, this pleasant kid, bawling across the dark waters

strange nautical words with disciplined deliberation that carried in them the very strength of the
sea itself, the strong matured words of the Captain of his own ship, saying, "Aye, aye, sir. If
there is any change I will use my own judgment
and report to you again at dawn. Goodnight,
sir."

Then the whole darkness enveloped the American armada. Not a pinpoint of light showed from
those hundreds of ships as they surged on
through the night toward their destiny, carrying
across this ageless and indifferent sea tens of
thousands of young men of new professions,
fighting for . . . for . . . well, at least for each other.

July 22, 1943

The prototypical Pyle hero.

"My Personal Hero"

IN ITALY — The company commander said to
me, "Every man in this company deserves the
Silver Star."

We walked around in the olive grove where the
men of the company were sitting on the edges of
their foxholes, talking or cleaning their gear.

"Let's go over here," he said. "I want to introduce you to my personal hero."

I figured that the Lieutenant's own "personal
hero," out of a whole company of men who deserved the Silver Star, must be a real soldier
indeed.

Then the company commander introduced me to Sergt. Frank Eversole, who shook hands sort of timidly and said, "Pleased to meet you," and then didn't say any more.

I could tell by his eyes and by his slow and courteous speech when he did talk that he was a Westerner. Conversation with him was sort of hard, but I didn't mind his reticence for I know how Westerners like to size people up first.

The Sergeant wore a brown stocking cap on the back of his head. His eyes were the piercing kind. I noticed his hands — they were outdoor hands, strong and rough.

Later in the afternoon I came past his foxhole again, and we sat and talked a little while alone. We didn't talk about the war, but mainly about our West, and just sat and made figures on the ground with sticks as we talked.

We got started that way, and in the days that followed I came to know him well. He is to me, and to all those with whom he serves, one of the great men of the war.

Frank Eversole's nickname is "Buck." The other boys in the company sometimes call him "Buck Overshoes," simply because Eversole sounds a bit like "overshoes."

Buck was a cowboy before the war. He was born in the little town of Missouri Valley, Ia., and his mother still lives there. But Buck went West on his own before he was 16, and ever since has worked as a ranch hand. He is 28, and unmarried.

He worked a long time around Twin Falls, Idaho, and then later down in Nevada. Like so many cowboys, he made the rodeos in season. He was never a star or anything. Usually he just rode the broncs out of the chute for pay — $7.50 a ride. Once he did win a fine saddle. He has ridden at Cheyenne and the other big rodeos.

Like any cowboy, he loves animals. Here in Italy one afternoon Buck and some other boys were pinned down inside a one-room stone shed by terrific German shellfire. As they sat there, a frightened mule came charging through the door. There simply wasn't room inside for men and mule both, so Buck got up and shooed him out the door. Thirty feet from the door a direct hit killed the mule. Buck has always felt guilty about it.

Another time Buck ran onto a mule that was down and crying in pain from a bad shell wound. Buck took his .45 and put a bullet through its head. "I wouldn't have shot him except he was hurtin' so," Buck says.

Buck Eversole has the Purple Heart and two Silver Stars for bravery. He is cold and deliberate in battle. His commanders depend more on him than any other man. He has been wounded once, and had countless narrow escapes. He has killed many Germans.

He is the kind of man you instinctively feel safer with than with other people. He is not help-less like most of us. He is practical. He can improvise, patch things, fix things.

His grammar is the unschooled grammar of the plains and the soil. He uses profanity, but never violently. Even in the familiarity of his own group his voice is always low. He is such a confirmed soldier by now that he always says "sir" to any stranger. It is impossible to conceive of his doing anything dishonest.

After the war Buck will go back West to the land he loves. He wants to get a little place and feed a few head of cattle, and be independent.

"I don't want to be just a ranch hand no more," he says. "It's all right and I like it all right, but it's a rough life and it don't get you nowhere. When you get a little older you kinda like a place of your own."

Buck Eversole has no hatred for Germans. He kills because he's trying to keep alive himself. The years roll over him and the war becomes his only world, and battle his only profession. He armors himself with a philosophy of acceptance of what may happen.

"I'm mighty sick of it all," he says very quietly, "but there ain't no use to complain. I just figure it this way, that I've been given a job to do and I've got to do it. And if I don't live through it, there's nothing I can do about it."

February 21, 1944

IN ITALY — Buck Eversole is a platoon sergeant in an infantry company. That means he has charge of about 40 front-line fighting men.

He has been at the front for more than a year. War is old to him and he has become almost the master of it. He is a senior partner now in the institution of death.

His platoon has turned over many times as battle whittles down the old ones and the replacement system brings up the new ones. Only a handful now are veterans.

"It gets so it kinda gets you, seein' these new kids come up," Buck told me one night in his slow, barely audible Western voice, so full of honesty and sincerity.

"Some of them have just got fuzz on their faces, and don't know what it's all about, and they're scared to death. No matter what, some of them are bound to get killed."

We talked about some of the other old-time non-coms who could take battle themselves, but had gradually grown morose under the responsibility of leading green boys to their slaughter. Buck spoke of one sergeant especially, a brave and hardened man, who went to his captain and asked him to be reduced to a private in the lines.

"I know it ain't my fault that they get killed," Buck finally said. "And I do the best I can for them, but I've got so I feel like it's me killin' 'em instead of a German. I've got so I feel like a murderer. I hate to look at them when the new ones come in."

Buck himself has been fortunate. Once he was shot through the arm. His own skill and wisdom have saved him many times, but luck has saved him countless other times.

One night Buck and an officer took refuge from shelling in a two-room Italian stone house. As they sat there, a shell came through the wall of the far room, crossed the room and buried itself in the middle wall with its nose pointing upward. It didn't go off.

Another time Buck was leading his platoon on a night attack. They were walking in Indian file. Suddenly a mine went off, and killed the entire squad following Buck. He himself had miraculously walked through the mine field without hitting a one.

One day Buck went stalking a German officer in close combat, and wound up with the German on one side of a farmhouse and Buck on the other. They kept throwing grenades over the house at each other without success. Finally Buck stepped around one corner of the house, and came face to face with the German, who'd had the same idea.

Buck was ready and pulled the trigger first. His slug hit the German just above the heart. The German had a wonderful pair of binoculars slung over his shoulders, and the bullet smashed them to bits. Buck had wanted some German binoculars for a long time.

The ties that grow up between men who live savagely and die relentlessly together are ties of great strength. There is a sense of fidelity to each other among little corps of men who have endured so long and whose hope in the end can be but so small.

One afternoon while I was with the company Sergt. Buck Eversole's turn came to go back to rest camp for five days. The company was due to attack that night.

Buck went to his company commander and said, "Lieutenant, I don't think I better go. I'll stay if you need me."

The lieutenant said, "Of course I need you, Buck, I always need you. But it's your turn and I want you to go. In fact, you're ordered to go."

The truck taking the few boys away to rest camp left just at dusk. It was drizzling and the valleys were swathed in a dismal mist. Artillery of both sides flashed and rumbled around the horizon. The encroaching darkness was heavy and foreboding.

Buck came to the little group of old-timers in the company with whom I was standing, to say goodbye. You'd have thought he was leaving forever. He shook hands all around, and his smile seemed sick and vulnerable. He was a man stalling off his departure.

He said, "Well, good luck to you all." And then he said, "I'll be back in just five days." He said goodbye all around and slowly started away. But he stopped and said goodbye all around again, and he said, "Well, good luck to you all."

I walked with him toward the truck in the dusk. He kept his eyes on the ground, and I think he would have cried if he knew how, and he said to me very quietly:

"This is the first battle I've ever missed that this battalion has been in. Even when I was in the hospital with my arm they were in bivouac. This will be the first one I've ever missed. I sure do hope they have good luck."

And then he said:

"I feel like a deserter."

He climbed in, and the truck dissolved into the blackness. I went back and lay down on the ground among my other friends, waiting for the night orders to march. I lay there in the darkness thinking — terribly touched by the great simple devotion of this soldier who was a cowboy — and thinking of the millions far away at home who must remain forever unaware of the powerful fraternalism in the ghastly brotherhood of war.

February 22, 1944

This was Pyle's first report from Omaha Beach after D-Day. The column was "pooled" — made available to all newspapers and news agencies. It gave American readers their first detailed description of what the invasion of Normandy had been like.

A Pure Miracle

NORMANDY BEACHHEAD — Due to a last-minute alteration in the arrangements, I didn't arrive on the beachhead until the morning after D-day, after our first wave of assault troops had hit the shore.

By the time we got here the beaches had been taken and the fighting had moved a couple of miles inland. All that remained on the beach was some sniping and artillery fire, and the occasional startling blast of a mine geysering brown sand into the air. That plus a gigantic and pitiful litter of wreckage along miles of shoreline.

Submerged tanks and overturned boats and burned trucks and shell-shattered jeeps and sad little personal belongings were strewn all over these bitter sands. That plus the bodies of soldiers lying in rows covered with blankets, the toes of their shoes sticking up in a line as though on drill. And other bodies, uncollected, still sprawling grotesquely in the sand or half hidden by the high grass beyond the beach. That plus an intense, grim determination of work-weary men to get this chaotic beach organized and get all the vital supplies and the reinforcements moving more rapidly over it from the stacked-up ships standing in droves out to sea.

Now that it is over it seems to me a pure miracle that we ever took the beach at all. For some of our units it was easy, but in this special sector where I am now our troops faced such odds that our getting ashore was like my whipping Joe Louis down to a pulp.

In this column I want to tell you what the opening of the second front in this one sector entailed, so that you can know and appreciate and forever be humbly grateful to those both dead and alive who did it for you.

Ashore, facing us, were more enemy troops than we had in our assault waves. The advantages were all theirs, the disadvantages all ours. The Germans were dug into positions that they had been working on for months, although these were not yet all complete. A 100-foot bluff a couple of hundred yards back from the beach had great concrete gun emplacements built right into the hilltop. These opened to the sides instead of to the front, thus making it very hard for naval fire from the sea to reach them. They could shoot parallel with the beach and cover every foot of it for miles with artillery fire.

Then they had hidden machine-gun nests on the forward slopes, with crossfire taking in every inch of the beach. These nests were connected by networks of trenches, so that the German gunners could move about without exposing themselves.

Throughout the length of the beach, running zigzag a couple of hundred yards back from the shoreline, was an immense V-shaped ditch 15 feet deep. Nothing could cross it, not even men on foot, until fills had been made. And in other places at the far end of the beach, where the ground is flatter, they had great concrete walls. These were blasted by our naval gunfire or by explosives set by hand after we got ashore.

Our only exits from the beach were several swales or valleys, each about 100 yards wide.

The Germans made the most of these funnel-like traps, sowing them with buried mines. They contained, also, barbed-wire entanglements with mines attached, hidden ditches, and machine guns firing from the slopes.

This is what was on the shore. But our men had to go through a maze nearly as deadly as this before they even got ashore. Underwater obstacles were terrific. The Germans had whole fields of evil devices under the water to catch our boats. Even now, several days after the landing, we have cleared only channels through them and cannot yet approach the whole length of the beach with our ships. Even now some ship or boat hits one of these mines every day and is knocked out of commission.

The Germans had masses of those great six-pronged spiders, made of railroad iron and standing shoulder-high, just beneath the surface of the water for our landing craft to run into. They also had huge logs buried in the sand, pointing upward and outward, their tops just below the water. Attached to these logs were mines.

In addition to these obstacles they had floating mines offshore, land mines buried in the sand of the beach, and more mines in checkerboard rows in the tall grass beyond the sand. And the enemy had four men on shore for every three men we had approaching the shore.

And yet we got on.

Beach landings are planned to a schedule that

is set far ahead of time. They all have to be timed, in order for everything to mesh and for the following waves of troops to be standing off the beach and ready to land at the right moment.

As the landings are planned, some elements of the assault force are to break through quickly, push on inland, and attack the most obvious enemy strong points. It is usually the plan for units to be inland, attacking gun positions from behind, within a matter of minutes after the first men hit the beach.

I have always been amazed at the speed called for in these plans. You'll have schedules calling for engineers to land at H-hour plus two minutes, and service troops at H-hour plus 30 minutes, and even for press censors to land at H-hour plus 75 minutes. But in the attack on this special portion of the beach where I am — the worst we had, incidentally — the schedule didn't hold.

Our men simply could not get past the beach. They were pinned down right on the water's edge by an inhuman wall of fire from the bluff. Our first waves were on that beach for hours, instead of a few minutes, before they could begin working inland.

You can still see the foxholes they dug at the very edge of the water, in the sand and the small, jumbled rocks that form parts of the beach.

Medical corpsmen attended the wounded as best they could. Men were killed as they stepped out of landing craft. An officer whom I knew got a bullet through the head just as the door of his landing craft was let down. Some men were drowned.

The first crack in the beach defenses was finally accomplished by terrific and wonderful naval gunfire, which knocked out the big emplacements. They tell epic stories of destroyers that ran right up into shallow water and had it out point-blank with the big guns in those concrete emplacements ashore.

When the heavy fire stopped, our men were organized by their officers and pushed on inland, circling machine-gun nests and taking them from the rear.

As one officer said, the only way to take a beach is to face it and keep going. It is costly at first, but it's the only way. If the men are pinned down on the beach, dug in and out of action, they might as well not be there at all. They hold up the waves behind them, and nothing is being gained.

Our men were pinned down for a while, but finally they stood up and went through, and so we took that beach and accomplished our landing. We did it with every advantage on the enemy's side and every disadvantage on ours. In the light of a couple of days of retrospection, we sit and talk and call it a miracle that our men ever got on at all or were able to stay on.

Before long it will be permitted to name the units that did it. Then you will know to whom this glory should go. They suffered casualties.

And yet if you take the entire beachhead assault, including other units that had a much easier time, our total casualties in driving this wedge into the continent of Europe were remarkably low — only a fraction, in fact, of what our commanders had been prepared to accept.

And these units that were so battered and went through such hell are still, right at this moment, pushing on inland without rest, their spirits high, their egotism in victory almost reaching the smart-alecky stage.

Their tails are up. "We've done it again," they say. They figure that the rest of the army isn't needed at all. Which proves that, while their judgment in this regard is bad, they certainly have the spirit that wins battles and eventually wars.

June 12, 1944

Just before leaving the European theater, Pyle wrote this piece as an epilogue to Brave Men, *his collection of columns from Sicily, Italy and France. The end of the war against Germany was widely expected to come soon; in fact, the fighting would last nine more months.*

An Exhaustion of the Spirit

This final chapter is being written in the latter part of August, 1944; it is being written under an apple tree in a lovely green orchard in the interior of France. It could well be that the European war will be over and done with by the time you read this book. Or it might not. But the end is inevitable, and it cannot be put off for long. The German is beaten and he knows it.

It will seem odd when, at some given hour, the shooting stops and everything suddenly changes again. It will be odd to drive down an unknown road without that little knot of fear in your stomach; odd not to listen with animal-like alertness for the meaning of every distant sound; odd to have your spirit released from the perpetual weight that is compounded of fear and death and dirt and noise and anguish.

The end of the war will be a gigantic relief, but it cannot be a matter of hilarity for most of us. Somehow it would seem sacrilegious to sing and dance when the great day comes — there are so many who can never sing and dance again. The war in France has not been easy by any manner of means. True, it has gone better than most of us had hoped. And our casualties have been fewer than our military leaders had been willing to accept. But do not let anyone lead you to believe that they have been low. Many, many thousands of Americans have come to join the ones who already have slept in France for a quarter of a century.

For some of us the war has already gone on too long. Our feelings have been wrung and drained; they cringe from the effort of coming alive again. Even the approach of the end seems to have brought little inner elation. It has brought only a tired sense of relief.

I do not pretend that my own feelings is the spirit of our armies. If it were, we probably would not have had the power to win. Most men are stronger. Our soldiers still can hate, or glorify, or be glad, with true emotion. For them death has a pang, and victory a sweet scent. But for me war has become a flat, black depression without highlights, a revulsion of the mind and an exhaustion of the spirit.

The war in France has been especially vicious because it was one of the last stands for the enemy. We have won because of many things. We have won partly because the enemy was weakened from our other battles. The war in France is our grand finale, but the victory here is the result of all the other victories that went before. It is the result of Russia, and the western desert, and the bombings, and the blocking of the sea. It is the result of Tunisia and Sicily and Italy; we must never forget or belittle those campaigns.

We have won because we have had magnificent top leadership, at home and in our Allies and with ourselves overseas. Surely America made its two perfect choices in General Eisenhower and General Bradley. They are great men — to me doubly great because they are direct and kind.

We won because we were audacious. One could not help but be moved by the colossus of our invasion. It was a bold and mighty thing, one of the epics of all history. In the emergency of war our nation's powers are unbelievable. The strength we have spread around the world is appalling even to those who make up the individual cells of that strength. I am sure that in the past two years I have heard soldiers say a thousand times, "If only we could have created all this energy for something good." But we rise above our normal powers only in times of destruction.

We have won this war because our men are brave, and because of many other things — because of Russia, and England, and the passage of time, and the gift of nature's materials. We did not win it because destiny created us better than all other peoples. I hope that in victory we are more grateful than we are proud. I hope we can rejoice in victory — but humbly. The dead men would not want us to gloat.

The end of one war is a great fetter broken from around our lives. But there is still another to be broken. The Pacific war may yet be long and bloody. Nobody can foresee, but it would be disastrous to approach it with easy hopes. Our next few months at home will be torn between the new spiritual freedom of half peace and the old grinding blur of half war. It will be a confusing period for us.

Notes

The following abbreviations are used throughout the Notes:

   EP Ernie Pyle
 EPSHS Ernie Pyle State Historic Site, Dana, IN
  FDRL Franklin Delano Roosevelt Library, Hyde Park, NY
   GP Geraldine "Jerry" Pyle
  LBL Lucy B. Livingstone
  LGM Lee G. Miller
   LL Lilly Library, Indiana University, Bloomington, IN
   PC Paige Cavanaugh
  SHSW State Historical Society of Wisconsin, Madison, WI
  WDN *Washington Daily News*
  WJL Weil Journalism Library, Indiana University, Bloomington, IN

PROLOGUE

1. Pyle in death, Alexander Roberts to LGM, 9/26/45, Joseph B. Coolidge to LGM, 12/16/45, Miller papers, EPSHS.
2. Pyle's appearance, Lee Miller, "Ernie

Pyle," *Redbook*, Pyle scrapbooks, LL; Cecelia Ager, "War Correspondent Ernie Pyle," *PM*, 9/24/44; Arthur Miller, *Situation Normal* (New York: Reynal & Hitchcock, 1944), 164.

3. Reactions to Pyle's death, *New York Times*, 4/19/45; WDN, 4/18/45; Lee G. Miller, *Story of Ernie Pyle* (New York: Viking Press, 1950), 427.

4. "GBP's radio tribute to Ernie," Miller papers, EPSHS.

5. Pyle's V-E Day column, copy of Pyle's handwritten draft, Ernie Pyle Branch, Albuquerque Public Library.

CHAPTER 1

1. "that long, sad wind," column, 9/23/35.

2. "meek and no trouble," EP to Paige and Edna Cavanaugh, 9/1/37, Pyle mss. 1929–42, LL.

3. Pyle's memories of his father, column, 9/24/35.

4. "a woman of unusual character," T. K. Hooker to LGM, 12/16/45, Miller Papers, EPSHS.

5. Memories of Will and Maria Pyle, Edmon Goforth, author's interview, July 1994; Nellie Kuhns Hendrix, author's interview, May 1994.

6. "She wore the pants," Goforth interview.

7. Young Ernie and the snake, column, 9/23/35.

8. Aunt Mary Bales, column, 9/26/35.

9. Pyle as farm boy, column, 1/16/39.

10. Fred Painton, "The Hoosier Letter-Writer," *Saturday Evening Post*, 10/2/43.

11. "Aw, hell . . . ," T. K. Hooker to LGM, 12/16/45, Miller Papers, EPSHS.

12. Teeth-cleaning, Edwin Bland, author's interview.

13. Pyle on the farm, column, 9/24/35; Painton, "Hoosier Letter-Writer"; EP to LGM, 6/1/38, Miller Papers, EPSHS; "Ernie Pyle's War," *Time*, 7/17/44.

14. Pyle's view of outside world, "Ernie Pyle's War," *Time*, 7/17/44; Miller, *Story of Ernie Pyle*, 8; EP to Lowell Mellett [c. 1933], Pyle mss. 1929–42, LL.

15. Pyle's feelings about Indianapolis 500, column, 6/26/36.

16. Pyle's desire to enlist, column, 3/2/36.

17. "He always had big ideas," Nellie Kuhns Hendrix, author's interview.

18. "Ernie had a hero complex," quoted in Miller, *Story of Ernie Pyle*, 14–15.

19. Pyle's entrance into journalism, "All of Bloomington to See Ernie at I.U. 'Doctoring,' " *Indianapolis Times*, 11/10/44; "Ernie Pyle's First Step into Journalism," *Orange County Register*, date unknown, clipping at EPSHS.

20. "He had such a memory," Joel Benham to

LGM, 10/16/45, Miller Papers, EPSHS.

21. "he had periods of mental lowness," D. C. Crowder to LGM, 2/21/46, Miller Papers, EPSHS.

22. "He was a shy boy," Wilbur B. Cogshall to LGM, 10/2/45, Miller Papers, EPSHS.

23. Pyle's response to Kirke Simpson's account of the Unknown Soldier, John Hohenberg, ed., *The Pulitzer Prize Story* (New York: Columbia University Press, 1959); Painton, "Hoosier Letter-Writer," *Saturday Evening Post*, 10/2/43.

24. "I wish I was a good ball player," EP to Mary Bales, c. 1920, Pyle mss. II, LL.

25. College travel, Paige Cavanaugh, "Ernie Pyle," unpublished manuscript, EPSHS.

26. EP to Pyles, 4/20/22, EP to Pyles, undated, Pyle mss. II, LL; Miller, *Story of Ernie Pyle*, 15–16.

27. "Small, frail and sandy-haired . . ." "Data on Ernie Pyle" by Ray E. Smith, attached to letter, H. Stewart Badger to LGM, 9/21/45, Miller Papers, EPSHS.

28. Pyle in LaPorte, "How Ernie Got First Job Here," *LaPorte [Ind.] Herald-Argus*, 4/18/45; "Data on Ernie Pyle" by Ray E. Smith, attached to letter, H. Stewart Badger to LGM, 9/21/45, Miller papers, EPSHS.

29. Cavanaugh's warning, Lincoln Barnett, "Ernie Pyle," *Life*, 4/2/45.

30. Pyle and Harriett Davidson, "Data on Ernie Pyle" by Ray E. Smith, attached to

letter, H. Stewart Badger to LGM, 9/21/45, Miller Papers, EPSHS.

31. Pyle's hiring by *Washington Daily News*, "Ernie Pyle, Times Writer, Globe Trotter, Even as Student at Bloomington," *Indianapolis Times*, c. 1936, Pyle scrapbooks, WJL.

32. Pyle's arrival in Washington, D.C., Nelson Poynter to LGM, 11/28/45, Miller Papers, EPSHS.

33. "sand in his shoes," "Data on Ernie Pyle" by Ray E. Smith, attached to letter, H. Stewart Badger to LGM, 9/21/45, Miller Papers, EPSHS.

34. Earle Martin's plans, Emerson "Abe" Martin, "Home Town Slants," *Elkhart [Ind.] Daily Truth*, 11/22/43 (typescript in Miller Papers, EPSHS); Miller, *Story of Ernie Pyle*, 27–28.

35. "a damn good story," Emerson "Abe" Martin to LGM, 10/29/45, Miller Papers.

36. Pyle as a copy editor, Lee Miller, "Foxhole Historian," *Redbook* (February 1945); Emerson "Abe" Martin to LGM, 10/29/45, Miller Papers, EPSHS.

37. "A good man," "Ernie Pyle's War," *Time*, 7/17/44.

38. "wondrous hypochondria," Leonard Hall, "Ernie Pyle," (letters column), *Time*, 8/14/44.

39. "What's *that?*" Miller, *Story of Ernie Pyle*, 32.

40. Jerry Pyle's "stubborn . . . non-conformism," *ibid.*, 34.
41. Jerry Pyle before her marriage, Harriet Hendrixson, author's interview; Miller, *Story of Ernie Pyle*, 34.
42. "They were young," Cavanaugh, "Ernie Pyle," unpublished manuscript, EPSHS.
43. The Pyles in New York, column, 8/13/35.
44. Lee Miller rehires Pyle, Lee Miller, "Foxhole Historian," *Redbook* (February 1945).
45. After eight-hour shift, Miller, *Story of Ernie Pyle*, 41.
46. Pyle as aviation reporter, "Ernie Pyle Leads Them All — Notes," *U.S. Air Forces* (July 1943), Pyle scrapbooks, WJL.
47. "Hiram Bingham Jr., son of the Senator," column, WDN, 11/26/28.
48. "If you follow the movements," column, WDN, 10/23/29.
49. Mail pilots, Roger E. Bilstein, *Flight in America, 1900–1983* (Baltimore: Johns Hopkins University Press, 1984), 48–53.
50. "He has never been to the North Pole," column, WDN, 6/30/29.
51. "He found that . . . he had a gift," David Nichols, ed., *Ernie's War: The Best of Ernie Pyle's World War II Dispatches* (New York: Random House, 1986), 7.
52. "With a bow to my many friends," column, WDN, 1/8/29.
53. Noted aviation columns included WDN 9/6/29, 9/16/29, 3/3/31, 2/27/30 and 10/10/30.

54. Meeting with Amelia Earhart, Miller, *Story of Ernie Pyle*, 42.

55. "They were so concerned," Hendrixson, author's interview.

56. "Ernie and Jerry did live for each other," Cavanaugh, "Ernie Pyle," EPSHS.

57. Pyle's fear of becoming "old, sour-pussed," *ibid.*

58. "don't ever let 'em make you editor," EP to LGM, 3/1/38, Miller Papers, EPSHS.

59. Pyle's memo to staff, EP to "The Staff," c. March 1933, Pyle mss. 1929–42, LL.

60. Jerry's Pyle's mood; Pyle's fears of a suicide attempt, Cavanaugh, "Ernie Pyle," EPSHS; EP to LGM, 10/31/44, Miller Papers, EPSHS.

61. Jerry Pyle's abortion, Harriet Hendrixson, Shirley Mount Hufstedler, author's interviews.

62. "I . . . have failed," EP to Eugene Uebelhardt, c. 1935, quoted in Miller, *Story of Ernie Pyle*, 50.

63. "my idea of a good newspaper job," Abe Martin, "Home Town Slants," *Elkhart [Ind.] Daily Truth*, 11/22/43, typescript in Miller Papers, EPSHS.

64. "one of the few . . . happiest three weeks," column, 10/5/37.

65. "had a sort of Mark Twain quality," "Ernie Pyle's War," *Time*, 7/17/44.

66. Parker approves Pyle's plan for travel column, column, 11/1/40.

67. "I didn't like the inside work," "So Bert Says to Ernie and Ernie Says to Bert . . . ," *Knoxville News-Sentinel*, 1/26/37.

CHAPTER 2

1. "It wasn't flashy," George Carlin to Jack Alexander, 7/1/43, Walker Stone Papers, SHSW.
2. "The trouble with these column guys," John O'Rourke to EP, 6/9/38, Pyle mss. 1929–42, LL.
3. "Kids, Civil War veterans," Walter Morrow to EP, 5/31/38, Pyle mss. 1929–42, LL.
4. Kids and Civil War veterans, Walter Morrow to EP, 5/31/38, Pyle mss. 1929–42, LL; Evansville teenagers, Frank Ford to EP, 6/1/38, Pyle mss. 1929–42, LL; Pittsburgh college students, E. T. Leech to EP, 6/3/38; El Paso police chief, Edward M. Pooley to EP, 5/31/38, Pyle mss, 1929–42, LL.
5. Pyle as "president," Louis Seltzer to EP, 6/5/39, Pyle mss. 1929–42, LL.
6. Death Valley, column, 3/23/38; Oklahoma City, column, 1/26/37; Tamazunchale, column, 4/4/36; Indiana village, column, 8/9/40; "I know within five minutes," column, 5/1/38; New York, column, 8/14/35; Atlantic seaboard, column 8/27/35; "Chamber of Commerce mouthpiece," EP to EHS, 6/8/38, Shaffer Papers,

EPSHS; conditions in Ohio, column, 7/26/38.

7. "Goddam all big shots," EP to LGM, 11/28/37, Miller Papers, EPSHS.

8. Harry Hopkins's press conference, column, 10/26/35.

9. "the ordinary human being," John T. O'Rourke to EP, 6/9/38, Pyle mss. 1929–42, LL; "Everyday doings of simple people," Alvin H. Goldstein, "Union Writer's Africa Dispatches Win Acclaim," *Sacramento Union*, 7/18/43.

10. Columns of December 1935 and June 1936, 12/11/35, 12/28/35; 6/15/36, 6/18/36.

11. Pyle defends "the 'little stuff,' " EP to LGM, 9/6/36, Miller Papers, EPSHS.

12. "writing like a man talking," "Ernie Pyle With Invasion Force . . . ," WDN, 6/9/44.

13. "pink flagpoles," column, 8/17/39.

14. "the sand-laden wind," column, 6/6/36.

15. Montana's historical signboards, column, 10/9/36.

16. "You'll probably think I've gone nuts," EP to LGM, 9/6/36, Miller Papers, EPSHS.

17. Meditation in the Berkshires, column, 10/1/38.

18. Powder River country, column, 7/23/36.

19. Pyle's pleasure in starting trips, columns, 2/8/37, 1/21/39.

20. Drought in the upper plains, column, 7/27/36.

21. "Roaming Kalaupapa," column, 1/8/38.
22. "a nation's art is greatest," quoted in Charles Alexander, *Nationalism in American Thought, 1930–1945* (Chicago: Rand-McNally, 1969), 68.
23. ". . . gain new strength for the struggles ahead," Malcolm Cowley, "The Puritan Legacy," *New Republic*, 8/26/36.
24. "their primary emphasis," Stott, *Documentary Expression and Thirties America* (New York: Oxford University Press, 1973), 241.
25. Extra items in the Pyles' car, column, 6/20/38.
26. The Pyles' eclectic clothes, column, 2/9/37.
27. High-priced hotels, column, 2/6/37.
28. Choosing hotels, Pyles' AAA *Hotel Directories*, WJL.
29. Eight hundred hotels, "The Roving Reporter," *Pittsburgh Press*, 9/5/43.
30. "just like getting home," EP to PC, 8/8/39, Pyle mss. 1929–42, LL.
31. Breakfast on the road, columns, 9/5/37, 11/7/39.
32. Costs on the first day of traveling, Miller, *Story of Ernie Pyle*, 54.
33. Jerry's disinterest in *"things,"* Harriet Hendrixson, author's interview, May 1994.
34. "that terrible 'lost' feeling," column, 2/8/38.
35. "One story a day," column, 3/18/36.
36. "Five halves to every day," "Rover Boy With Typewriter," *Newsweek*, 2/15/43.

37. ". . . harder now than when I began," "So Bert Says to Ernie and Ernie Says to Bert . . . ," *Knoxville News-Sentinel*, 1/26/37.
38. Pyle's Four Corners output, EP to LGM, 6/29/39, Miller Papers, EPSHS; "Goddam lousy," EP to Shaffers, 6/25/39, Shaffer Papers, EPSHS.
39. "he sits down to write," "Mr. Ernie Pyle Gets Interview With Himself," *Evansville Press*, 5/26/36.
40. "This is a very fine boat," LGM, 7/8/36, Miller Papers, EPSHS.
41. "About one day in six months," column, 8/1/36.
42. "sell out and go back to the farm," EP to LGM, 3/24/36, Miller Papers, EPSHS.
43. "YOUR STUFF EXCELLENT," Lowell Mellett, LGM and George Parker to EP, 3/25/36, Miller Papers, EPSHS.
44. "That was grand of you," EP to Lowell [Mellett] and Lee [Miller], 3/25/36, Miller Papers, EPSHS.
45. "I'm not trying to be any prima donna," EP to LGM, 9/6/36, Miller Papers, EPSHS.
46. "inconceivably rotten," EP to Shaffers, 12/7/38, Shaffer Papers, EPSHS.
47. "The thing is so damned hard," EP to LGM, 3/1/38, Miller Papers, EPSHS.
48. List of minor maladies, EP to Shaffers, 3/28/38, Shaffer Papers, EPSHS.
49. "anguish and lonesomeness," EP to PC, 6/27/38, Pyle mss. 1929–42, LL.

50. "I've been so damn homesick," EP to GP, 6/18/38 [Miller's copy], Miller Papers, EPSHS.
51. Pyle's South American "doldrums," EP to Shaffers, 12/7/38, Shaffer Papers, EPSHS.
52. "The little dog in the manger," EP to Shaffers, 8/27/37, Shaffer Papers, EPSHS.
53. "all written out," *ibid.*
54. "As a writer McIntyre was not in Ernie's class," John Sorrells to LGM, 2/16/38, Pyle mss. 1929–42, LL.
55. Parker's approach to Pyle about syndication, EP to LGM, 3/1/38, Miller Papers, EPSHS.
56. "I don't know what the hell to do," EP to LGM, 3/1/38, Miller Papers, EPSHS.
57. "afraid of stepping into the big-time stuff," EP to LGM, 3/2/38, Miller Papers, EPSHS.
58. "Although I'm afraid of the consequences," EP to LGM, 4/11/38, Miller Papers, EPSHS.
59. Discussion of syndication with George Carlin, Miller, *Story of Ernie Pyle*, 95.
60. "two old people . . . almost broke my heart," EP to Pyles, 3/4/39, Pyle mss. II, LL.
61. "Honest to Christ," EP to PC, 3/6/39, Pyle mss. 1929–42, LL; EP to Shaffers, 3/7/39, Shaffer Papers, EPSHS.
62. "I believe things will pick up now . . . ," EP to GP, 6/8/39, EPSHS.

63. "Things are so black," EP to Pyles, 8/24/39, Pyle mss. II, LL.
64. "All these crises," EP to Lee and Katie Miller, 8/27/39, Miller Papers, EPSHS.
65. "and we'll become famous war correspondents," *ibid.*
66. "Personally, I'm just about to bust," EP to PC, 9/11/39, Pyle mss., 1929–42, LL.
67. "trying not to think," EP to PC, 9/30/39, Pyle mss. 1929–42, LL.
68. "my kind of war stuff," EP to LGM, 11/12/39, Miller Papers, EPSHS.
69. "As for Panama," EP to LGM, 12/13/39, Miller Papers, EPSHS.

CHAPTER 3

1. "I have been lower," EP to PC, 4/4/40, Pyle mss. 1929–42, LL.
2. "Europe is OUT," quoted in EP to PC, 5/22/40, Pyle mss. 1929–42, LL.
3. "Can't think of anything else," EP to LGM, 5/14/40, Miller Papers, EPSHS.
4. "if I must be a self-analyst," EP to Shaffers, 5/19/40, Shaffer Papers, EPSHS.
5. "The birds sing all night," column, 6/12/40.
6. "empty and meaningless," EP to GP, 3/15/42 [Miller's copy], Miller Papers, EPSHS.
7. "It didn't matter to Jerry," Paige Cavanaugh, "Ernie Pyle," EPSHS.
8. Jerry's references to herself, GP to Lee and

Katie Miller, 9/26/38, Miller Papers; GP to ES, 11/1/37; GP to Shaffers, 8/14/39; GP to Shaffers, 11/5/40, Shaffer Papers, EPSHS.

9. "Jerry has had her battle out," EP to LGM, 12/22/39, Miller Papers, EPSHS.
10. "I have a feeling," EP to PC, 9/17/40, Pyle mss. 1929–42, LL.
11. "the situation seems to me," GP to Shaffers, 11/5/40, Shaffer Papers, EPSHS.
12. "The war is beginning to get me down," EP to PC, 9/19/40, Pyle mss. 1929–42, LL.
13. "greatly moved," EP to Shaffers, 10/29/40, Shaffer Papers, EPSHS.
14. "It seemed to me that in London," *Ernie Pyle in England* (New York: Robert M. McBride, 1941), xi.
15. "the gabled buildings," column, 12/26/40.
16. Pyle's plan for London coverage, EP to LGM, 12/28/40, Miller Papers, EPSHS.
17. "a ghostly whoo-isshhh," column, 1/6/41; "damn near scared me to death," EP to LGM, 12/16/40, Miller Papers, EPSHS.
18. "As for myself," EP to LGM, 12/28/29, Miller Papers, EPSHS.
19. "For on that night . . . has always been there" column, 12/30/40.
20. "True, the destruction has been immense," column, 12/30/40.
21. " 'Is that because they like guns?' " column, 1/22/41.
22. Air-raid warden, column, 1/9/41.
23. Sandbags, column, 2/6/41.

24. "Such an ending is inconceivable," column, 1/10/41.
25. "marvelous stuff," EP to GP, 1/12/41, Pyle mss. 1929–42, LL.
26. "Until last week Ernie Pyle," "Tourist in War Zone," *Time*, 1/13/41.
27. "YOUR STUFF NOT ONLY GREATEST," Roy W. Howard to EP, 1/10/41, Pyle mss. 1929–42, LL.
28. "Isn't that the damnedest thing," EP to GP, 1/12/41, Pyle mss. 1929–42, LL.
29. Miller's defense of Pyle's style, LGM to Roy W. Howard, 3/25/41, Miller Papers, EPSHS.
30. "from grocery boys to the city rabbi," EP to LGM, 3/30/41, Miller Papers, EPSHS.
31. "The damn place," EP to Beatrice Bales, 4/6/41, Pyle mss. II, LL.
32. "All kinds of wires," EP to LGM, 3/30/41, Miller Papers, EPSHS.
33. "any renewal of acquaintanceship," EP to LGM, 3/30/41, Miller Papers, EPSHS.
34. "the most ironic touch," *ibid.*
35. "he found roving around," Shirley Mount Hufstedler, author's interview, June 1994.
36. "work up much blood pressure," EP to LGM, 4/9/41, Miller Papers, EPSHS.
37. "The long trip home is done" . . . "out of your mind," *Ernie Pyle in England*, 227–28.
38. "Trying to get the columns started," quoted in Miller, *Story of Ernie Pyle*, 165.
39. "a time of constant worry and bewilder-

ment," EP to LGM, 10/28/41, Miller Papers, EPSHS.

40. "Nobody can help," EP to PC, 11/8/41, Pyle mss. 1929–42, LL.

41. "If can't get to Orient," EP to LGM, 11/29/41, Miller Papers, EPSHS.

42. "bitter and disgusted," EP to LGM, 12/1/41, Miller Papers, EPSHS.

43. "since feeling of war intimacy," EP to LGM, 12/8/41, Miller Papers, EPSHS.

44. "jitterier and gloomier" and "When the rumor came," EP to PC, 12/10/41, Pyle mss. 1929–42, LL.

45. "tight, swollen up feeling," EP to GP, 1/15/42, Pyle mss. 1929–42, LL.

46. "Instead of being grim and deadly," EP to Shaffers, 12/26/41, Shaffer Papers, EPSHS.

47. "a torture," EP to GP, 1/10/42, Pyle mss. 1929–42, LL.

48. "shrivelled up . . . mentally," EP to GP, 12/17/41, Pyle mss. 1929–42, LL.

49. "I had a nice letter from Deac," EP to LGM, 1/14/42, Miller Papers, EPSHS.

50. "under the present set-up," EP to Shaffers, 3/12/42, Shaffer Papers, EPSHS.

51. "I can't attempt any longer," EP to GP, 3/14/42, EPSHS.

52. News item on Pyles' divorce, "Ernie Pyle Divorced; Traveling Reporter," *Washington Times Herald*, 4/15/42.

53. Readers write about Pyles' divorce, "Union Writer's Africa Dispatches Win Acclaim,"

Sacramento Union, 7/18/43.

54. "a necessary and last-hope form," EP to LGM, George Parker and Walker Stone, 4/14/42, Miller Papers, EPSHS.

55. "under the impression that I've gone," EP to GP, 5/8/42, Pyle mss. 1929–42, LL.

56. "The worth of what you are doing," George B. Parker to EP, 3/21/42, Walker Stone Papers, SHSW.

57. "I got to thinking," EP to PC, 5/27/42, Pyle mss. 1929–42, LL.

58. "wanted to die," EP to GP, 6/9/42, Miller Papers, EPSHS.

59. Pyle's plan on eve of overseas trip, *ibid.*

60. "I really feel that I can never be successful," EP to GP, 6/21/42, Miller Papers, EPSHS.

61. "silly little pool-table game," EP to GP, 10/29/42, Pyle mss. 1929–42, LL.

62. "just dainty and whimsical enough," EP to Lucy B. Livingstone, 5/1/44, Cooper/Livingstone Papers.

63. "Today is my birthday," EP to LGM, 8/3/42, Miller Papers, EPSHS.

64. "sort of an adopted unofficial biographer," EP to LGM, 8/3/42, Miller Papers, EPSHS.

65. "homey touches," column, 7/27/42.

66. Columns on servicemen in Britain, 9/18/42, 9/19/42.

67. "Folks with 'boys' over there," John Sorrells to Walker Stone, 11/21/42, Miller Papers, EPSHS.

68. "Every new arrival," EP to GP, 10/11/42, Pyle mss., 1929–42, LL.
69. "could do more good over here," EP to LGM, 9/9/42, Miller Papers, EPSHS.
70. "Somehow I feel," EP to GP, 10/29/42, Pyle mss. 1929–42, LL.
71. "I told somebody the other day," *ibid.*
72. "It isn't impossible," EP to LGM, 9/25/42, Miller Papers, EPSHS.
73. "what readers want," EP to LGM, 12/4/42, Miller Papers, EPSHS.
74. How Pyle got story of Vichy influence, Miller, *Story of Ernie Pyle*, 220.
75. "people at home think," column, 1/4/43.
76. "soft-gloving snakes in our midst," column, 1/4/43.
77. "The censors are so bored," column, 12/19/42.
78. Account of how Pyle's column on collaborationists went uncensored, "Union Writer's Africa Dispatches Win Acclaim," *Sacramento Union*, 7/18/43.
79. "It wouldn't bring me home," EP to GP, 11/26/42, Pyle mss. 1929–42, LL.
80. Remarriage proxy, Miller, *Story of Ernie Pyle*, 220.
81. "I have no feeling at all," EP to GP, 12/8/42, Pyle mss. 1929–42, LL.
82. "the Germans obviously know," column, 1/19/43.
83. Returning bomber series, 1/19, 1/20, 1/21/43.

84. "a proper son-of-a-bitch," LGM to EP, 1/27/43, Miller Papers, EPSHS.

CHAPTER 4

1. Riddleberger's conversation with Pyle, Patrick Riddleberger, author's interview.
2. Night convoy columns, February 16–18, 1943.
3. "I'm sorry to leave the Air Corps . . . ," EP to GP, 1/25/43, Pyle mss., 1943–45, LL.
4. "The goddam weather," EP to GP, 1/25/43, Pyle mss. 1943–45, LL.
5. Clothes and gear in Tunisia, EP to GP, 1/25/43, Pyle mss. 1943–45, LL.
6. "really a swell apple," quoted in "Pyle Praised as 'One of the Boys' " *New York World-Telegram*, 6/17/43.
7. Pyle with soldiers and press in Africa, Horace Miner to LGM, 1/1/46, Miller Papers, EPSHS.
8. "feeling . . . of being in the heart," column, 4/8/43.
9. Generals' frankness with correspondents, *ibid.*
10. "five-gallon gasoline tin," column, 2/17/43.
11. "From one corner of the farmyard," Jack Thompson to LGM, 9/6/45, Miller Papers, EPSHS.
12. "It was the coziest place," column, 2/16/43.
13. "The danger comes in spurts," *ibid.*
14. "You don't have appointments to keep,"

column, 4/8/43.

15. "Some of this stuff out of Tunisia," LGM to George Carlin, 2/10/43, Walker Stone Papers, SHSW.
16. "the strong personal feeling the little guy . . . had," Noland Norgaard to LGM, 10/22/45, Miller Papers, EPSHS.
17. "Awful nights of fleeing," column, 2/27/43.
18. "You get so interested," EP to GP, 2/21/43, Pyle mss. 1943–45, LL.
19. "damned humiliating," column, 2/24/43; "complete melee," column, 2/25/43.
20. "You need feel no shame"; "We had too little to work with," column, 2/24/43.
21. "I thought this was odd," column, 2/26/43.
22. "I'm terribly disappointed," EP to GP, 3/2/43, Pyle mss. 1943–45, LL.
23. "Is war dramatic, or isn't it?" column, 3/10/43.
24. "It's a minor Washington," EP to LGM, 2/27/43, Miller Papers, EPSHS.
25. "never felt so good," *ibid.*
26. "so wonderfully simple," EP to PC, 2/28/43, Pyle mss. 1943–45, LL.
27. "You are in the heart of everything," column, 4/8/43.
28. Pyle's plan for central African trip, EP to GP, 3/2/43, Pyle mss. 1943–45, LL.
29. Report of proxy remarriage, Miller, *Story of Ernie Pyle*, 243–44.
30. "I can't tell you how relieved and glad . . . I am," EP to GP, 3/13/43, Pyle mss.

1943–45, LL.

31. Washington fund for Pyle, "Ernie Moves Admirers to Raising Fund for Yanks," WDN, 3/24/43; "More About Those Guys Who Gave $52 for Ernie," WDN, 4/5/43.

32. Readers contribute to cigarette fund, "Cigaret Money Keeps Pouring in for Ernie," WDN, 4/12/43.

33. "How come they do that?" EP to LGM, 4/24/43, Miller Papers, EPSHS.

34. Pyle's circulation figures, "Man About the World," *Time*, 5/1/43; LGM to EP, 3/23/43, Miller Papers, EPSHS.

35. Praise from Seltzer and Sorrells, LGM to EP, 3/25/43, Miller Papers, EPSHS.

36. Popularity in London, LGM to EP, 4/8/95, Miller Papers, EPSHS.

37. Publishing proposals, LGM to EP, 3/23/43, Miller Papers, EPSHS.

38. "I'm not coming home," EP to LGM, 3/26/43, Miller Papers.

39. Conversion to war spirit, column, 4/19/43.

40. "When I sit alone," column, 4/22/43.

41. Spooky night with Chris Cunningham, column, 4/22/43.

42. Advance with First Division, EP to LGM, 5/2/43, Miller Papers, EPSHS.

43. "one of those days," column, 5/5/43.

44. Writing in foxholes, EP to LGM, 5/2/43, Miller Papers, EPSHS.

45. "an incredible week," EP to LGM, 5/2/43, Miller Papers, EPSHS.

46. New consensus about role of war correspondents, Joseph J. Mathews, *Reporting the Wars* (Minneapolis: University of Minnesota Press, 1957), 175–78.

47. "The American public seems more interested," Harry C. Butcher, *My Three Years with Eisenhower* (New York: Simon and Schuster, 1946), 282.

48. "a pretty disheartening picture," EP to LGM, 4/8/43, Miller Papers, EPSHS.

49. "no matter how hard," column, 5/2/43.

50. Men marching at night, column, 5/1/43.

51. Columns on night march, rest and attack, 5/1, 5/3, 5/3/43 (*sic*).

CHAPTER 5

1. "utter exhaustion," column, 5/21/43.

2. Chaotic journey to Algiers, EP to GP, 5/19/43, Pyle mss. 1943–45, LL.

3. "Always a place of strange mixtures," John Steinbeck, *Once There Was a War* (New York: Viking, 1958), 122–23.

4. "tightness in the back of the head," EP to GP, 5/19/43, Pyle mss. 1943–45, LL.

5. Camp at Zeralda, Pyle, *Here Is Your War* (New York: Henry Holt, 1943), 302.

6. Comments on Pyle in *Time*, "Man About the World," *Time*, 5/1/43.

7. "the No. 1 correspondent of the war," EP to Will Pyle and Mary Bales, 6/8/43, Pyle mss. 1943–45, LL.

8. Hollywood's interest, LGM to EP, 5/11/43, Miller Papers, EPSHS.

9. "Christ, if something doesn't happen," EP to LGM, 5/14/43, Miller Papers, EPSHS.

10. "Sometimes it seems wrong," EP to Pyles, 5/14/43, Pyle mss. II, LL.

11. "I'll just drift with the war," *ibid.*

12. Columns addressed to readers in response to mail, 6/23, 6/24/43.

13. Pyle's guest column in *Stars and Stripes* was excerpted by Scripps-Howard in Pyle's regular run of subscribed columns, 7/9/43.

14. Epilogue to *Here Is Your War*, 295–304.

15. George Biddle's description of Pyle, *Artist at War* (New York: Viking, 1944), 44.

16. "I think I ought to do something on the Navy," EP to LGM, 5/14/43, Miller Papers, EPSHS.

17. "If you were suddenly offered," column, 7/9/43.

18. "they laughed with amusement," column, 7/12/43.

19. "I never heard anybody say anything patriotic," column, 7/13/43.

20. "an irresistible egoism," column, 7/13/43.

21. "out of nowhere, a rolling little subchaser," column, 7/22/43.

22. "the worst exhaustion," EP to GP, 7/11/43, Miller Papers, EPSHS.

23. "a world that is orderly," column, 7/12/43.

24. "a strange delight," column, 8/4/43.

25. "I find myself more and more reluctant,"

EP to GP, 8/15/43, Miller Papers, EPSHS.

26. Meeting with Matthew Ridgway, Raymond
    Clapper, "A Night in Sicily," WDN,
    8/5/43; Matthew B. Ridgway, *Soldier* (New
    York: Harper & Row, 1956), 77–79.

27. "It seemed sad to leave him there," Ray-
    mond Clapper, "With Press in Sicily,"
    WDN, 8/6/43.

28. "battlefield fever," column, 8/6/43.

29. Pyle's decision to return home, EP to
    Scripps-Howard Newspapers, 8/21/43; EP
    to LGM, 8/20/43, Miller Papers, EPSHS.

30. Euphemisms in war reports, Paul Fussell,
    *Wartime: Understanding and Behavior in the
    Second World War* (New York: Oxford Uni-
    versity Press, 1989), 147.

31. Description of infantry casualties, John
    Ellis, *The Sharp End: The Fighting Man in
    World War II* (New York: Scribner's,
    1980), 109, 174–75.

32. "battle . . . if it is sufficiently severe," David
    Marlowe, "The Human Dimension of
    Battle and Combat Breakdown," in
    Richard Gabriel, ed., *Military Psychiatry*
    (Westport, CT: Greenwood Press, 1986),
    12.

33. Stages of battle fatigue, Lawrence
    Ingraham and Frederick Manning, "Amer-
    ican Military Psychiatry," in Gabriel, ed.,
    Military Psychiatry, 42.

34. "The key to understanding," J. W. Appel et
    al, "Preventive Psychiatry: An Epidemio-

logical Approach," *JAMA*, 8/18/46, 1469–75, quoted in Marlowe, "The Human Dimension of Battle and Combat Breakdown," in Gabriel, ed., *Military Psychiatry*.

35. "Ernie . . . hated Patton's guts," Don Whitehead to LGM, 10/26/45, Miller Papers, EPSHS.

36. "go and discover Bradley," Butcher, *My Three Years with Eisenhower*, 298.

37. Hansen's pitch to Bradley, Omar N. Bradley, *A Soldier's Story* (New York: Henry Holt, 1951), 147.

38. Pyle describing men in hospital, columns, 8/9, 8/11, 8/13/43.

39. "It couldn't help," column, 8/9/43.

40. Pyle's attempt to write about battle fatigue, Ralph G. Martin, author's interview, October 1994.

41. "I know the longer we stay," quoted in Don Whitehead to LGM, 10/26/45, Miller Papers, EPSHS.

42. "walking and fighting all that time," column, 8/25/43.

43. "It is true we don't fight on," column, 8/25/43.

44. "The mind gets so complicated," EP to GP, 8/14/43, Miller Papers, EPSHS.

45. "Battles differ from one another," column, 9/11/43.

46. Why Steinbeck would do well as war correspondent, column, 9/14/43.

47. "you don't have any idea," Graham Hovey, author's interview, February 1992.

CHAPTER 6

1. Pyle's arrival, LGM to PC, 8/29/44, Stone Papers, SHSW.
2. Pyle's reception in New York, "Pyle's 'Vice President' Gives Up . . . ," WDN, 9/20/43; "Ernie Pyle, Back in U.S., Just Wants to Sit and Sit," WDN, 9/8/43; "Ernie Pyle Going to the Far East," *Editor and Publisher*, 9/11/43.
3. "No statesman . . . or general," "Where's Ernie Now?" WDN, Pyle scrapbooks, LL.
4. "Ernie Pyle, America's Favorite War Correspondent," *Look*, 9/7/43.
5. Polls on "people . . . not taking the war seriously," U.S. Office of Facts and Figures, "Survey of Intelligence Materials No. 11," February 23, 1942, box 172, President's Secretary's File, FDRL; U.S. Office of Public Opinion Research, "The Nature of the Enemy," August 13, 1942, box 1837, Records of the Office of Government Reports, Record Group 44, National Archives.
6. "In these crucial days," Mrs. B. B. Bailey to FDR, 8/10/42, Official File 5015 misc., FDRL.
7. Gallup Poll on opinion about the war's purpose, George H. Gallup, *The Gallup Poll:*

Public Opinion, 1935–1971. Vol. 1, *1935–1948* (New York: Random House, 1972), 359.

8. Business details on *Here Is Your War*, LGM to EP, 3/18/43; LGM to EP, 4/14/43; LGM to EP, 8/4/43, Miller Papers, EPSHS.

9. Orders for *Here Is Your War*, LGM to EP, 8/4/43, Miller Papers, EPSHS.

10. "a grin like a canteloupe slice," Arthur Miller, *Timebends: A Life* (New York: Harper & Row, 1987), 278.

11. "show the world something," Col. Curtis Mitchell to Lester Cowan, 7/12/45, Paige Cavanaugh materials, EPSHS.

12. "If you want to learn about the infantry," " 'GI Joe' Producer Says It's Pyle's, Not His," *New York World-Telegram*, 8/13/45.

13. Liberal interpretations of the war effort, James Tobin, "Why We Fight: Versions of the American Purpose in World War II" (Ph.D. diss., University of Michigan, 1986), 38–80.

14. "I had merely brushed shoulders," Miller, *Situation Normal*, 163.

15. "chary of implanting any 'theme,' " entry from Arthur Miller diary, October 19 [1943], Walker Stone Papers, SHSW.

16. Arthur Miller's conversations with Pyle about the war's meaning, Miller, *Situation Normal*, 178–80.

17. "sensed a little fear in him," Arthur Miller diary, October 19 [1943], Walker Stone

Papers, SHSW.

18. "universally credited with telling the truth," Miller, *Situation Normal*, 164–65.
19. "she was reaching into the sea," Miller, *Timebends*, 278.
20. "Don't, don't do anything," *ibid.*, 283.
21. "She just went to pieces," EP to LGM, 10/20/43, Miller Papers, EPSHS.
22. "Her will to control herself," EP to PC, 10/21/43, Pyle mss. 1943–45, LL.
23. "I wake up and lie awhile," EP to LGM, 10/15/43, Miller Papers, EPSHS.
24. "I know my leaving was mighty tough," EP to GP, 10/27/43, EPSHS.
25. Pyle's visit to Dana, column, 11/10/43.
26. Publisher's printings of *Here Is Your War*, EP to GP, 11/1/43, EPSHS.
27. "A full-length, deeply human portrait," Edward Streeter, "Ernie Pyle's Story of G.I. Joe," *New York Times Book Review*, 10/31/43.
28. "the sensitiveness of this man Pyle," Hal Borland, "A War Fought by Humans," *Saturday Review*, 10/30/43.
29. "If you could have been there," advertisement, "Take It From One Who's Been There," Pyle scrapbooks, LL.
30. Pyle's lunch with Roy Howard, EP to GP, 11/6/43, Pyle mss. 1943–45, LL; offers from competitors, LGM to George B. Parker, 11/10/43, Miller Papers, EPSHS.
31. "a mob scene!" Lucy B. Livingstone to

John S. Cooper, 7/16/90, Cooper/Livingstone Papers.

32. Pyle's thoughts on "the bolt of fame," column, 11/8/43.

33. "an adoring relationship," John S. Cooper, author's interview, August 1994.

34. Henry Kaiser's visit, Eleanor Roosevelt's appointment book, FDRL.

35. Pyle's visit to the White House is described in his column, 11/12/43.

36. "It is one of our popular heroic myths," column, 11/8/43.

37. "But I am going back," "Ernie Pyle Going Back to Cover War He Hates," *Miami Herald*, 11/20/43.

38. "I leave that sort of thing," Pvt. Bernard Freeman, "Errant Ernie, No Desk General, Mum on War," Pyle scrapbooks, LL.

39. Pyle's arrival in Algiers, EP to GP, 11/28/43 [Miller's copy], Miller Papers, EPSHS.

40. Pyle's letters to wife and mistress from Algiers, EP to Lucy B. Livingstone, 11/28/43, Cooper/Livingstone Papers; EP to GP, 11/28/43 [Miller's copy], Miller Papers, EPSHS.

41. "something happened," column, 12/15/43.

CHAPTER 7

1. "the kids up there," EP to GP, 1/1/44, Pyle mss. 1943–45, LL.

2. "They live and die so miserably," column, 1/14/44.
3. Tidwell-Pyle meeting, Riley Tidwell, author's interview, May 1994.
4. "I got back to base camp," EP to GP, 12/19/43, Pyle mss. 1943–45, LL.
5. Pyle's composition of Waskow column, Edwin Bland, author's interview, June 1994.
6. Waskow column, 1/10/44.
7. Voice-cast of Waskow column, Wallace Irwin, Jr., to the author, 4/12/94.
8. "When the war is over," Grove Patterson, "The Way of the World," *Toledo Blade*, 1/13/44.
9. "praying for a curse upon war," "A Masterpiece," *Salida Daily Mail*, 1/12/44.
10. "silently dedicated themselves," "Ray Clapper," *Washington Post*, 2/4/44.
11. Criticism of Waskow column, Fussell, *Wartime*, 287–88; soldier attitudes toward officers, Samuel A. Stouffer et al., *The American Soldier: Adjustment During Army Life*, vol. 1 (Princeton, NJ: Princeton University Press, 1949), 366–67.
12. Veteran's memory of Waskow, W. B. Slaughter, author's interview, June 1994.
13. Critiques of war correspondents, Steinbeck, *Once There Was a War*, ix–xxi; Fussell, *Wartime*, 287; Fletcher Pratt, "How the Censors Rigged the War," *Harper's* (February 1946), 97–105; Phillip

Knightley, *The First Casualty* (New York: Harcourt Brace Jovanovich, 1975), 332–33.

14. "huge and gassy thing called the War Effort," Steinbeck, *Once There Was a War*, xi–xii.

15. Richard Tregaskis, *Guadalcanal Diary* (New York: Random House, 1943), 111, 263.

16. "The tendency was to write," Ralph G. Martin, author's interview, October 1994.

17. "a division of particularly high morale," David Marlowe, "The Human Dimension of Battle and Combat Breakdown," in Gabriel, ed., *Military Psychiatry*, 13.

18. Company E's status and position, John J. Sheehy to LGM, 9/17/45, Miller Papers, EPSHS.

19. Jack Pierson and Junior, column, 2/17/44.

20. "a warrior-type person," Vincent "Pete" Conners, author's interview, September 1994.

21. "I couldn't see why he picked me," Frank Eversole to LGM, 10/30/45, Miller Papers, EPSHS.

22. The anxiety Eversole suffered over the men under his command was called "old sergeant's syndrome" by military psychiatrists, a species of battle fatigue in which high-performing veterans expressed a conviction that they were not sick but "changed, using phrases like 'I'm no good

anymore,' 'all burned out,' or 'I'll just get us all killed.' " Such soldiers contributed to the emerging medical view in World War II that "every man has his breaking point." Lawrence Ingraham and Frederick Manning, "American Military Psychiatry," in Gabriel, ed., *Military Psychiatry*, 39.

23. "The ties that grow between men. . . ." This passage is quoted from the text of *Brave Men* (New York: Henry Holt, 1944), 197, the collection of Pyle's columns from Sicily, Italy and France. It differs slightly from the original as printed in newspapers, which was: "The ties that grow up between men who live savagely and die relentlessly together are ties of great strength." Though the book manuscript does not survive, and thus cannot be checked, I believe Pyle himself, not Lee Miller or one of his book editors, made the change, as he reviewed the text of *Brave Men* before publication. Though the difference may strike the reader as unimportant, I have used the edited version because it apparently reflects Pyle's considered judgment that "communing with Death" conveyed his meaning more clearly than to "die . . . together." The former makes it clear that it was the constant nearness of death that encouraged such close comradeship among the living. After all, those who "die together" no longer share anything.

24. Eversole columns, 2/21–22/44.
25. The series on Company E's night march was released for publication February 16–18, 1944.
26. Company E casualties, John J. Sheehy to LGM, 9/17/45, Miller Papers, EPSHS.

CHAPTER 8

1. "I'm just floored by it . . . ," EP to LGM, 2/4/44, Miller Papers, EPSHS.
2. "Then, it seemed, I would sense," Tom Treanor, " 'What Did You See, Tom?' " *Vogue*, 10/44.
3. Artillery barrage and rainbow, Pyle, *Brave Men*, 116.
4. "There was something in him," Pyle's introduction to Raymond Clapper, *Watching the World* (New York: McGraw-Hill, 1944), vii.
5. "a sound man," *ibid.*
6. "I had been very low," EP to Lucy B. Livingstone, 2/6/44, Cooper/Livingstone Papers.
7. "You're a damned fool" and "He would tell you," Don Whitehead to LGM, 10/26/45, Miller Papers, EPSHS.
8. "We called it 'Shell Alley,' " Pyle, *Brave Men*, 246–47.
9. Pyle's narrow escape at Anzio, three columns dated 3/20–3/21/44.
10. "just purposely to get my nerve back," EP

to PC, 3/24/44, Pyle mss. 1943–45, LL; Anzio bombing, "Ernie Pyle Has Narrow Escape . . . ," *Washington Star*, 3/16/44; "4 U.S. Writers Injured by Bomb Blast at Anzio," *New York Times*, 3/18/43.

11. "They apparently never saw a guy," EP to LGM, 4/13/44, Miller Papers, EPSHS; column, 5/10/44.

12. " 'Dog News,' " column, 5/11/44.

13. London in April 1944, column, 5/10/44.

14. " 'crossed' and blurry," EP to GP, 5/7/44; "and after the winter's months of beastliness . . . ," EP to Lucy B. Livingstone, 4/16/44, Cooper/Livingstone Papers.

15. "I find that after the beachhead," EP to LGM, 4/13/44, Miller Papers, EPSHS.

16. "a soldier whose sister I met," EP to LBL, 5/1/44, Cooper/Livingstone Papers.

17. "acknowledge receipt of your nomination," Carl W. Ackerman to LGM, 1/28/38, Miller Papers, EPSHS.

18. "it has been suggested," Carl W. Ackerman to George Carlin, 1/20/44, Walker Stone Papers, SHSW.

19. "My stuff just doesn't fit their rules," EP to LGM, Miller Papers, EPSHS.

20. "Wanna bet?" LGM to EP, 3/20/44; "I hereby bet you," LGM to EP, 4/17/44, Miller Papers, EPSHS.

21. Pyle gets news of Pulitzer, Don Whitehead to LGM, 10/26/45, Miller Papers, EPSHS.

22. "I didn't realize," EP to LGM, 5/2/44,

Miller Papers, EPSHS.

23. "a hard guy to be jealous of," Chalmer Roberts, author's interview, July 1994.
24. Clark Lee's plea for whiskey, Clark Lee to LGM, 11/1/45, Miller Papers, EPSHS.
25. "I never did think the Bible," Clark Lee to LGM, 11/1/45, Miller Papers, EPSHS.
26. Jerry's condition, EP to PC, 3/24/44, Pyle mss. 1943–45, LL.
27. "I feel so goddam sorry for her," EP to PC, 3/24/44, Pyle mss. 1943–45, LL.
28. "The more I thought about it," Elizabeth Shaffer's report to Miller, ES to LGM, 4/9/44, Miller Papers, EPSHS.
29. "a lovely place," column, 5/17/44.
30. "It's a funny war," John Mason Brown, *Many a Watchful Night* (New York: McGraw-Hill, 1944), 80.
31. Spaatz's anger at German bombers, "These English are beginning to act," column, 5/13/44.
32. Son of coffee-shop owner, column, 6/2/44; husband of Dana neighbor, column, 5/31/44; Arthur McCollum, column, 5/12/44.
33. "when our trails cross again," column, 6/3/44.
34. "Your Katie is full of war ideologies," EP to LGM, 4/28/44, EPSHS.
35. "Half of them not even newspapermen," EP to LGM, 5/26/44, Miller Papers, EPSHS.
36. "Line of Press Flow Copy," records of the

Public Relations Division, SHAEF, Record Group 331, National Archives.

37. "the first hammer blow," message to "AGWAR for Combined Chiefs of Staff" from "Unity Signed Eisenhower," May 31, 1944, RG SHAEF PRD, 0007-1, National Archives.

38. "queer vague pains," EP to GP, 5/7/44, Pyle mss. 1943–45, LL.

39. Press briefings, Bradley's and Eisenhower's remarks to war correspondents, "450 Reporters Covering Invasion of Europe," *U.S. Air Services*, July 1944, and untitled speech, records of the Public Relations Division, SHAEF, Record Group 331, National Archives.

40. Pyle's broken typewriter, EP to LGM, 4/13/44, Miller Papers, EPSHS.

41. Liquor for D-Day, EP to LGM, 5/26/44, Miller Papers, EPSHS; "I believe in nothing," EP to LBL, 4/16/44, Cooper/Livingstone Papers.

42. "Obviously I can't go into," EP to LGM, 5/21/44, Miller Papers, EPSHS.

43. "Tied up in knots," EP to PC, 5/26/44, Pyle mss. 1943–45, LL.

44. "For Christ's sake take it easy," LGM to EP, 3/5/44, Miller Papers, EPSHS.

45. "I have not yet made plans," EP to LBL, 4/16/44, Cooper/Livingstone Papers.

46. "something like an invitation," EP to GP, 7/1/44, Pyle mss. 1943–45, LL.

47. "I would say that the war correspondent," Robert Capa, *Slightly Out of Focus* (New York: Henry Holt, 1947), 143–44.

48. "I guess all of us feel that way," EP to LGM, 5/21/44, Miller Papers, EPSHS.

49. "All the time fear lay," column, 6/10/44.

50. "but we knew inside ourselves," column, 6/10/44.

51. "a cab drew up," Don Whitehead to LGM, 10/26/45, Miller Papers, EPSHS.

52. "how does it feel to be an assault correspondent?" column, 6/10/44.

53. "clothing impregnated against gas attack," column, 6/10/44.

54. "We had got a little soft," column, 6/10/44.

55. "They have no great faith," Stephen E. Ambrose, *D-Day* (New York: Simon & Schuster, 1994), 162.

56. Pyle's change of D-Day plans, Samuel L. Myers, "Notes on the Activities of Ernie Pyle . . . ," Miller Papers, EPSHS.

57. "the secret the whole world had waited years," column, 6/12/44.

CHAPTER 9

1. "Even if it meant I had to die," quoted in Ambrose, *D-Day*, 500.

2. "a lot of smoke," *ibid.*, 490.

3. Hicks's D-Day broadcast, quoted in Joseph Persico, *Edward R. Murrow: An American Original* (New York: Dell, 1988), 323.

4. "about ready to commit mass hari-kiri," Harold Boyle to Frances Boyle, 6/29/44, Hal Boyle Papers, SHSW.

5. "simply because the fatheads," Harold Boyle to Frances Boyle, 6/18/44, Hal Boyle Papers, SHSW.

6. "The correspondents sent some 700,000 words," Knightley, *The First Casualty*, 322.

7. "It was too much to describe," Tom Treanor, *Washington Post*, 6/8/44.

8. "I couldn't help them," Treanor, " 'What Did You See, Tom?' " *Vogue*, 10/44.

9. "Indeed it will be some time," column, 6/10/44.

10. Jack Thompson, *Chicago Tribune*, 6/11/44.

11. "There is a helluva battle," Leonard Mosley, Associated Press, 6/8/44.

12. "very tired [and] very sad," Samuel L. Myers, "Notes on the Activities of Ernie Pyle . . . ," Miller Papers, EPSHS.

13. Omaha Beach, columns, 6/16/44 and 6/17/44.

14. "It's getting so you," LGM to EP, 6/19/44, Miller Papers, EPSHS.

15. "I think America," EP to LGM, 7/1/44, Miller Papers, EPSHS.

16. "When we leave here," Pyle, *Here Is Your War*, 304.

17. "Instead of getting used to it," "Ernie Pyle's War," *Time*, 7/17/44.

18. "so noisy that it's almost impossible," EP to LGM, 6/29/44, Miller Papers, EPSHS.

19. "constant tenseness," EP to GP, 6/16/44, Pyle mss. 1943–45, EPSHS.
20. "I find I cant take as much," EP to LGM, 7/16/44, Miller Papers, EPSHS.
21. "Not publicity in the manufactured sense . . . ," column, 7/11/44; "I completely lost 24 hours," EP to LGM, 6/29/44, Miller Papers, EPSHS.
22. "He could have had a limousine," Don Whitehead to LGM, 10/26/45, Miller Papers, EPSHS.
23. Pyle's popularity with soldiers in Normandy, "Pyle Called Biggest Thing in War," *New York World-Telegram*, 8/9/44.
24. "Ernie had to fake a little," Lee Miller, "Foxhole Historian," *Redbook* (February 1945).
25. "Please wire Mrs. Murray Hughes," EP to LGM, 7/10/44, Miller Papers, EPSHS.
26. Soldiers leave positions to see Pyle, "Pyle Called Biggest Thing in War," *New York World-Telegram*, 8/9/44.
27. "Soldiers like to read about themselves," EP to LGM, 8/20/43, Miller Papers, EPSHS; "Your average doughfoot," column, 7/11/44.
28. "jubilant interpretations," "Army Writer Hits 'Hopped-up' Italy War News," *Editor and Publisher*, 10/28/44.
29. "a guy who knows how it is," Sgt. Mack Morriss, "Friend of the GIs," *New York World-Telegram* [reprinted from *Yank*],

10/30/44; "Most of these news men over here," quoted in letter from A. E. Bush to EP, 1/7/44, Miller Papers, EPSHS.

30. "brilliantly naive," LGM to EP, 1/17/44; "I wish the cocksucker," EP to LGM, 2/9/44, Miller Papers, EPSHS.

31. "I can not say much about the war," "Indorse Ernie Pyle as GI's Representative," *New York World-Telegram*, 8/28/44.

32. "usually German planes were over," column, 7/11/44.

33. "the rotating band," column, 7/11/44.

34. "so much like the Hollywood sets," column, 7/19/44.

35. Cherbourg street, columns, 7/13–7/17/44.

36. "too much death," EP to GP, 7/16/44, Pyle mss. 1943–45, LL.

37. "The country is lovely," EP to GP, 6/15/44, Pyle mss. 1943–45, LL.

38. "Although I don't often stick my neck out," EP to LGM, 6/29/44, Miller Papers, EPSHS.

39. "This hedge to hedge stuff," EP to LBL, 6/30/44, Cooper/Livingstone Papers.

40. "We feel pretty badly," EP to GP, 7/1/44, Pyle mss. 1943–45, LL.

41. Front too exhausting, EP to GP, 8/1/44, Pyle mss. 1943–45, LL.

42. "the early part of the invasion," EP to GP, 8/1/44, Miller Papers, EPSHS.

43. "The layman doesn't hear much" and extracts that follow, column, 7/25/44.

44. "The country . . . must have gone nuts," EP to LGM, 6/29/44, Miller Papers, EPSHS.

45. "They say I'm to be," EP to PC, 6/30/44, Pyle mss. 1943–45, LL.

46. "Ain't that colossal?" EP to GP, 7/1/44, Pyle mss. 1943–45, LL.

47. "soft-pedal the divorce," EP to GP, 7/18/44, Pyle mss. 1943–45, LL.

48. *Time* cover story, "Ernie Pyle's War," *Time*, 7/17/44.

49. "on the whole a really marvelous job," LGM to EP, 7/14/44, Miller Papers, EPSHS.

50. "eliminate all monkey business," EP to LGM, 7/28/44, Miller Papers, EPSHS.

51. "They had to try," EP to GP, 7/18/44, Pyle mss. 1943–45, LL.

52. "I was *so hurt*," GP to LGM, 8/2/44, Miller Papers, EPSHS.

53. "It wouldn't be fair," EP to GP, 8/1/44, Miller Papers, EPSHS.

54. "This is no limited-objective drive," column, 8/5/44.

55. "a not uncommon practice," Max Hastings, *Overlord* (New York: Simon & Schuster, 1984), 253.

56. Pyle's series on the Saint-Lô bombardment, columns, 8/5–8/10/44.

57. "the enduring appeals of battle," J. Glenn Gray, *The Warriors: Reflections on Men in Battle* (New York: Harper & Row, 1959), 33–36.

58. "It was hell," quoted in Carlo D'Este, *Decision in Normandy* (New York: Harper-Collins, 1983), 402.
59. "Maddened men," Hastings, *Overlord*, 254.
60. "Terribly upset," *ibid.*, 255.
61. "a hell of a period of depression," EP to LGM, 8/9/44, Miller Papers, EPSHS.
62. "a 'collapse' reaction," EP to LGM, 8/9/44, Miller Papers, EPSHS.
63. "coming over the rim," EP to GP, 8/9/44, Pyle mss. 1943–45, LL.
64. "not with a crash," column, 8/14/44.
65. Shock cases, column, 8/15/44.
66. "the worst experience of all," column, 8/19/44.
67. "a sweet old stone village," column, 8/21/44.
68. Radio correspondents' explanations, Larry Lesueur to Ernest Dupuy, Paul Manning to Ernest Dupuy, RG 331 SHAEF PRD File 000.73, National Archives.
69. "Any G.I. who doesn't get laid," Andy Rooney, *My War* (New York: Times Books, 1995), 208–9.
70. "I am glad you share," EP to Reed Switzer, 3/1/45, Miller Papers, EPSHS.
71. "I damn near had a war neurosis," Lincoln Barnett, "Ernie Pyle," *Life*, 4/2/45.
72. "I've been immersed in it too long," column, 9/7/44.

CHAPTER 10

1. "Would you Be So Kind . . ." P. D. Don-nelly to EP, 4/15/43, Miller Papers, EPSHS.
2. "I know it is a 1000 to 1 shot . . ." D. O. Sparnon to EP, 8/17/43, Miller Papers, EPSHS.
3. "Mr Pyle my sweetheart," Marty Hankinson to EP, Miller Papers, EPSHS.
4. "silly as it may seem," LGM to William Sloane, 6/20/44, Walker Stone Papers, SHSW.
5. "I don't ever expect," Mrs. John Goodnow to EP, 2/18/43, Miller Papers, EPSHS.
6. "The illusion that he was a personal friend," Randall Jarrell, "Ernie Pyle," *Nation*, 5/18/45.
7. "as much a part," Fidelis Rice, review of *Brave Men*, 4/4/45, Pyle scrapbooks, LL.
8. "The photographic eye," Diana Trilling, "What Has Happened to Our Novels?" *Harper's*, May 1944.
9. "no mere intellectual comprehension," Janet Underhill to LGM, Miller Papers, EPSHS.
10. "a noble soul," "Adding to Admiration of Correspondent Pyle," *New York World-Telegram*, 8/23/44; "90 percent heart," "TWJ Newsletter," 5/8/43, Pyle Scrap-books, WJL.
11. "a frail old poet," Lincoln Barnett, "Ernie

Pyle," *Life*, 4/2/45.

12. "sweet and kind," Cecelia Ager, "War Correspondent Ernie Pyle," *PM*, 9/24/44.

13. "little homey facts [that] matter even more," Mrs. John Goodnow to EP, 2/18/43, Miller Papers, EPSHS.

14. "God is in Ernie's column," "Profanity Is Elsewhere Than in Ernie's Story," WDN, 2/8/44.

15. "average, in antecedents," unsigned letter to EP, 10/5/43, Miller Papers, EPSHS.

16. Pyle's appearance, "TWJ Newsletter," 5/8/43, Pyle Scrapbooks, LL; "Adding to Admiration of Correspondent Pyle," *New York World-Telegram*, 8/23/44; Robert St. John, NBC radio script, 12/10/43, Pyle scrapbooks, LL; Cecelia Ager, "War Correspondent Ernie Pyle," *PM*, 9/24/44.

17. "The nice thing about you," Marty Hankinson to EP, 4/1/43, Miller Papers, EPSHS.

18. Pyle's jacket auctioned, LGM to EP, 1/14/44, EP to LGM, 2/9/44, Miller Papers.

19. "He is what Americans," *New York Sun*, 4/5/35, quoted in Ben Yagoda, *Will Rogers* (New York: Knopf, 1993), xi.

20. Pyle's reception on New York street corner, Cecelia Ager, "War Correspondent Ernie Pyle," *PM*, 9/24/44.

21. "Not for *your* money," LGM to EP, 7/3/44, Miller Papers, EPSHS.

22. "I know his reason," EP to LGM, 4/13/44, Miller Papers, EPSHS.
23. "These things are so damned hard," EP to LGM, 10/10/43, Miller Papers, EPSHS.
24. Murrow's radio invitation, EP to LGM, 9/18/42, Miller Papers, EPSHS.
25. Miller's concerns about *Cavalcade of America* script, LGM to Keith Jennison, 12/26/43, Walker Stone Papers, SHSW.
26. "You can't trust," LGM to EP, 1/14/44, Miller Papers, EPSHS.
27. "a damned nice piece of income," LGM to EP, 4/17/44, Miller Papers, EPSHS.
28. "I'm still scared," EP to LGM, 5/21/44, Miller Papers, EPSHS.
29. Diminish Ernie's value, LGM to G. B. Parker (copy), 5/29[44], Walker Stone Papers, SHSW.
30. "no program could possibly catch the spirit," John Sorrells to LGM, 5/8/44, Walker Stone Papers, SHSW.
31. "tend to make Ernie into a Boy Scout," LGM to Maurice J. Speiser, 5/24/44, Walker Stone Papers, SHSW.
32. Miller's endorsement of Westinghouse proposal, LGM to EP, 5/31/44, Walker Stone Papers, SHSW.
33. Howard's opposition, LGM to "GBP, RWH, JHS, WS," 5/29/44, Walker Stone Papers, SHSW.
34. "It is perfectly true," *ibid.*
35. Worries about radio show's reception

among Pyle fans, William W. Hawkins to Deac Parker, 5/31/44, Walker Stone Papers, SHSW.

36. "I have never heard you," G. B. Parker to EP, 6/1/44, EPSHS.

37. "Roy is a little free," EP to LGM, 6/16/44, Miller Papers, EPSHS.

38. "Maybe I'm making a mistake," EP to GP, 6/15/44, Pyle mss. 1943–45, LL.

39. "Have downturned so much," EP to LGM, 6/24/44, Miller Papers, EPSHS; "relieved," EP to LGM, 6/29/44, Miller Papers, EPSHS.

40. "I hope you elect," RWH to EP, 7/1/44, Walker Stone Papers, SHSW.

41. "visions of an extra three grand," LGM to Russ Johnston, Walker Stone Papers, SHSW.

42. "Hollywood's first gesture," press release, 3/11/44, Walker Stone Papers, SHSW.

43. "we could see millions of fingers," Lester Cowan to Col. Curtis Mitchell, 6/28/44, Walker Stone Papers, SHSW.

44. "eternally grateful," *ibid.*

45. Candidates for role of Pyle, "Rowswell (Who Looks Like Pyle!) Gets Screen Test for Film Role," *Pittsburgh Press*, 8/20/44; "Meredith Cast as Pyle," *New York Herald Tribune*, 10/27/44.

46. "Get him the hell out," EP to PC, 3/31/44, Pyle mss. 1943–45, LL.

47. Choice of lead actor, Lester Cowan to Gen.

A. D. Surles, 7/3/44, Walker Stone Papers, SHSW.

48. "Like Ernie," Lincoln Barnett, "Ernie Pyle," *Life*, 4/2/45.

49. "People find it easy," Irving Rubine to LGM, 4/27/44, Walker Stone Papers, SHSW.

50. Meredith's account of getting Pyle role, Burgess Meredith, *So Far, So Good: A Memoir* (New York: Little, Brown, 1994), 153–53.

51. "For God's sake," Don Whitehead to LGM, 10/26/45, Miller Papers, EPSHS.

52. Cunningham's report on Pyle, "Interview with Chris Cunningham on Ernie Pyle," 6/4/44, Cavanaugh materials, LL.

53. "writes better than any of us," Lester Cowan to Col. Curtis Mitchell, 6/28/44, Walker Stone Papers, SHSW.

54. "I see the thing now," quoted in Miller, *Story of Ernie Pyle*, 370.

55. "the progress to *commitment*," "Memo on Character and Story of Ernie Pyle," Cavanaugh materials, LL.

56. Developing script for *The Story of G.I. Joe*. This summary is derived from memos and synopses written by Cowan's scriptwriters in June 1944. The sequence and content of scenes vary slightly from one version to the next, but the plan and themes remain essentially the same. Paige Cavanaugh materials, LL; Cowan's copy of script of part of Act I,

labeled "Draft 'C' — June 26, 1944," EPSHS.

57. "extremely dissatisfied," LGM to Lester Cowan, 7/11/44, Walker Stone Papers, EPSHS.

58. "You and I and a lot of others," Lowell Mellett to LGM, 7/11/44, Walker Stone Papers, SHSW.

59. "I've lost all interest," EP to LGM, 6/16/44, Miller Papers, EPSHS.

60. "I turned down," EP to LGM, 10/8/44, Miller Papers, EPSHS.

61. Pyle's first days in Albuquerque, EP to LGM, 10/8/44, Miller Papers, EPSHS.

62. Jerry's condition, EP to LGM, 10/8/44, Miller Papers, EPSHS.

63. "apparently a delayed reaction," quoted in Miller, *Story of Ernie Pyle*, 369.

64. "I think everybody," EP to GP, 11/11/43, Pyle mss. 1943–45, LL.

65. "But what can I do," EP to LGM, 10/17/44, Miller Papers, EPSHS.

66. "Ernie's visit here," Lester Cowan to LGM, 10/25/44, Walker Stone Papers, SHSW.

67. "how antiwar he was," Meredith, *So Far, So Good*, 153.

68. "letters from soldiers I know," EP to LGM, 10/31/44, Miller Papers, EPSHS.

69. Jerry's suicide attempt, *ibid.*

70. Jerry's treatment, *ibid.*

71. "I've long ago given up hope," EP to LGM, 11/7/44, Miller Papers, EPSHS.

72. Pyle's honorary degree, "Ernie Becomes 'Doctor of Humane Letters' . . . ," *Indianapolis Times*, 11/13/44; "Ernie Pyle, G.I. Joe's Personal Reporter, Becomes Doctor at I.U.," *Indianapolis Star*, 11/14/44; "Ernie Pyle gets a degree," *PM*, 11/26/44.

73. Pyle's trip to Dana, Nellie Hendrix, author's interview, May 1994.

74. Pyle's encounter with Madeline Markman and breakup with Moran Livingstone, Lucy B. Livingstone to John Cooper, 7/16/90, Cooper/Livingstone Papers.

75. Jerry's plea; Pyle's reply, EP to GP, 1/10/45, Miller Papers, EPSHS.

CHAPTER 11

1. First day in Honolulu, column, 2/15/45.
2. "an awful inner horror," EP to GP, 2/2/45, Pyle mss. 1943–45, LL.
3. "with a big embrace," column, 2/15/45.
4. Flight across Pacific, column, 2/17/45.
5. "just as bad," EP to GP, 2/2/45, Pyle mss. 1943–45, LL.
6. Reception in Guam, column, 2/21/45.
7. "He isn't exactly a nephew," column, 2/26/45.
8. "out of the personal world," EP to Walker Stone, 1/22/45, Walker Stone Papers, SHSW; "the one-tracked mental world," EP to GP, 2/2/45, Pyle mss. 1943–45, LL.
9. "I felt I just never," EP to GP, 2/2/45, Pyle mss., 1943–45, LL.

10. Diversions in Marianas, column, 3/13/45.
11. "The islands are a paradise," column, 2/22/45.
12. "It's quantity and not quality," EP to GP, 2/2/45, Pyle mss. 1943–45, LL.
13. Pyle's stay with Bales and comrades, Jack Bales, author's interview, November 1995.
14. Pyle's conversation with Red Valens on Saipan, Valens's unpublished memoir, Valens Papers, copy in author's possession.
15. Bales "had been on more missions," column, 2/26/45.
16. "pretty fearful" about Jack Bales, EP to GP, 2/2/45, Pyle mss. 1943–45, LL.
17. Conversation with Jack Bales on Saipan, Bales interview.
18. "my friends fighting on the German border," column, 2/17/45.
19. "you guys don't know what war is about," Bales interview.
20. "the calm and repose," column, 3/26/45.
21. "the methods of war," column, 2/16/45.
22. Differences between Pacific and European wars, *ibid.*
23. Description of task force, column, 3/14/45.
24. "At Anzio, the Third Division," column, 2/16/45.
25. "a man doesn't have to be under fire," *ibid.*
26. "The boys ask you," column, 3/17/45.
27. "It was such a contrast," EP to GP, 2/26/43 [Miller's copy], Miller Papers, EPSHS.
28. "they are good boys," column, 3/17/45.

29. Navy caste system, Robert Sherwood to LGM, 2/22/49, Miller Papers, EPSHS.

30. "This war," EP to R. C. von Ripper, 3/1/45, Miller Papers, EPSHS.

31. "never close enough," EP to GP, 2/26/45, Pyle mss. 1943–45, LL.

32. "sort of enjoyed being at sea," EP to PC, 2/27/45, Pyle mss. 1943–45, LL.

33. "the way I like it," EP to GP, 2/26/45, Pyle mss. 1943–45, LL.

34. "Have no spot news," EP to Scripps-Howard Newspapers, 2/28/45, Walker Stone Papers, SHSW.

35. Pyle's letter about the Tokyo air strike, EP to Walker Stone, 3/1/45 (copy), Walker Stone Papers, SHSW.

36. "The rule had some basis," EP to GP, 2/5/45, Pyle mss. 1943–45, LL.

37. "to give the average guy's picture," EP to GP, 2/2/45, Pyle mss. 1943–45, LL.

38. Censorship problem, EP to GP, 2/5/45, Pyle mss. 1943–45, LL.

39. "I can hardly keep awake," EP to GP, 3/4/45, Pyle mss. 1943–45, LL.

40. "I honest didn't think *Ernie*," Valens memoir.

41. "sly high schoolish criticism," Max Miller to LGM, 1/2/46, Miller Papers, EPSHS; "throat-cutting and back-fence gossiping," EP to Max Miller [4/16/45], Miller Papers, EPSHS.

42. "Some of us are deeply concerned," Ross H. Snyder and N. S. Bullfield to EP, un-

dated, Miller Papers, EPSHS.

43. "I have a nephew," EP to Ross H. Snyder and N. S. Bullfield, 3/14/45, Miller Papers, EPSHS.

44. Criticism of Pyle in Air Corps magazine, copy in Valens memoir.

45. "So far you haven't been where you belonged," Valens memoir.

46. Pyle's exchange of letters with Eisenhower, Dwight D. Eisenhower to EP, 12/15/44, EP to Eisenhower, 2/27/45, Miller Papers, EPSHS.

47. "easy and unconcerned in spirit," EP to GP, 3/11/45, Pyle mss. 1943–45, LL.

48. "That you could ever become a victim," GP to EP, 3/19/45, Miller Papers, EPSHS.

49. "You know darling," EP to GP [date?], Pyle mss. 1943–45, LL.

50. "eyebrow-raising," Max Miller to LGM, 10/13/[45], Miller Papers, EPSHS.

51. "And the way I look at things," EP to PC [date?], Pyle mss. 1943–45, LL.

52. Encounter with Robert Sherwood, Robert Sherwood to LGM, 2/22/49, Miller Papers, EPSHS.

53. Unopposed Okinawa invasion, column, 4/4/45.

54. "I've got almost a spooky feeling," EP to Max Miller, 3/15 [4/16/45], Miller Papers, EPSHS.

55. "And so it is over," copy of Pyle's handwritten draft, Ernie Pyle Branch, Albu-

querque Public Library.

56. Accounts of Pyle's death, Joseph Coolidge to LGM, 12/16/45, Miller Papers, EPSHS; Edwin H. Randle, "The End of Ernie Pyle," *American Legion Magazine* (December 1955).

EPILOGUE

1. Halberstam-Krulak argument, William Prochnau, *Once Upon a Distant War* (New York: Times Books, 1995), 394–95.
2. "the most imitated writer," "a stock figure," A. J. Liebling, "Pyle Set the Style," *The New Yorker*, 9/2/50.
3. "Ernie Pyle was telling the truth," Ira Wolfert, "Why the U.S.A. has fallen for this guy Pyle," Pyle scrapbooks, LL.
4. "what you write is never, never good enough," interview with Martha Gellhorn in "War Reporters," Peter Williams, reporter and producer, TVS, 1987, Films for the Humanities, 1991.

APPENDIX

1. Mike Harden and Evelyn Hobson, eds., *On A Wing And A Prayer: The Aviation Columns of Ernie Pyle* (Friends of Ernie Pyle: 1995), pp. 113–14.
2. *Brave Men* (New York, Henry Holt, 1943), 464–66.

A Note on Sources

Jerry Pyle once told a friend that "what seems to confuse everybody about Ernie is his simple, direct honesty — everybody who tries to explain him, I mean." I found him direct and honest but not at all simple — thus the challenge of making sense of the large public and private record he left behind. These remarks on the principal sources I used may help those who wish to understand and explain him further.

NEWSPAPER COLUMNS

Pyle was his own best biographer, however much of the story he chose to leave out of his writings. Anyone interested in him should get to know him first-hand and at length. Luckily, this is perfectly feasible.

Typescripts of every column Pyle wrote for the Scripps-Howard newspapers from August 1935 until his death in April 1945 are housed at the Lilly Library at Indiana University. These are not Pyle's original typescripts, few if any of which survive. They are the wire copy that was sent from the Scripps-Howard Newspaper Alliance in Washington, D.C., to subscribing newspapers. Unless otherwise noted, these are the texts from which I quoted. After his first couple of years as a travel columnist Pyle seldom complained about being edited, so it is safe to assume these documents are perhaps 99 percent original Pyle material. Microfilm copies of the entire run of columns also are housed at the Lilly Library.

Published versions of Pyle's column as it appeared in the *Washington Daily News* and some other papers are contained in scrapbooks at the Lilly Library. Copies of many of Pyle's columns as Scripps-Howard's aviation editor from 1928 to 1932 are housed at the Ernie Pyle State Historic Site in Dana, Indiana. A selection of these appear in Mike Harden and Evelyn Hobson, eds., *On a Wing and a Prayer: The Aviation Columns of Ernie Pyle* (Friends of Ernie Pyle, 1995).

Five Pyle collections were published in the 1940s: *Ernie Pyle in England* (New York: Robert M. McBride, 1941); *Here Is Your War* (New York: Henry Holt, 1943), which covers Pyle's time in North Africa; *Brave Men* (New York: Henry Holt, 1944), which covers the campaigns in Sicily, Italy and France; *Last Chapter* (New York: Henry Holt, 1946), which covers Ernie's months in the Pacific; and *Home Country* (New York: William Sloane, 1947), a selection of Pyle's travel columns from the 1930s and early '40s. These books are out of print, but used copies can be found in many second-hand book stores. *Here Is Your War*, *Brave Men* and *Last Chapter* include nearly every column Pyle wrote about the war, but the books' editors made numerous small changes in the texts, and the order is rearranged. Two excellent Pyle collections with biographical essays were published more recently: David Nichols, ed., *Ernie's War: The Best of Ernie Pyle's World War II Dispatches* (New York: Random House, 1986), and Nichols, ed., *Ernie's America: The Best of Ernie Pyle's 1930s Travel Dispatches* (New York: Random House, 1989). Selections of some of Pyle's best work appear in *Reporting World War II, Parts I and II* (New York: Library of America, 1995).

MANUSCRIPT SOURCES

Ernie Pyle State Historic Site, Dana, Indiana

The papers of Lee Graham Miller, Pyle's editor and friend for many years, comprise the most valuable collection for the study of the reporter's career. Pyle wrote often and at length to Miller, who also served as his business agent, on subjects professional and personal. Miller's papers include many of his own letters and memoranda, both to Pyle and others, covering various aspects of the reporter's career, including the making of *The Story of G.I. Joe.* Pyle's financial records are a part of the series, as are a few letters from Jerry Pyle and copies of some Pyle letters to Jerry. Letters from other Scripps-Howard executives also appear, as do letters from Pyle fans. Of particular value are the letters Miller solicited for his biography, *The Story of Ernie Pyle* (New York: Viking, 1950). Confidants and acquaintances of Pyle, writing shortly after the correspondent's death, shared many vivid memories with Miller. His notes for the biography are also a part of the collection.

Pyle's correspondence with his friend E. H. Shaffer, editor of the *Albuquerque Tribune*, and Shaffer's wife, Elizabeth, is especially helpful for an understanding of the Pyles' marriage.

The Historic Site contains many other valuable materials: clippings, photographs, books and memorabilia. That they are stored at the house where Pyle was born gives them a special verisimilitude.

Lilly Library, Indiana University

Pyle manuscripts here are contained in two principal collections: letters that Pyle wrote to his mother, father and aunt (in which Pyle minimized revealing details); and scores of letters he wrote to his wife, Geraldine, and to his lifelong friend, Paige Cavanaugh. The letters to Jerry Pyle are a sad but beautifully written record of a tragic marriage. Those to Cavanaugh are of a sort that one man rarely writes to another — highly frank and self-revealing, often obscene and sophomoric, but filled with the intimate stuff of Pyle's extraordinary life: his frustrations, exhilarations, depressions, hypochondria, boredom, extra-marital affairs and wit. The

Cavanaugh letters are better for the pre-war than the wartime period, though they contain much material on *The Story of G.I. Joe*, for which Cavanaugh served as a consultant.

Throughout much of Pyle's career, various friends maintained scrapbooks about him; these are now at the Lilly Library. Packed with hundreds of clippings from newspapers and magazines, the scrapbooks were an invaluable source for tracking Pyle's rising public star.

State Historical Society of Wisconsin, Madison

The papers of Walker Stone, who served in high editorial positions at Scripps-Howard before, during and after World War II, include many letters that document the chain's handling of "the Pyle phenomenon."

Two other collections contain materials of interest: the papers of newspaperman Harold "Hal" Boyle, a close friend of Ernie's in North Africa and Europe, and of Tom Waller, a publicity agent for *The Story of G.I. Joe*.

Weil Journalism Library, Indiana University; and Library of Congress

The Roy Wilson Howard papers at both sites contain few letters to or from Ernie Pyle, but they comprise a treasure trove for a study of the newspaper business of the era.

Cooper/Livingstone materials

These comprise seventeen letters Ernie Pyle wrote to his friend Lucy Bennett Livingstone from 1942 to 1945 in which Pyle reveals many of his most private feelings about the war. There is also a long letter of reminiscences about Pyle which Mrs. Livingstone wrote to her son, John S. Cooper, in 1990. Mr. Cooper generously provided copies to the author. Mrs. Livingstone died in 1993.

SELECTED BIBLIOGRAPHY

Books

Alexander, Charles C. *Nationalism in American Thought, 1930–1945.* Chicago: Rand-McNally, 1969.

Ambrose, Stephen E. *D-Day: The Climactic Battle of World War II.* New York: Simon and Schuster, 1994.

Bilstein, Roger E. *Flight in America, 1900–1983.* Baltimore: The Johns Hopkins University Press, 1984.

Capa, Robert. *Slightly Out of Focus.* New York: Henry Holt and Co., 1947.

Desmond, Robert W. *Tides of War: World News Reporting, 1931–45.* Iowa City: University of Iowa Press, 1984.

D'Este, Carlo. *Bitter Victory: The Battle for Sicily, 1943.* New York: HarperCollins, 1988.

————. *Decision in Normandy*. New York: William Collins and Sons, 1983.

————. *Fatal Decision: Anzio and the Battle for Rome*. New York: HarperCollins, 1991.

Ellis, John. *The Sharp End: The Fighting Man in World War II*. New York: Charles Scribner's Sons, 1980.

Fussell, Paul. *Wartime: Understanding and Behavior in the Second World War*. New York: Oxford University Press, 1989.

Gwynn-Jones, Terry. *Farther and Faster: Aviation's Adventuring Years, 1909–1939*. Washington: Smithsonian Institution Press, 1991.

Hastings, Max. *Overlord: D-Day, June 6, 1944*. New York: Simon and Schuster, 1984.

Kennett, Lee. *G.I.: The American Soldier in World War II*. New York: Charles Scribner's Sons, 1987.

Knightley, Phillip. *The First Casualty: From the Crimea to Vietnam: The War Correspondent as Hero, Propagandist, and Myth Maker*. New York: Harcourt, Brace, Jovanovich, 1975.

Koppes, Clayton R., and Gregory D. Black. *Hollywood Goes to War*. New York: Free Press, 1987.

Liebling, A. J. *Mollie and Other War Pieces*. New York: Ballantine Books, 1964.

Lingeman, Richard. *Don't You Know There's a War On? The American Home Front, 1941–45*. G.P. Putnam's Sons, 1970.

Mathews, Joseph J. *Reporting the Wars*. Minneapolis: University of Minnesota Press, 1957.

Mauldin, Bill. *Back Home.* New York: William Sloane Associates, 1947.

———. *The Brass Ring.* New York: W.W. Norton and Co., 1971.

———. *Up Front.* New York: Henry Holt and Co., 1945.

Melzer, Richard. *Ernie Pyle in the American Southwest.* Santa Fe: Sunstone Press, 1995.

Meredith, Burgess. *So Far, So Good: A Memoir.* New York: Little, Brown, 1994.

Miller, Arthur. *Situation Normal.* New York: Reynal & Hitchcock, 1944.

———. *Timebends: A Life.* New York: Harper and Row, 1987.

Miller, Lee G. *An Ernie Pyle Album.* New York: William Sloane Associates, 1946.

———. *The Story of Ernie Pyle.* New York: Viking Press, 1950.

O'Neill, William L. *A Democracy at War: America's Fight at Home and Abroad in World War II.* New York: Free Press, 1993.

Pells, Richard H. *Radical Visions and American Dreams.* New York: Harper and Row, 1973.

Perrett, Geoffrey. *Days of Sadness, Years of Triumph: The American People, 1939–45.* New York: Coward, McCann & Geoghegan, 1973.

Persico, Joseph E. *Edward R. Murrow: An American Original.* New York: Bantam Doubleday Dell, 1988.

Prochnau, William. *Once Upon a Distant War.* New York: Times Books, 1995.

Roeder, George H., Jr. *The Censored War: Amer-*

ican *Visual Experience During World War Two.* New Haven: Yale University Press, 1993.

Steinbeck, John. *Once There Was a War.* New York: The Viking Press, 1958.

Stott, William. *Documentary Expression and Thirties America.* New York: Oxford University Press, 1973.

Stouffer, Samuel, Edward A. Suchman, Leland C. De Vinney, Shirley A. Star and Robin M. Williams, Jr. *The American Soldier. Vol. 1, Adjustment During Army Life.* Princeton: Princeton University Press, 1949.

Voss, Frederick. *Reporting the War: The Journalistic Coverage of World War II.* Washington: Smithsonian Institution Press, 1994.

The screenplay for *Ernie Pyle's Story of G.I. Joe* appears in John Gassner and Dudley Nichols, eds., *Best Film Plays — 1945.* New York: Crown Publishers, 1946.

Articles

Ager, Cecelia. "War Correspondent Ernie Pyle," *PM,* 9/24/44. [In Pyle scrapbooks, LL.]

Barnett, Lincoln. "Ernie Pyle," *Life,* 4/2/45.

"Ernie Pyle, America's Favorite War Correspondent," *Look,* 9/7/43.

"Ernie Pyle's War," *Time,* 7/17/44.

Ingraham, Lawrence, and Frederick Manning. "American Military Psychiatry," in Richard Gabriel, ed., *Military Psychiatry.* Westport: Greenwood Press, 1986.

Jarrell, Randall. "Ernie Pyle," *Nation*, 5/19/45.

Liebling, A. J. "Pyle Set the Style," *The New Yorker*, 9/2/50.

"Man About the World," *Time*, 5/1/43.

Marlowe, David. "The Human Dimension of Battle and Combat Breakdown," in Richard Gabriel, ed., *Military Psychiatry*. Westport: Greenwood Press, 1986.

Miller, Lee. "Foxhole Historian," *Redbook*, February 1945.

Painton, Frederick C. "The Hoosier Letter-Writer," in *More Post Biographies*. Athens, Ga.: University of Georgia Press, 1947.

Pratt, Fletcher. "How the Censors Rigged the News," *Harper's*, February 1946.

"Rover Boy With Typewriter," *Newsweek*, 2/15/43.

Shaffer, E. H. "Chasing a Story with Ernie Offers Many Real Thrills," WDN, 7/19/39.

Sweeney, Michael S. "Appointment at Hill 1205: Ernie Pyle and Captain Henry T. Waskow." Unpublished paper, Ohio University.

Treanor, Tom. " 'What Did You See, Tom?' " *Vogue*, 10/44.

Wolfert, Ira. "Why the U.S.A. Has Fallen for This Guy Pyle," Pyle scrapbooks, LL.

Dissertation

Tobin, James. "Why We Fight: Versions of the American Purpose in World War II." Ph.D. dissertation, University of Michigan, 1986.

Acknowledgments

Researching and writing this book has been my own private adventure story replete with wise mentors, skilled helpers, trusted allies and well-wishers along the road. It is a pleasure to thank them.

First comes Evelyn Hobson, who deserves the Silver Star and a couple of Purple Hearts for her work in preserving the memory of Ernie Pyle. As curator of the Ernie Pyle State Historic Site in Dana, Indiana, she has assembled a vast cache of Pyle materials that otherwise would surely have been lost. Her ebullient interest in Pyle was contagious. She repeatedly stole time from her busy schedule to help me. She steered me into fruitful paths of research and filled in many blanks in my knowledge. She was a warm hostess in Dana and an able ambassador for her entire neck of the woods, the pretty, pastoral landscape of west central Indiana.

It was my good fortune to begin my research just as the Pyle Historic Site — thanks to Mrs. Hobson, David Nichols and Rosemary and Devon Miller — took custody of the voluminous papers of Lee Graham Miller, Pyle's editor, friend and first biographer. A biographer seldom gets to crib from the research of a predecessor. I wish I could thank Lee Miller, and I hope he would have liked the result.

Several archivists and librarians gave skilled assistance: at Indiana University, Frances Wilhoit and Dawn Hornbeck of the Weil Journalism Library; Rebecca Campbell Cape and Heather Munro of the Lilly Library; and Faye Mark of the Indiana University Archives; at the National Archives, John Taylor, Richard Boylan and Edward Reese; at the Franklin D. Roosevelt Library, Nancy Snedeker; at the Michigan Historical Collections, Nancy Bartlett; and at the Ernie Pyle Branch of the Albuquerque Public Library, Susan Sultemeier and Kenneth Perez. For research assistance, I thank Joshua Ranger, Heather Burch and especially Elizabeth Dawson Jacobs, a good friend throughout.

Many people generously shared memories, personal letters and memorabilia. I am especially grateful to several who went well out of their way to give assistance: Harriet Hendrixson, George and Nancy Shaffer, John and Ann Cooper, Alma Pyle Cowan, Dan Thomassen, Susan Nall Bales, Cecil Byrd, Michael S. Sweeney, who sent me his fine paper on Pyle and Captain Henry Waskow, and Jim Hughes, the biographer of the great photographer W. Eugene Smith, who shared vital materials from the estate of Red Valens.

One of the project's main pleasures was to correspond and speak with people who knew Ernie. I'm indebted to all those who responded to my requests for information: Walter and Vivian Ainslie, Robert Albrecht, Russell F. Anderson, Bob Audette, Jack Bales, Marshall Becker, Loren Beckley, Lawrence Bennett, Mr. and Mrs. Leonard Bessman, Bill Bielec, Thomas Bitsas, Edwin Bland, Jr., Arthur Bonwell, William Cullen Bryant II, Richard Burrage, J. V. Campbell, Martin Clayton, Vince "Pete" Conners, W. J. Danforth, Russell Darkes, John Dolney, Jack Foisie, Henry Fowzer, Roy Goad, Edmon Goforth, Iz Goldstein, Frank Graf, Jack Gross, Chester Hansen, F. F. Harder, Evelyn Helt, Nellie Hendrix, Graham Hovey, Shirley Mount Hufstedler, William Jayne, Murray Juvelier, Conrad Kersch, R. J. Laughlin, Frank and Luigi Liberatore, Gainor Lindsey, Boardman Lockwood, Ralph G. Martin, Burgess Meredith, Rosemary Miller, Robert Moore, Louis Nilsen, Joseph Palmieri, Wendell Phillippi, Earl Richert, Patrick Riddleberger, Freeland Riles, Babette Robb, Chalmers Roberts, Gerald Robinson, Maurice Rosch, Joseph Routledge, Carl Sadler, Helen Scherer, Arthur Schunck, Edward Shaffer, W. B. Slaughter, Ann Sudduth, Zeb Sunday, Reed Taylor, Riley Tidwell, Russ Tornabene, Urban Vachon, June Wandrey, Herman Wells, Horace West, Len Wilkerson, James Williams, William Wilson and John Wozniak.

Gordon Prepsky and Dr. Jonathan Metzl shared their insights on psychological aspects of the Pyles' lives.

I thank the Scripps Howard Foundation for permission to quote from the published works of Ernie Pyle, and the Ball Brothers Foundation for a research grant.

At the Free Press, Bruce Nichols has been a discerning and supportive editor whose good judgment led to many improvements in the text. I'm grateful to Ann Adelman for careful and skillful copyediting, and to Joyce Seltzer, now of Harvard University Press, for seeing merit in the project at the outset.

Among many current and former colleagues at the *Detroit News* who gave encouragement and good advice, I wish to thank Ben Burns, Shanna Flowers, Bryan Gruley, Thomas Hardin, Hugh McCann, Patricia McCaughan and Flora Rathburn. I am especially indebted to Scott Vance, Judy Diebolt and George Bullard for their patience and support.

The generosity of Robert H. Giles, editor and publisher of the *Detroit News*, made it possible for me to write this book. A journalism scholar himself, Bob Giles knew there was a good story to be told about Ernie Pyle, and I have always felt flattered that he thought I could tell it. If he had not granted my requests for two paid leaves of absence from the *News*, the book never could have been completed — at least, not within the lifetime of anyone who might wish to read it.

Three superb historians have helped me a great deal. Jonathan Marwil's penetrating mind, exacting editorial eye and broad knowledge of

528

the intellectual history of war have influenced every page; I am especially grateful to him for a searching critique of the entire manuscript. Gerald Linderman shared his profound understanding of men at war and his faith that Ernie Pyle was worth a book. The book's roots lie in a doctoral dissertation directed by Sidney Fine, whose friendship and guidance have been among my chief blessings for many years.

I owe much to family and friends who advised, urged and reassured: Dick Tobin and Peggy Wilson; Melanie and Bob LaFave; Kim Browning and Gordon Prepsky; Dave Farrell; Jim Mitzelfeld. Special thanks are due my Wednesday night writing comrades — John U. Bacon, Richard Campbell, Randy H. Milgrom and Robert Pasick — who provided valuable critiques of various drafts. My thanks go also to Dr. Thomas Horner. Elizabeth Tobin provided the balm of unquestioning faith that surely her dad knew what he was doing, and her sister, Claire, offered frequent comic relief.

James and Dorothy Tobin and Floyd and Elizabeth Erickson gave of themselves at every turn and in every way. They enjoyed the project as much as I and shared their memories of World War II whenever I asked, which was often. The book is in some sense an homage to these two men, who fought on either side of the world for my generation, and to the two beautiful women who waited for them. My obligations to them are beyond telling.

A book is a houseguest invited by only one member of a family, and it takes a seat in the corner and stays for a long, long time. Leesa Erickson Tobin bore this guest with extraordinary patience and grace, even long after it wore out its welcome. Without her encouragement, her savvy, her skills as a professional archivist and her energy as a researcher, the project would have died a-borning. Then, year after year, she gave me the gift of time when it was least affordable. To say I am grateful does justice neither to the gift nor to my feelings.

James Tobin
October 1996

The employees of G.K. Hall hope you have enjoyed this Large Print book. All our Large Print titles are designed for easy reading, and all our books are made to last. Other G.K. Hall books are available at your library, through selected bookstores, or directly from us.

For information about titles, please call:

(800) 257-5157

To share your comments, please write:

Publisher
G.K. Hall & Co.
P.O. Box 159
Thorndike, ME 04986